Gun Safety and America's Cities

ALSO OF INTEREST AND FROM MCFARLAND

Keeping Schools Safe: Case Studies and Insights,
edited by Joaquin Jay Gonzalez III and Roger L. Kemp (2023)

Climate Change and Disaster Resilience:
Challenges, Actions and Innovations in Urban Planning,
edited by Joaquin Jay Gonzalez III, Roger L. Kemp
and Alan R. Roper (2022)

Syringe Exchange Programs and the Opioid Epidemic:
Government and Nonprofit Practices and Policies,
edited by Joaquin Jay Gonzalez III and Mickey P. McGee (2022)

Gun Safety and America's Cities: Current Perspectives and Practices,
edited by Joaquin Jay Gonzalez III, Roger L. Kemp (2022)

Brownfields Redevelopment: Case Studies
and Concepts in Community Revitalization,
edited by Joaquin Jay Gonzalez III,
Tad McGalliard and Ignacio Dayrit (2021)

Cities and Homelessness: Essays and Case Studies
on Practices, Innovations and Challenges,
edited by Joaquin Jay Gonzalez III and Mickey P. McGee (2021)

Senior Care and Services: Essays and Case Studies
on Practices, Innovations and Challenges,
edited by Joaquin Jay Gonzalez III,
Roger L. Kemp and Willie Lee Brit (2020)

Veteran Care and Services: Essays and Case Studies
on Practices, Innovations and Challenges,
edited by Joaquin Jay Gonzalez III,
Mickey P. McGee and Roger L. Kemp (2020)

Legal Marijuana: Perspectives on Public Benefits,
Risks and Policy Approaches,
edited by Joaquin Jay Gonzalez III
and Mickey P. McGee (2019)

Cybersecurity: Current Writings on Threats and Protection,
edited by Joaquin Jay Gonzalez III and Roger L. Kemp (2019)

Gun Safety and America's Cities

Current Perspectives and Practices

Edited by Joaquin Jay Gonzalez III
and Roger L. Kemp

McFarland & Company, Inc., Publishers

Jefferson, North Carolina

ISBN (print) 978-1-4766-8285-3
ISBN (ebook) 978-1-4766-4892-7

Library of Congress and British Library
cataloguing data are available

Library of Congress Control Number 2023018107

Front cover: New York City skyline (Shutterstock/Greens87);
bullseye target with bullets and gun (Shutterstock/Prath)

Printed in the United States of America

*McFarland & Company, Inc., Publishers
Box 611, Jefferson, North Carolina 28640
www.mcfarlandpub.com*

Jay dedicates this book to grandson Aiden
and all gun safety advocates.

* * *

Roger dedicates this book to his granddaughter,
Kieran, the best and the brightest.

Acknowledgments

We are grateful for the support of the Mayor George Christopher Professorship at Golden Gate University, and GGU's Pi Alpha Alpha Chapter. We appreciate the encouragement from President David Fike, Provost Brent White, Deans Bruce Magid and Nate Hinerman, Dr. Mick McGee, and our wonderful colleagues at the GGU Edward S. Ageno School of Business, the Department of Public Administration, and the Executive MPA Program.

Our heartfelt "THANKS!" goes to the contributors listed in the back section and the individuals, organizations, and publishers below for granting permission to reprint the material in this volume and the research assistance, support, and inspiration. All waived fees as an expression of their support for practical research and information sharing that benefits our community and country.

Alan R. Roper
American Society for Public Administration
California Attorney General's Office
California Department of Justice
City of Lafayette, Colorado
The Conversation
Ian Smith
International City/County Management Association
Kaiser Health News
Kamille Sarmiento
League of Minnesota Cities
Meghan Reilly

National Shooting Sports Foundation
The New Republic
PA Times
PM Magazine
ProPublica
State of Connecticut
U.S. Bureau of Alcohol, Tobacco, Firearms and Explosives
United States Congress
U.S. Department of Justice
Utah Department of Public Safety
Veronica Rose
Washington State Office of Superintendent of Public Instruction

Table of Contents

Part III: The Future

Appendices

Preface

The subject of guns and public safety in the United States is very controversial, dynamic, and evolving. This is basically due to the gun-rights provision of the Constitution or also known as the Second Amendment. This Constitutional Amendment states that *"A well regulated Militia, being necessary to the security of a free State, and the right of the people to keep and bear Arms, shall not be infringed."* And thus, firearms will always be part and parcel of American society, culture, as well as the economy. Politically, Second Amendment rights drive the never-ending heated debates and policy changes on our cities, states, and nation's gun laws, regulations, and practices.

Mitigating the challenges and concerns associated with "guns" will always be an evolving feature of American politics. However, one solution that unifies the messaging and actions from advocates and supporters from all sides of the political spectrum is the concern for PUBLIC SAFETY. We share with you our colorful finds on this theme in this compilation. Our research covers many old and new safety laws, regulations, restrictions, and practices from the federal to municipal levels of governance.

The research resulting from this volume is explained in detail below.

Part I—Introduction. This section contains six essays which focus on our Nation's Second Constitutional Amendment, the fact that most citizens believe that our nation should have gun regulations, the history of the National Firearms Act, a definition of "firearms" under the National Firearms Act, information on the social costs of firearms which is a new approach to gun control, and the last essay of this section, which deals with the definition of "guns," which should not include "assault weapons."

Part II—Challenges and Solutions. This section has nearly fifty essays in it, which have been divided into several sections to make it easier for the reader to reference and research these topics. The sections are as follows: Section A—Federal Safety Regulations; Section B—State Safety Regulations; Section C—Cities and Communities; Section D—Firearms Industry and Associations; Section E—Schools and Children; Section F—Active Shooters, Mass Shootings, and Homicides; Section G—Mental Health and Suicide; and Section H—Covid Pandemic. The various reports and articles contained in these sections are divided and categorized into these eight sections for reference purposes.

Part III—The Future. The various topics and subjects contained in this section include what makes a "Smart Gun" smart, do American's want to buy "Smart Guns," and a review of gun licenses and regulations. The focus of this essay is that it would make guns safer if they were regulated like cars were. Another essay focuses on people who shoot guns and their exposure to unhealthy levels of lead. The last essay of this section focuses on the use of the internet to explore the gun control debate, which is now taking place in our nation.

Appendices. The book concludes with four appendices, which have been included for the reader's reference. The topics of these appendices include a glossary of terms and acronyms, a copy of the proclamation declaring June 4, 2021, as "National Gun Violence Awareness Day," the U.S. Congress' support for the designation of June 4, 2021, as "National Gun Violence Awareness Day," and June 2021, as "National Gun Violence Awareness Month." The last appendix is a Model Policy for Prohibiting Firearms at Work.

We decided that the best time to "end" the writing for this book was when there was a ceasefire in gun-related incidents in our country. This lull never came. We thought the Covid-19 pandemic lockdowns, fewer people on city streets and most businesses closed would bring this on naturally. We were wrong. Every time, we thought there was much-needed peace and tranquility—grief and sadness followed. Between Thanksgiving of 2021 and the 2022 New Year, as we began finalizing the manuscript, a 15-year-old was being charged with the killing of four classmates at his Michigan high school. Along with his mother, his father, who had just bought the 9mm Sig Sauer pistol their kid used at a Black Friday special, was being charged with involuntary manslaughter for failing to prevent this tragedy from happening. Within days, in Colorado, a drive-by shooting wounded six students at a high school. Before the end of 2021, in Ohio, a dad shot dead his teenage daughter after mistaking her for an intruder.

The racial and age demographics are alarming! The Children's Defense Fund reports that African American children and teenagers were four times more likely than whites to be fatally shot. *USA Today* reports that for kids ages 11 and younger, gun violence deaths in 2020 were up 50 percent over the year before. Overall numbers for children were also up for 2021 at the time of this writing. According to the Pew Research Center, National Safety Council, University of California–Davis, and Violence Policy Center, six-in-ten gun-related deaths in the U.S. were suicides. Thus, it is not surprising that the United States breaks gun violence records year after year.

Guided by the Second Amendment, the responses to gun safety vary across states given their unique cultures, experiences, and practices. On one end of the spectrum are California, New Jersey, Massachusetts, Hawaii, and New York, which have enacted the most restrictive regulations in the nation. While at the other end, Arizona, Idaho, Alaska, Kansas, and Oklahoma have the least restrictive policies. Passionate discussions revolve around the Right-to-Carry, access to "Black Rifles," excessive use-of-force, Castle Doctrine, and more as we demonstrated here.

It was an honor for us to prepare this reference book on guns and public safety for citizens, public officials, businesses, and students, to help them understand the details and complexity of this important subject. We hope that this leads to new and better life saving messaging, actions, advocacies, activism, and justice.

We hope that everyone has a great read from this book on the evolving and dynamic topic of our Second Amendment Rights for a safer America!

PART I

Introduction

1. Second Amendment*

Emily Costa

As perhaps the most iconic Amendment to the Constitution, America's right to bear arms may be the most cited Amendment of the last 20 years. We all know it, so I will not quote it or restate it here. As my lens is a historical one, I see no real confusion as to the founder's intention and to the technology at the time of its writing. Today however, there is something very wrong with our relationship to guns and our American society.

We always look to see the good in people. Why? Is it because we assume humans are innately bad? The right to self-protection is inalienable and should be. The right to be fearful is human. The right to inflict carnage is a weakness of our species. Historically, we have never been able to escape this. Throughout the context of time, our species has been at war with one another over ideas, which are usually outdated. There has never been peace on earth, not once.

I feel some level of fear every day, as I'm sure everyone does. I am not sure if the media makes this worse or if I am hypersensitive. I strongly fear the future of our Democracy and the lives of the residents that will inhabit it. I am happy we are becoming more inclusive and eco-conscious, but I worry deeply about our country's mental integrity and how it affects everyone living here.

What is bizarre and unprecedented is why children are walking into schools and killing other children with reckless abandon. These are not personal disputes being handled with a deadly weapon—these are just randomized acts of terror meant to cause shock and panic. For years, I've blamed the weapons. I really felt that gun availability was responsible. But now, I am starting to feel our society must hold some blame as well. Children have been shooting their parents weapons, but this is a new phenomenon. It happens primarily in America and has lasted for a twenty-year period. It is mostly white boys who commit the act, and they are mostly from the middle class.

Someone close to me recently said "it's hard for men because there's no new territory to conquer." I haven't forgotten this because I thought it was strange. I have never entertained that thought before. The concept that our lackluster world is over-explored, that there is nothing new out there.... It brings me to my original point about our species. Perhaps our human need for violence bears some responsibility for the epidemic of school shootings. Maybe these boys felt bored and unheard too, so they decided to inflict pain on others. Our species' past does not make this sound impossible.

*Originally published as Emily Costa, "Second Amendment," *PA Times*, https://patimes.org/second-amendment/ (March 23, 2018). Reprinted with permission of the publisher.

5

The post–World War II decades were good to most of us. Middle class kids got TV's and many pairs of shoes. They had plenty to eat and parents who indulged them more times than they didn't. Generation X and Millennials have grown up with some hiccups, but they've never had it too bad. They generally go to school and graduate. They have never been drafted into the military. They also have had a lot of support from their families without too far to fall when they're in trouble.

I had a conversation about adversity the other day and what it means to personality development. We were talking about our own experiences, people who have it worse and people who've had it better. What we realized is that sometimes adversity makes people great, or more creative, or leaders. There is something to be said for how our minds develop when we are facing difficult choices. A person who has never paid a heating bill cannot understand why another wouldn't just turn up the thermostat, or why someone begging for money just doesn't get a job. A child that has never seen real violence doesn't understand what killing unarmed classmates really means. I gather that when they do, they usually commit suicide.

School shootings aren't directly caused by any one problem facing American kids. They are caused by a portfolio of problems that have infested American society and the people living here. Technology and our settlement into the industrial, digital world has led to many unexpected consequences. We are both hyper-stimulated and bored, all from the comfort of our living rooms. It is also hard to manage the concept of human evolution when we are still killing people over ideas and hurt feelings. Generation X was the first generation to watch film representation of the trials of being a teenager. Millennials, myself included, still swoon over these today. Characters from movies like Pretty in Pink define teenage angst and embarrassment in a way that is relevant years later. Kids today have a lot to overcome. Still, I would like to believe they can turn their awkward teenage years into roots from which they grow from instead of platforms from which they kill from.

2. Most Americans Believe We Should Have Gun Regulation*

Ann Christiano *and* Annie Neimand

There is a segment of the American population who believes passionately that guns are critical for personal protection against both violent individuals and governmental intrusion. They believe nothing should prevent them from getting the guns they need to do that.

There is another, larger group of Americans who believes passionately that we have created an environment that makes it far too easy for those who intend to kill to have access to all the firepower they want.

How could groups who hold these disparate views ever agree?

What's more: If most Americans believe we should have some gun regulation, why are those who don't winning the debate?

People on each side agree the threat from violence is real, but support different responses to that threat—either regulate the sale of guns or make sure a gun is in the hand of every good guy.

Winning Hearts and Minds

According to Pew Research Center, "50 percent say it is more important to control gun ownership, just slightly more than the 47 percent who say it is more important to protect the right of Americans to own guns." However, 92 percent of Americans agree that there should be background checks for gun buyers. These numbers reveal a country deeply conflicted about the role guns play in keeping us safe.

No one wants to see more lives lost, and both sides make a case for public safety. Yet the discussion in support of commonsense gun laws tends to be shrouded in numbers, infographics, case studies and stories of lives lost, while those opposed make their case with powerful messages about threats to personal safety and liberty—messages that tap into cultural significance they associate with guns, as well as how they see themselves and their world.

---

*Originally published as Ann Christiano and Annie Neimand, "Most Americans Believe We Should Have Gun Regulation. Here Is Why Those Who Don't Are Winning the Debate," *The Conversation*, https://theconversation.com/most-americans-believe-we-should-have-gun-regulation-here-is-why-those-who-dont-are-winning-the-debate-61251 (July 4, 2016). Reprinted with permission of the publisher.

Jonathan Haidt, a moral psychologist, says in his book The Righteous Mind that people form beliefs not through careful consideration of evidence but with gut emotional reactions to experience. They seek facts that justify their beliefs.

This means that people's beliefs about gun control are founded not in their careful consideration of available data, but in how they see the world.

At the University of Florida, we're building a curriculum and an emerging discipline called public interest communications that will help movement builders do their work more effectively. We bring together scholars, change makers and funders at an annual gathering called frank where people share the best of what they know about how to drive positive social change that reflects what the science tells us is in the public's interest.

Effective, strategic communication in the public's interest must be based in research. We spend our time digging for the best science that can help people driving change do so better.

One of the major themes that we have found in literature across a range of disciplines is the importance of cultural worldviews in building support for an issue.

Moral and social psychologists have studied how worldviews—cultural values, norms and how an individual sees the world—affect people's perspectives on politically charged issues like gun control. What they are finding is that your worldviews—more than your race, your gender, if and how you pray, how much money you have, where you're from or how you vote—are the single most accurate predictor of how you feel about guns.

Different Worldviews

Researchers have discovered that people who are more liberal tend to support solutions framed with language of equality and protection from harm.

People who are more conservative tend to support solutions when they are presented in the context of protection for themselves and their families, respect for authority and preserving what is sacred.

This gulf isn't limited to gun control. It holds up across a range of issues from climate change to marriage equality to health care.

In one study, Donald Braman and Dan Kahan wanted to see if cultural worldviews influenced beliefs about who should have access to guns.

They built two scales to measure participants' worldviews:

The first assessed how much participants were inclined toward a hierarchical worldview, defined by deference to and respect for authority, or an egalitarian worldview, defined by distrust of social hierarchies and support for social equality.

The second scale assessed how inclined participants were toward an individualist worldview, defined by reverence for individual self-reliance, or a solidaric worldview, defined by valuing the good of a community over individual opportunity.

Once they understood participants' worldviews, the researchers examined the influence of those views, as well as factors like religion and geography, on their attitudes toward gun control. They asked questions like whether participants supported a law that would require people to get permits before they could buy guns.

Not surprisingly, those who were more egalitarian and solidaric were more likely to support gun control. Those who were more respectful of authority were twice as likely to oppose gun control. Those who were more individualistic were four times as likely to oppose gun control.

Here is the important part: the participants' views on authority or their individualism were three times more significant than their faith, fear of crime or where they were from. And cultural worldviews were four times more powerful than political affiliation.

While cultural worldviews are not the sole predictor of gun control beliefs, they may influence them more than anything else does. What's important here is that we cannot make assumptions that people who oppose gun control belong to a particular faith, religion, politics or region. Looking at cultural worldviews offers a more promising approach.

In another study from Braman and Kahan, they make the case that arguments based in empirical claims for public safety are destined to fail because they don't tap into the symbolic meaning people associate with guns.

They write:

[G]uns (at least for some) resonate as symbols of "freedom" and "self-reliance," associations that make opposition to gun control cohere with an individualist orientation…. While control opponents see guns as celebrating individual self-sufficiency, control supporters see them as denigrating solidarity: guns are often equated with a hyper masculine or "macho" personal style that many individuals, male as well as female, resent.

In other words, the gun debate is destined to stagnate as long as those waving their empirical evidence in the air continue to ignore the symbolic meaning guns have for so many Americans.

A Positive Example

Here's an example of how one cause got it right: When Brian Sheehan, director of Ireland's Gay Lesbian Equality Network, developed a strategy that led Ireland to be the first country to support marriage equality, he and his team didn't root their message in the values of the people who already supported the issue—values like equality, fairness and social justice. Instead, they built a campaign for a particular audience that would be fundamental to passing the marriage equality referendum: middle-aged, straight men. They crafted a message centered in this particular group's values of equal citizenship and family. Last May, Irish voters passed marriage equality by nearly two to one, making marriage equality real in a country where—just a decade earlier—it was a crime.

Imagine what the world could be like if we approached change by understanding the mindset of those who we hope to affect and engage them by talking about what matters to them. Could such an approach allow us to move forward as a society on the issues that will define us—even one as controversial and emotional as gun control?

3. History of the National Firearms Act*

U.S. Bureau of Alcohol, Tobacco, Firearms and Explosives

1.1.1 The National Firearms Act (NFA) of 1934. The NFA was originally enacted in 1934.[1] Similar to the current NFA, the original Act imposed a tax on the making and transfer of firearms defined by the Act, as well as a special (occupational) tax on persons and entities engaged in the business of importing, manufacturing, and dealing in NFA firearms. The law also required the registration of all NFA firearms with the Secretary of the Treasury. Firearms subject to the 1934 Act included shotguns and rifles having barrels less than 18 inches in length, certain firearms described as "any other weapons," machineguns, and firearm mufflers and silencers.

While the NFA was enacted by Congress as an exercise of its authority to tax, the NFA had an underlying purpose unrelated to revenue collection. As the legislative history of the law discloses, its underlying purpose was to curtail, if not prohibit, transactions in NFA firearms. Congress found these firearms to pose a significant crime problem because of their frequent use in crime, particularly the gangland crimes of that era such as the St. Valentine's Day Massacre. The $200 making and transfer taxes on most NFA firearms were considered quite severe and adequate to carry out Congress' purpose to discourage or eliminate transactions in these firearms. The $200 tax has not changed since 1934.

As structured in 1934, the NFA imposed a duty on persons transferring NFA firearms, as well as mere possessors of unregistered firearms, to register them with the Secretary of the Treasury. If the possessor of an unregistered firearm applied to register the firearm as required by the NFA, the Treasury Department could supply information to State authorities about the registrant's possession of the firearm. State authorities could then use the information to prosecute the person whose possession violated State laws. For these reasons, the Supreme Court in 1968 held in the *Haynes* case that a person prosecuted for possessing an unregistered NFA firearm had a valid defense to the prosecution—the registration requirement imposed on the possessor of an unregistered firearm violated the possessor's privilege from self-incrimination under the Fifth Amendment of the U.S. Constitution.[2] The *Haynes* decision made the 1934 Act virtually unenforceable.

1.1.2 Title II of the Gun Control Act of 1968. Title II amended the NFA to cure the constitutional flaw pointed out in *Haynes*.[3] First, the requirement for possessors of unregistered firearms to register was removed. Indeed, under the amended law, there

*Public document originally published as U.S. Bureau of Alcohol, Tobacco, Firearms and Explosives, "History of the National Firearms Act," https://www.atf.gov/firearms/national-firearms-act-handbook (2021).

is no mechanism for a possessor to register an unregistered NFA firearm already possessed by the person. Second, a provision was added to the law prohibiting the use of any information from an NFA application or registration as evidence against the person in a criminal proceeding with respect to a violation of law occurring prior to or concurrently with the filing of the application or registration.[4] In 1971, the Supreme Court reexamined the NFA in the *Freed* case and found that the 1968 amendments cured the constitutional defect in the original NFA.[5]

Title II also amended the NFA definitions of "firearm" by adding "destructive devices" and expanding the definition of "machinegun."

1.1.3 Firearm Owners' Protection Act. In 1986, this Act amended the NFA definition of "silencer" by adding combinations of parts for silencers and any part intended for use in the assembly or fabrication of a silencer.[6] The Act also amended the GCA to prohibit the transfer or possession of machineguns.[7]Exceptions were made for transfers of machineguns to, or possession of machineguns by, government agencies, and those lawfully possessed before the effective date of the prohibition, May 19, 1986.

Section 1.2 Meaning of Terms. Certain terms and abbreviations used in this book are defined as follows:

1.2.1 "AECA" means the Arms Export Control Act, 22 U.S.C. 2778.

1.2.2 "ATF" means the Bureau of Alcohol, Tobacco, Firearms and Explosives, U.S. Department of Justice.

1.2.3 "ATF Ruling" means a formal ruling published by ATF stating its interpretation of the law and regulations as applied to a specific set of facts.

1.2.4 "CFR" means the Code of Federal Regulations in which Federal firearms regulations are published.

1.2.5 "DIO" means an ATF Director of Industry Operations responsible for regulating the firearms industry within an ATF field division.

1.2.6 "FFL" means a Federal firearms licensee, person or entity having a license to import, manufacture, or deal in firearms under the GCA.

1.2.7 "FTB" means ATF's Firearms Technology Branch.

1.2.8 "GCA" means the Gun Control Act of 1968, 18 U.S.C. Chapter 44.

1.2.9 "NFA" means the National Firearms Act, 26 U.S.C. Chapter 53.

1.2.10 "NFRTR" means the National Firearms Registration and Transfer Record containing the registration of NFA firearms.

1.2.11 "SOT" means a special occupational taxpayer, a person or entity qualified to import, manufacture, or deal in NFA firearms by having paid the special (occupational) tax to do so under the NFA.

1.2.12 "U.S.C." means the United States Code in which Federal firearms laws are codified.

Section 1.3 Administration and Enforcement of Federal Firearms Laws

Until January 24, 2003, authority to administer and enforce Federal firearms laws was the responsibility of the Bureau of ATF within the U.S. Department of the Treasury. As a result of enactment of Section 1111 of the Homeland Security Act of 2002, ATF and its firearms authorities were transferred to the U.S. Department of Justice, effective

January 24, 2003. ATF's name was also changed to the Bureau of Alcohol, Tobacco, Firearms and Explosives. ATF continues to have the authority to administer and enforce Federal firearms laws. The Department of State retained its authority over the enforcement of the export provisions of the AECA that relate to firearms.

Section 1.4 What Are Regulations and Rulings?

1.4.1 Regulations. Regulations interpret the statutes (the law) and explain the procedures for compliance. The Administrative Procedure Act (APA) generally requires agencies to publish proposed regulations in the Federal Register as a notice of proposed rulemaking, giving the public the opportunity to comment on the proposals before they may be issued as final regulations. The APA provides no specific comment period for proposed rules under the NFA.[8] As specifically provided for in the GCA, GCA regulations require a comment period of at least 90 days.[9] An exception in the APA eliminates the need to provide any notice or comment period with respect to AECA regulations. Regulations have the force and effect of law. Courts will uphold a regulation if they find reasonable legal basis for it and if it generally is within the scope of the statute.

1.4.2 Rulings. ATF publishes rulings in its periodic bulletins and posts them on the ATF website. These contain ATF's interpretation of the law and regulations as they pertain to a particular fact situation. Rulings do not have the force and effect of law but may be cited as precedent with respect to substantially similar fact situations. Courts will recognize and apply such rulings if they are determined to correctly interpret the law and regulations.

Section 1.5 Other ATF Publications

1.5.1 ATF's Internet Website. This is the best source for up-to-date information on ATF's firearms administration and enforcement activities, including amendments to the law, rulings, regulations, and open letters to firearms industry members. The website address is http://www.atf.gov.

1.5.2 ATF P 5300.4. This is ATF's publication, "Federal Firearms Regulations Reference Guide."

ATF supplies the publication to all FFLs and SOTs. It contains all Federal firearms laws and regulations (except those pertaining to the firearms and ammunition excise tax and State Department export regulations), ATF firearms rulings, articles on various firearms issues, and questions and answers. The publication can be found on ATF's website, http://www.atf.gov, and downloaded.

Section 1.6 ATF Points of Contact

Chief, National Firearms Act Branch
Bureau of Alcohol, Tobacco, Firearms and Explosives 244 Needy Road
Martinsburg, West Virginia 25405

Phone: (304) 616-4500
Fax: (304) 616-4501

Chief, Federal Firearms Licensing Center
Bureau of Alcohol, Tobacco, Firearms and Explosives 244 Needy Road
Martinsburg, West Virginia 25405
Phone: (304) 616-4600 or 1-866-662-2750
Fax: (304) 616-4501 or 1-866-257-2749

Chief, Firearms & Explosives Imports Branch
Bureau of Alcohol, Tobacco, Firearms and Explosives 244 Needy Road
Martinsburg, West Virginia 25405
Phone: (304) 616-4550
Fax: (304) 616-4551

Chief, Firearms Technology Branch
Bureau of Alcohol, Tobacco, Firearms and Explosives 244 Needy Road
Martinsburg, West Virginia 25405
Phone: (304) 260-5476
Fax: (304) 260-1701

Section 1.7 ATF Forms

ATF forms may be ordered from ATF's Distribution Center by use of the Center's order form on ATF's website at http://www.atf.gov. After entering the website, click on "Forms." They may also be obtained by calling the Center at (301) 583-4696 or writing the ATF Distribution Center at 1519 Cabin Branch Drive, Landover, Maryland 20785-3816.

NOTES

1. National Firearms Act, Public Law 474, approved June 26, 1934.
2. Haynes v. U.S., 390 U.S. 85 (1968).
3. Gun Control Act of 1968, Public Law 90-618, approved October 22, 1968.
4. 26 U.S.C. 5848.
5. U.S. v. Freed, 401 U.S. 601 (1971).
6. Firearm Owners' Protection Act, Public Law 99-308, approved May 19, 1986.
7. 18 U.S.C. 922(o).
8. 5 U.S.C. 552.
9. 18 U.S.C. 926(b).

4. What Are "Firearms" Under the National Firearms Act?*

U.S. Bureau of Alcohol, Tobacco, Firearms and Explosives

Section 2.1 Types of NFA Firearms

The NFA defines the specific types of firearms subject to the provisions of the Act. These definitions describe the function, design, configuration and/or dimensions that weapons must have to be NFA firearms. In addition to describing the weapon, some definitions (machine gun, rifle, shotgun, any other weapon) state that the firearm described also includes a weapon that can be readily restored to fire. A firearm that can be readily restored to fire is a firearm that in its present condition is incapable of expelling a projectile by the action of an explosive (or, in the case of a machinegun, will not in its present condition shoot automatically) but which can be restored to a functional condition by the replacement of missing or defective component parts. Please be aware that case law is not specific but courts have held that the "readily restorable" test is satisfied where a firearm can be made capable of renewed automatic operation, even if it requires some degree of skill and the use of tools and parts.

2.1.1 Shotgun. A shotgun is a firearm designed to be fired from the shoulder and designed to use the energy of the explosive in a fixed shotgun shell to fire through a smooth bore either a number of projectiles or a single projectile for each pull of the trigger.[1] A shotgun subject to the NFA has a barrel or barrels of less than 18 inches in length.

The ATF procedure for measuring barrel length is to measure from the closed bolt (or breech-face) to the furthermost end of the barrel or permanently attached muzzle device. Permanent methods of attachment include full-fusion gas or electric steel-seam welding, high-temperature (1100°F) silver soldering, or blind pinning with the pin head welded over. Barrels are measured by inserting a dowel rod into the barrel until the rod stops against the bolt or breech-face. The rod is then marked at the furthermost end of the barrel or permanently attached muzzle device, withdrawn from the barrel, and measured.

2.1.2 Weapon made from a shotgun. A weapon made from a shotgun is a shotgun type weapon that has an overall length of less than 26 inches or a barrel or barrels of less than 18 inches in length.

*Public document originally published as U.S. Bureau of Alcohol, Tobacco, Firearms and Explosives, "What Are 'Firearms' Under the National Firearms Act?," https://www.atf.gov/firearms/national-firearms-act-handbook (2021).

The overall length of a firearm is the distance between the muzzle of the barrel and the rearmost portion of the weapon measured on a line parallel to the axis of the bore.

2.1.3 Rifle. A rifle is a firearm designed to be fired from the shoulder and designed to use the energy of an explosive in a fixed cartridge to fire only a single projectile through a rifled barrel for each single pull of the trigger.[2] A rifle subject to the NFA has a barrel or barrels of less than 16 inches in length.

The ATF procedure for measuring barrel length is to measure from the closed bolt (or breech-face) to the furthermost end of the barrel or permanently attached muzzle device. Permanent methods of attachment include full-fusion gas or electric steel-seam welding, high-temperature (1100°F) silver soldering, or blind pinning with the pin head welded over. Barrels are measured by inserting a dowel rod into the barrel until the rod stops against the bolt or breech-face. The rod is then marked at the furthermost end of the barrel or permanently attached muzzle device, withdrawn from the barrel, and measured.

2.1.4 Weapon made from a rifle. A weapon made from a rifle is a rifle type weapon that has an overall length of less than 26 inches or a barrel or barrels of less than 16 inches in length.

The overall length of a firearm is the distance between the muzzle of the barrel and the rearmost portion of the weapon measured on a line parallel to the axis of the bore.

2.1.5 Any other weapon. Firearms meeting the definition of "any other weapon" are weapons or devices capable of being concealed on the person from which a shot can be discharged through the energy of an explosive. Many "any other weapons" are disguised devices such as pen guns, cigarette lighter guns, knife guns, cane guns and umbrella guns.

Also included in the "any other weapon" definition are pistols and revolvers having smooth bore barrels designed or redesigned to fire a fixed shotgun shell.

While the above weapons are similar in appearance to weapons made from shotguns, they were originally manufactured in the illustrated configuration and are not modified from existing shotguns. As a result, these weapons do not fit within the definition of shotgun[3] or weapons made from a shotgun.[4]

The "any other weapon" definition also includes specifically described weapons with combination shotgun and rifle barrels 12 inches or more but less than 18 inches in length from which only a single discharge can be made from either barrel without manual reloading. The firearm most commonly associated with this portion of the definition is the Marble's Game Getter.

Note: One version of the Marble's Game Getter was produced with 18-inch barrels and a folding shoulder stock. This model of the Game Getter, as manufactured, is not subject to the provisions of the NFA because it has barrels that are 18 inches in length and the overall length of the firearm, with stock extended, is more than 26 inches. *However, if the shoulder stock has been removed from the 18-inch barrel version of the Game Getter, the firearm has an overall length of less than 26 inches and is an NFA weapon.* Specifically, the firearm is classified as a weapon made from a rifle/shotgun.

The "any other weapon" definition excludes weapons designed to be fired from the shoulder that are not capable of firing fixed ammunition or a pistol or revolver having a rifled bore. However, certain alterations to a pistol or revolver, such as the addition of a second vertical handgrip, create a weapon that no longer meets the definition of pistol or revolver.[5] A pistol or revolver modified as described is an "any other weapon" subject to the NFA because the weapon is not designed to be fired when held in one hand.

As stated above, a pistol or revolver having a rifled bore does not meet the definition of "any other weapon" and is not subject to the NFA. It is important to note that any pistol or revolver having a barrel without a rifled bore does not fit within the exclusion and is an "any other weapon" subject to the NFA.

2.1.6 Machinegun. Firearms within the definition of machinegun include weapons that shoot, are designed to shoot, or can be readily restored to shoot, automatically more than one shot without manual reloading by a single function of the trigger.

Of all the different firearms defined as NFA weapons, machineguns are the only type where the receiver of the weapon by itself is an NFA firearm. As a result, it is important that the receiver of a machinegun be properly identified. Many machineguns incorporate a "split" or "hinged" receiver design so the main portion of the weapon can be easily separated into upper and lower sections. Additionally, some machineguns utilize a construction method where the receiver is composed of a number of subassemblies that are riveted together to form the complete receiver.

The following table lists specific models of machineguns incorporating the above designs and the portion of the weapon that has been held to be the receiver. This list is not all-inclusive. For information concerning a split or hinged receiver type machinegun not listed below, contact FTB at (304) 260-1699.

Model	Receiver
Armalite AR10	lower
Armalite AR15 (all variations)	lower
Armalite AR18	lower
Beretta AR70	lower
British L1A1	upper
Browning M1917	right side plate
Browning M1919 (all variations)	right side plate
Browning M2 & M2HB	right side plate
Colt M16 (all variations)	lower
Czech Vz 61	lower
FN FNC	lower

Model	Receiver
FN CAL	upper
FN FAL	upper
French MAT 49	upper
German MP38 & MP40	upper
H&K G3 (all variations)	upper
H&K MP5 (all variations)	upper
IMI UZI	upper
M61 Vulcan	outer housing

Model	Receiver
M134 Minigun	outer housing
Maxim MG08 and 08/15	right side plate
SIG AMT	upper
SIG STG 57	upper
SIG 550 Series (all variations)	upper
Soviet PPsH 41	upper
Soviet PPS 43	upper
Steyr MPi 69	upper
Steyr MPi 81	upper
Thompson submachinegun (all variations)	upper
Vickers water cooled machineguns	right side plate

The "designed to shoot automatically more than one shot without manual reloading by a single function of the trigger" portion of the definition relates to the characteristics of the weapon that permit full automatic fire. ATF has also held that the "designed" definition includes those weapons which have not previously functioned as machineguns but possess design features which facilitate full automatic fire by simple modification or elimination of existing component parts. ATF has published rulings concerning specific firearms classified as machineguns based on this interpretation of the term "designed."[6]

Included within the definition of machinegun is any part designed and intended solely and exclusively, or combination of parts designed and intended, for use in converting a weapon into a machinegun. This portion of the machinegun definition addresses what are commonly referred to as conversion kits. The "any part designed and intended solely and exclusively" language refers to a part that was produced for no other reason than to convert a weapon into a machinegun.

The parts are designed solely and exclusively for use in converting a weapon into a machinegun and are classified as machineguns.

The "combination of parts designed and intended for use in converting a weapon into a machinegun" language refers to a group of parts designed and intended to be used in converting a weapon into a machinegun. A typical example is those M2 carbine parts that are only used to permit fully automatic fire in a U.S. Carbine M1 or M2.

The parts consist of an M2 selector lever, selector lever spring, disconnector lever assembly, M2 disconnector, disconnector spring, disconnector plunger and M2 hammer are classified as a machinegun. These parts are used specifically for fully automatic fire and have no application in a semiautomatic carbine. While other parts such as an M2 sear, operating slide, trigger housing and stock are used in the fully automatic carbine, these parts are also appropriate for use in semiautomatic M1 carbines.[7]

Therefore, the M2 sear, operating slide, trigger housing and stock are not a combination of parts designed and intended for use in converting a weapon into a machinegun. Other commonly encountered conversion kits include modified trigger housings and/or trigger paks for Heckler & Koch (HK) type semiautomatic firearms. As originally manufactured, semiautomatic HK firearms (HK, 41, 43, 91, 93 and SP89) were specifically designed such that they will not accept fully automatic trigger housings or trigger paks for HK selective fire weapons such as the G3 and MP5. If selective fire trigger paks or trigger housings are modified so that they will function with semiautomatic HK firearms, the modified components are classified as parts designed and intended solely and exclusively, or combination of parts designed and intended for use in converting a weapon into a machinegun. These modified parts are also machineguns as defined.

Note: Standard selective fire HK trigger housings and trigger paks as originally manufactured are component parts for machineguns. These unmodified parts, in and of themselves, are not subject to the NFA. However, when adapted to function with a semiautomatic HK firearm the modified parts have been redesigned and are intended for use in converting a weapon into a machinegun.

For the conversion sear to function the trigger or the trigger pak must be modified to increase the rearward travel of the trigger. When the trigger is modified a notch is cut into the trailing leg to provide more travel before the trigger contacts the upper trigger stop. When the trigger pak is modified, the upper trigger stop is either removed or relocated.

Important Note: Should the conversion sear be removed from the trigger pak and the modified pak left in the firearm, the weapon will still be capable of fully automatic fire. Therefore, it is important that registered HK conversion sears be kept with their respective trigger paks. This is particularly important in instances where HK type firearms are sold as being "sear ready" or "sear host guns." If these weapons contain semiautomatic trigger paks modified to function with conversion sears the firearms are capable of fully automatic fire (without the conversion sear) and as such are machineguns as defined.

Concerning the installation of conversion kits in semiautomatic firearms, it must be pointed out that the receiver of the firearm may not be modified to permit fully automatic fire. Such modification results in the making of a machinegun which is prohibited by 18 U.S.C. 922(o).

The definition of machinegun also includes a combination of parts from which a machinegun can be assembled if such parts are in the possession or under the control of a person. An example of a firearm meeting this section of the definition is a semiautomatic AR15 rifle possessed with an M16 bolt carrier, hammer, trigger, disconnector and selector. If the semiautomatic AR15 is assembled with the described M16 parts and the rifle is capable of fully automatic fire, the weapon possessed in conjunction with the M16 parts, whether assembled or not, is a machinegun as defined.[8]

An additional example of a combination of parts from which a machinegun can be assembled is a STEN submachinegun "parts kit" possessed with a length of metal tube to be used as a replacement receiver and instructions for assembling the parts into a functional machinegun. The parts kit as sold does not contain a firearm receiver although remnants of the destroyed receiver may be present. A machinegun parts kit in this condition is not subject to the GCA or the NFA.

Unfinished receiver tubes with instructions and/or templates for use in the assembly of a functional machinegun are also commercially available. These tubes with instructions/templates, in and of themselves, are not subject to the GCA or NFA.

When the parts kit is possessed in conjunction with the above described unfinished receiver tube, a combination of parts from which a machinegun can be assembled exists and is a machinegun as defined.

2.1.7 Silencer. A firearm silencer and a firearm muffler are defined as any device for silencing, muffling, or diminishing the report of a portable firearm.[9] Firearm silencers are generally composed of an outer tube, internal baffles, a front-end cap, and a rear end cap.

The definition of a silencer also includes any combination of parts, designed or redesigned, and intended for use in assembling or fabricating a firearm silencer or firearm muffler.

The following illustration depicts parts that are designed and intended for use in assembling a firearm silencer. Another example of parts redesigned and intended for use in assembling or fabricating a firearm silencer are automotive engine freeze plugs that have been modified by drilling a hole through their center to permit passage of a bullet.

Also included within the silencer definition is any part intended only for use in the assembly or fabrication of a firearm silencer.

Note: The language in the definition of silencer contains no provisions that permit an owner of a registered silencer to possess spare or replacement components for the silencer. However, licensed manufacturers who are SOTs may possess spare silencer components in conjunction with their manufacturing operations.

2.1.8 Destructive device. The destructive device definition contains different categories that address specific types of munitions. Each category describes the devices subject to the definition based on the material contained in the item, the dimensions of the bore of certain weapons, and a combination of parts for use in converting the described items into destructive devices.

2.1.8.1 Explosive devices. The first portion of the definition deals with explosive, incendiary and poison gas munitions. The definition specifies that any explosive, incendiary or poison gas bomb, grenade, mine or similar device is a destructive device. This portion of the definition includes a rocket having a propellant charge of more than four ounces and a missile (projectile) having an explosive or incendiary charge of more than one-quarter ounce.

Note: Missiles (projectiles) less than caliber 20 mm generally are not large enough to accommodate more than one-quarter ounce of explosive or incendiary material. In the case of 20 mm high explosive (HE) or high explosive incendiary (HEI) projectiles, it is imperative to determine the model designation of the specific item as some 20 mm HE and HEI projectiles contain more than one-quarter ounce of explosive or incendiary material and are destructive devices. Other 20 mm HE and HEI projectiles do not contain more than one-quarter ounce of explosive and are not destructive devices. Therefore, it is incumbent upon persons interested in 20 mm HE and HEI ammunition to determine the amount of explosives contained in a specific projectile. HE and HEI missiles (projectiles) larger than 20 mm generally contain more than one-quarter ounce of explosive or incendiary material and are destructive devices.

2.1.8.2 Large caliber weapons. The second section of the definition states that any type of weapon by whatever name known which will, or which may be readily converted to, expel a projectile by the action of an explosive or other propellant, the barrel or barrels of which have a bore diameter of more than one-half inch in diameter is a destructive device. This portion of the definition specifically excludes a shotgun or shotgun shell which the Attorney General finds is generally recognized as particularly suitable for sporting purposes. ATF has issued rulings classifying specific shotguns as destructive devices because they have a bore of more than one half inch in diameter and were found to not be particularly suitable for sporting purposes.[10]

The majority of weapons covered by this portion of the destructive device definition are large caliber military weapons such as rocket launchers, mortars and cannons.

It is important to note that the large caliber firearms covered by this section are defined as weapons that expel a projectile by the action of an explosive or other propellant. This is the only place in the GCA and NFA where a propellant other than an explosive must be considered when classifying a weapon. Examples of weapons having a bore diameter of more than one-half inch in diameter and that expel a projectile by means other than an explosive are mortars that utilize compressed air as a propellant and some rocket launchers.

Certain destructive devices may also meet the definition of machinegun because in addition to having a bore diameter of more than one-half inch the weapons are capable of fully automatic fire. ATF treats NFA firearms of this type as both machineguns and destructive devices. The weapons are coded as machineguns in the NFRTR with an annotation that they are also destructive devices. Any such weapons manufactured on or after May 19, 1986, are subject to 18

U.S.C. 922(o). In instances where a weapon of this type is being transferred, it is imperative that State and local laws where the weapon is being transferred do not prohibit possession of destructive devices or machineguns.

In addition to defining destructive devices, the definition also specifically excludes certain items from that classification. As previously stated, any shotgun or shotgun shell which the Attorney General finds is generally recognized as particularly suitable for sporting purposes is not a destructive device. Additionally, the following items are also excluded from the definition:

- Any device which is neither designed nor redesigned for use as a weapon.
- Any device, although originally designed for use as a weapon, which is redesigned for use as a signaling, pyrotechnic, line throwing, safety or similar device.
- Surplus ordnance sold, loaned or given by the Secretary of the Army pursuant to the provisions of 10 U.S.C. 4684(2), 4685, or 4686.
- Any other device which the Attorney General finds is not likely to be used as a weapon, or is an antique, or is a rifle which the owner intends to use solely for sporting purposes.

It should not be assumed that any device meeting the above descriptions is automatically excluded from the definition of a destructive device. ATF has ruled that certain pyrotechnic devices are destructive devices.[11] ATF should be contacted to confirm the classification of any items that appear to meet the above exclusions. Additionally, many of the items excluded from the definition of destructive device may contain a firearm receiver and would still be a firearm as defined in the GCA.

2.1.9 Unserviceable firearm. An unserviceable firearm is a firearm that is incapable of discharging a shot by the action of an explosive and is incapable of being readily restored to a firing condition. The most common method for rendering a firearm unserviceable, and that recommended by ATF, is to weld the chamber of the barrel closed and weld the barrel to the receiver.[12] The chamber of the barrel should be plug welded closed and all welds should be full fusion, deep penetrating, and gas or electric steel welds. In instances where the above procedure cannot be employed to render a firearm unserviceable, FTB should be contacted for alternate methods.

It is important to remember that rendering a firearm unserviceable does not remove it from the definition of an NFA firearm. An unserviceable NFA firearm is still subject to the import, registration, and transfer provisions of the NFA. However, there is no tax imposed on the transfer of an unserviceable firearm as a "curio or ornament." See 26 U.S.C. 5852(e).

Note: "curio or ornament" is only descriptive of unserviceable firearms transferred exempt from transfer tax. An unserviceable firearm transferred as a "curio or ornament" is not necessarily a "curio or relic" firearm for purposes of the GCA unless the weapon is classified as a curio or relic under the GCA. For further information on curio or relic classification see section 2.2.

Section 2.2 Antique firearms. Firearms defined by the NFA as "antique firearms" are not subject to any controls under the NFA.[13] The NFA defines antique firearms based on their date of manufacture and the type of ignition system used to fire a projectile. Any firearm manufactured in or before 1898 that is not designed or redesigned for using rimfire or conventional center fire ignition with fixed ammunition is an antique firearm. Additionally, any firearm using a matchlock, flintlock, percussion cap or similar type ignition system, irrespective of the actual date of manufacture of the firearm, is also an antique firearm.

NFA firearms using fixed ammunition are antique firearms only if the weapon was actually manufactured in or before 1898 and the ammunition for the firearm is no longer manufactured in the United States and is not readily available in the ordinary channels of commercial trade. To qualify as an antique firearm, a fixed cartridge firing NFA weapon must meet both the age and ammunition availability standards of the definition.

Concerning ammunition availability, it is important to note that a specific type of fixed ammunition that has been out of production for many years may again become available due to increasing interest in older firearms. Therefore, the classification of a specific NFA firearm as an antique can change if ammunition for the weapon becomes readily available in the ordinary channels of commercial trade.

Section 2.3 Curios or relics. Curios or relics are firearms that are of special interest to collectors.[14] NFA firearms can be classified as curios or relics under the same criteria used to classify conventional firearms as curios or relics.[15]

An NFA firearm that is recognized as a curio or relic is still an NFA "firearm" and is still subject to the registration and transfer provisions of the NFA. The primary impact of a curio or relic classification is that a properly registered NFA firearm classified as a curio or relic may be lawfully transferred interstate to, or received interstate by, a person licensed as a collector of curios or relics under the GCA.

Section 2.4 Applications to Remove Firearms from the Scope of the NFA as Collector's Items

Certain NFA weapons can be removed from the provisions of the NFA as collector's items.[16] The procedures for requesting removal of an NFA firearm are the same as used for requesting a destructive device determination.[17] An NFA firearm removed from the NFA as a collector's item is no longer subject to any of the provisions of the NFA. In most cases, the weapon will still be a firearm as defined in the GCA and subject to regulation under the GCA. In some situations, the weapon that is removed from the NFA as a collector's item will be an antique firearm as defined in the GCA.[18] In these instances, the weapon would no longer be a firearm as defined in Federal law.

The Attorney General does not have the authority to remove a machinegun or a destructive device from the provisions of the NFA as collector's items.[19] Therefore, applications to remove machineguns or destructive devices from the NFA as collector's items cannot be approved.

Section 2.5 Removal of Firearms from the Scope of the NFA by Modification/Elimination of Components

Firearms, except machineguns and silencers, that are subject to the NFA fall within the various definitions due to specific features. If the particular feature that causes a firearm to be regulated by the NFA is eliminated or modified, the resulting weapon is no longer an NFA weapon.

For example, a shotgun with a barrel length of 15 inches is an NFA weapon. If the 15-inch barrel is removed and disposed of, the remaining firearm is not subject to the NFA because it has no barrel. Likewise, if the 15-inch barrel is modified by permanently attaching an extension such that the barrel length is at least 18 inches and the overall length of the weapon is at least 26 inches, the modified firearm is not subject to the NFA.

Note: An acceptable method for permanently installing a barrel extension is by gas or electric steel seam welding or the use of high temperature silver solder having a flow point of 1100 degrees Fahrenheit.

A shot pistol ("any other weapon") such as an H&R Handy Gun may be removed from the NFA by either disposing of the smooth bore barrel or permanently installing a rifled sleeve chambered to accept a standard pistol cartridge into the smooth bore barrel. Modified by sleeving the barrel, an H&R Handy Gun is no longer an NFA weapon because it now has a rifled bore.

Large caliber destructive devices that are not also machineguns can be removed from the NFA by disposing of the barrel. If the barrel of a 37 mm cannon is removed and disposed of, the remaining weapon has no barrel or bore diameter. As an alternative, the barrel of a destructive device may be functionally destroyed. To destroy the barrel of a destructive device the following operations must be performed:

- Cut a hole, equal to the diameter of the bore, on a 90-degree angle to the axis of the bore, through one side of the barrel in the high pressure (chamber) area.
- Weld the barrel to the receiver of the weapon.
- Weld an obstruction into the barrel to prevent the introduction of a round of ammunition.

2.5.1 Removal of machineguns and silencers from the scope of the NFA. Machineguns are defined to include the receiver of a machinegun and the definition of silencer includes each component of a silencer. Therefore, to remove these weapons from the provisions of the NFA, the receiver of a machinegun or all the components of a silencer must be destroyed.

The preferred method for destroying a machinegun receiver is to completely sever the receiver in specified locations by means of a cutting torch that displaces at least one-quarter inch of material at each cut location. ATF has published rulings concerning the preferred destruction of specific machineguns.[20]

A machinegun receiver may also be properly destroyed by means of saw cutting and disposing of certain removed portions of the receiver. To ensure that the proposed saw cutting of a particular machinegun receiver is acceptable, FTB should be contacted for guidance and approval of any alternative destruction proposal. *Note: a machinegun receiver that is not properly destroyed may still be classified as a machinegun, particularly in instances where the improperly destroyed receiver is possessed in conjunction with other component parts for the weapon.*

A silencer may be destroyed by completely severing each component by means of a cutting torch that has a tip of sufficient size to displace at least one-quarter inch of material at each cut location.

Concerning the outer tube(s) of a silencer, these components may be destroyed by crushing them flat in lieu of cutting with a torch.

Anyone interested in destroying an NFA weapon by means other than described above should contact FTB to discuss possible alternatives.

NOTES

1. 26 U.S.C. 5845(d).
2. 26 U.S.C. 5845(c).
3. 26 U.S.C. 5845(d).
4. 26 U.S.C. 5845(a)(2).
5. 27 CFR 479.11.
6. Appendix B (ATF Rulings 82-2, 82-8, 83-5).
7. TM9-1267, Cal. .30 Carbines M1, M1A1, M2, and M3, United States Government Printing Office, 1953.
8. ATF P 5300.4 (9/05), Federal Firearms Regulations Reference Guide—2005, p. 155.
9. 18 U.S.C. 921(a)(24).
10. Appendix B (ATF Rulings 94-1, 94-2).
11. Appendix B (ATF Ruling 95-3).
12. ATF Form 5 (5320.5), Instruction 6a.
13. 26 U.S.C. 5845(a), (g).
14. 27 CFR 478.11.
15. 27 CFR 478.26.
16. 26 U.S.C. 5845(a).
17. 27 CFR 479.24-479.25.
18. 18 U.S.C. 921(a)(16).
19. 26 U.S.C. 5845(a).
20. Appendix B (ATF Rulings 2003–1, 2003–2, 2003–3, 2003–4).

5. Quantifying the Social Cost of Firearms

A New Approach to Gun Control*

Timothy M. Smith

Another week in America, another week of sadness and hand-wringing prompted by gun violence.

While the most recent incidents are tinged by race, they also point to a country awash in guns and the too many deaths that result from their use (or abuse). But are these shootings any more likely to lead to some kind of meaningful action to address the problem?

Unfortunately, probably not. As long as the debate continues to be one of constitutionality (the right to bear arms) and control (regulation), little meaningful change is likely to address the 16 million new guns entering the U.S. market each year or the nearly 34,000 annual gun deaths.

A new dialogue is desperately needed among policymakers and the public. And it could begin by shifting our focus away from the regulation of guns toward understanding (and mitigating) the social costs of firearm fatalities.

My research examines ways to assess the social, environmental and health effects of new technologies to inform policymakers and companies. Though my focus at the University of Minnesota is on sustainability, similar analyses may also be useful for the political debate over gun control.

Firearm Fatalities

The current congressional debate focuses on the most violent actors (terrorists or those whose background check may not check out) and the most lethal guns (military-style rifles)—not necessarily the deadliest guns or those creating the greatest risks to society.

Despite the headlines, most guns never kill anyone, and military-style rifles are some of the least frequently used guns in firearm deaths. Each year, fewer than one firearm-related death occurs in the U.S. for every 10,000 guns in circulation, or 33,636 fatalities for an estimated 357 million guns. And about two-thirds of those deaths are suicides.

*Originally published as Timothy M. Smith, "Quantifying the Social Cost of Firearms: A New Approach to Gun Control," *The Conversation*, https://theconversation.com/quantifying-the-social-cost-of-firearms-a-new-approach-to-gun-control-62148 (July 13, 2016). Reprinted with permission of the publisher.

Gun deaths associated with mass shootings have surged dramatically in recent years, but are still rare compared with other gun violence. In just the first four months of 2016, 70 mass shootings have been reported (more than all of 2015), with 129 victim fatalities, according to Stanford University's Mass Shootings in America. Adding in Orlando and Dallas, mass shooting deaths in the first half of 2016 equal those of 2015 and are four times the annual average in recent years.

While this is alarming, such deaths represent just a fraction of the number of firearm-related homicides, about 1.6 percent. And military-style rifles were used in just 10 of the 136 mass shootings reported since January 2015.

Any policy to reduce the likelihood of these events should, therefore, reflect the very small probability of a military-style rifle being used in a mass shooting that targets the public—just one in 575,000 (about 50 deaths out of about 29 million rifles).

New regulation would need to be very restrictive. Millions of these guns would have to be removed from circulation to see any measurable effect on public safety, a politically impossible lift.

Price Tag of Saving a Life

A potential reframing of the issue might be to estimate the social cost of gun deaths, establish the burden borne by each weapon and seek policies that reflect it in the market for firearms.

Across many different areas of government, this kind of analysis is applied all the time when examining the benefits and costs of potential policies. When considering food handling or tracking systems, benefits of reducing the risk of illness and premature death are compared with the costs of implementing the policy. Policies to reduce harmful pollution, improve the safety of automobiles or add bicycle lanes to roads are evaluated in similar ways.

To get at a social cost of mortality, measures have been developed to assess how much people are willing to pay for small reductions in their risks of dying. In aggregate, these values are referred to as the "value of a statistical life" (VSL).

This is not how much an actual individual life is worth, but it is an estimate of how much, in total, a large group of people would be willing to pay to save one statistical life. For example, if the average response from a sample of 100,000 people indicated a willingness to pay US$100 to reduce their risk of dying by 0.001 percent, than the VSL would be $10,000,000. So, the total economic cost of mortality in a particular year equals the VSL times the number of premature deaths. Similarly, the economic benefit of a mitigating action becomes the same VSL multiplied by the number of lives saved.

That said, different federal agencies use various valuation methods and assumption. The Environmental Protection Agency's adjusted VSL for 2013 is $9.4 million, the Department of Transportation set its 2013 base year value at $9.1 million and the Department of Agriculture provides a midpoint estimate of $8.66 million.

From a purely economic perspective, the social costs of gun deaths likely exceed $300 billion annually. This is a staggering number, more than what the federal government spent on Medicaid in the same year. And that's not including the more than 80,000 nonfatal firearm injuries each year.

A Gun's Burden

Identifying guns' overall mortality risk burden doesn't exactly help inform legislation targeting certain types of guns used in certain types of homicides.

But, based on the previous analysis of military-style rifles used in mass shootings, these guns (in these situations) are some of the least costly from a VSL perspective. In fact, the social burden of a single military-style rifle is likely to be as little as $15.77 a year (or $455 million for all rifles based on 50 deaths and a $9.1 million VSL).

It is hard to see how this valuation could deter gun sales enough, or support the implementation of a robust screening and background check system, to make a difference. By comparison, handguns—which are implicated in nearly 70 percent of gun-related homicides—bear a disproportionate burden on society of $401 annually per handgun in circulation.

Policies reducing the burden of gun deaths (e.g., by reducing the number of guns or improving their safety) need to be compared against the additional costs of implementing them. These costs could come as regulations, increased taxes/fees or price increases.

In other words, applying a mortality risk valuation to handguns might cost as much every year as the initial cost to the gun owner. In the current climate, any form of tax or fee approaching this valuation would be a political nonstarter.

A Way Forward

So, if this analysis leads to societal burdens that are both so low (the case of rifles) and so high (the case of handguns) that neither are politically viable, one can easily understand the paralysis in Congress.

The automobile insurance market, where risks are pooled across geographies, types of vehicles and driving behavior, may provide some insights and a way forward.

Similar to guns, nearly 250 million personal vehicles (or their drivers) were associated with 27,507 deaths in 2013. These premature fatalities tally social costs of $250 billion.

A closer look at translating a social burden into a liability premium. CDC, FBI, Author provided

For illustrative purposes, if we assume that half of these damages are associated with no-fault third parties, the social burden for non-policy-holder deaths might be about $502 per vehicle, on average.

Unlike with guns, a robust system of vehicle registration and mandatory insurance requirements exists in this market. If we also assume that about half of each auto's liability policy (estimated at $519 in 2013) covers bodily injuries (not property), these insurance premiums represent about half of each vehicle's societal burden.

I'm not suggesting that these premiums are effective deterrents to poor driving or cover all an accident's damages to society. Rather, incorporating the external costs of mortality risks into the cost of ownership alters the number of cars on the road and how they are used.

Applying this relationship to firearms, an annual social price tag of $140 per gun might go a long way toward mitigating the mortality costs of gun-related homicide. This estimate is a weighted average of different types of guns, ranging from $15/year for rifles to $200/year for handguns.

Nobody likes new taxes or additional fees, and the gun lobby will certainly oppose even the hint of a disincentive on gun ownership. But there may be enough Republican and Democrat lawmakers open to the idea of market-based policies that don't directly restrict gun access, progressively impose higher costs to more dangerous guns and generate resources to improve the safety and security associated with guns in America.

Gun Reform Doesn't Have to Be Gun Control

This back-of-the-napkin analysis may be crude, but it does highlight the need and potential for shifting current arguments away from regulating guns to mitigating the social costs of gun-related deaths.

The devil is always in the details, and important debates will be needed around the imposition of new taxes, registration fees or mandatory insurance. It is unclear who should be affected (owners, retailers, manufacturers) or how to include all of the estimated 357 million guns in the U.S., not just the registered ones.

Policymakers should even consider the impact of these types of economic mechanisms on equity of gun ownership—maybe gun subsidies would be needed for low-income or first-time gun buyers. Most importantly, policymakers should have much-needed arguments about how to reduce gun deaths.

An $140 annual registration fee, applied only to the 23.1 million guns transacted each year, could generate over $3.2 billion in revenues annually. If nothing else, these resources could bolster local police and security budgets, improve access to gun safety training and education, incentivize new technologies that make guns less dangerous and compensate victims' families.

Anything to break the logjam and actually address the real costs of gun violence.

6. Analysis

I Was a Teenage Rifle Owner, Then an ER Doctor: Assault Weapons Shouldn't Count as "Guns"*

ELISABETH ROSENTHAL

Many who know me might be shocked by this: I shot my first pistol when I was 8 or 9, taught by my father, a physician, aiming at targets in our basement. At summer camp, I loved riflery the way some kids loved art. Staring through the sight, down the barrel, I proved an excellent shot, gathering ever more advanced medals from the National Rifle Association. As a reward, for my 13th birthday, my uncle gave me a .22 Remington rifle.

I did not grow up on a farm or in a dangerous place where we needed protection. I grew up in the well-off, leafy suburb of Scarsdale, New York.

When I entered high school in the 1970s, I joined the riflery team and often slung my cased gun over my shoulder on my mile-long walk to school for practice. It didn't seem dissonant that, on other mornings, I went to the train station to join protests against the Vietnam War.

Since then, the United States has undergone a cultural, definitional, practical shift on guns and what they are for.

Once mostly associated in the public mind with sport, guns in the United States are now widely regarded more as weapons to maim or kill—or to protect from the same. Guns used to be on a continuum with bows and arrows; now they seem better lumped in with grenades, mortars and bombs.

In the 1990s, by which time I was an emergency room doctor at a Level 1 trauma center in New York City, I became acquainted with the damage that small-caliber handguns could cause. When I started treating gunshot victims, I marveled at how subtle and clean the wounds often were, externally at least. Much cleaner than stabbings or car wreck injuries.

We searched for a tiny entrance wound and the larger exit wound; they were often subtle and hard to locate. If you couldn't find the latter, you would often see the tiny metal bullet, or fragments, lodged somewhere internally on an X-ray—often not worth retrieving because it was doing no damage.

These were people shot in muggings or in drug deals gone wrong. Most of these

*Originally published as Elisabeth Rosenthal, "Analysis: I Was a Teenage Rifle Owner, Then an ER Doctor. Assault Weapons Shouldn't Count as 'Guns,'" *Kaiser Health News*, April 14, 2021. Reprinted with permission of the publisher. *Kaiser Health News* is a nonprofit news service covering health issues. It is an editorially independent program of the Kaiser Family Foundation that is not affiliated with Kaiser Permanente.

patients had exploratory surgery, but so long as the bullet had not hit a vital organ or major vessel, people survived.

No one was blown apart.

An assault-style weapon was allegedly used last month to kill 10 people in a Boulder, Colorado, supermarket, just as one has been used in more than a dozen mass-casualty shootings, leaving four or more people dead, since 2017.

Guns and the devastating injuries they cause have evolved into things I don't recognize anymore. My Remington .22 has about as much in common with an assault-style weapon as an amoeba has with a human life. The injuries they produce don't belong under one umbrella of "gun violence." Though both crimes are heinous, the guy who shoots someone with an old pistol in a mugging is a different kind of perpetrator from the person who, dressed in body armor, carries a semiautomatic weapon into a theater, house of worship or school and commences a slaughter.

Certainly many American gun owners—maybe a majority of them—are still interested in skill and the ability to hit the bull's-eye of a target (or a duck or deer, if you're of the hunting persuasion). But the adrenaline in today's gun culture clearly lies in paramilitary posturing, signaling to the world the ability to bring mayhem and destruction. Add a twisted mind with the urge to actually bring mayhem and destruction, and tragedy awaits.

Before Congress passed an assault weapons ban in 1994, Americans owned about 400,000 AR-15s, the most popular of these military-style weapons. Today, 17 years after Congress failed to reauthorize the ban, Americans own about 20 million AR-15-style rifles or similar weapons.

Why this change in the nature of gun ownership? Was it because 9/11 made the world a much scarier place? Was it NRA scaremongering about the Second Amendment? The advent of violent video games?

Now, not just emergency rooms but also schools and offices stage active-shooter drills. When I was an ER doctor, we, too, practiced disaster drills. A bunch of surrogate patients would be wheeled in, daubed with fake blood. Those drills seem naive in 2021—we never envisioned the kinds of mass-shooting disasters that have now become commonplace.

And, frankly, no disaster drill really prepares an emergency room for a situation in which multiple people are shot with today's semiautomatic weapons. You might save a few people with careful triage and preparation. Most just die.

I gave up riflery as a teenager when other options—boys, movies, travel—came along. Maybe I'll take it up again someday, if assault-style weaponry is banned and the word "gun" again brings to mind sport and not a spinoff of war.

Part II

Challenges and Solutions

• A. *Federal Safety Regulations* •

7. Project Guardian and Project Safe Neighborhoods*

U.S. DEPARTMENT OF JUSTICE

Project Guardian is an initiative started in November 2019 designed to reduce gun violence and enforce federal firearms laws across the country.

Reducing gun violence and enforcing federal firearms laws have always been among the Department's highest priorities. In order to develop a new and robust effort to promote and ensure public safety, the Department reviewed and adapted some of the successes of past strategies to curb gun violence. Project Guardian draws on the Department's earlier achievements, such as the "Triggerlock" program, and it serves as a complementary effort to the success of Project Safe Neighborhoods (PSN). In addition, the initiative emphasizes the importance of using all modern technologies available to law enforcement to promote gun crime intelligence.

"Gun crime remains a pervasive problem in too many communities across America. Today, the Department of Justice is redoubling its commitment to tackling this issue through the launch of Project Guardian," said Attorney General William P. Barr. "Building on the success of past programs like Triggerlock, Project Guardian will strengthen our efforts to reduce gun violence by allowing the federal government and our state and local partners to better target offenders who use guns in crimes and those who try to buy guns illegally."

Project Guardian's implementation is based on five principles:

- **Coordinated Prosecution.** Federal prosecutors and law enforcement will coordinate with state, local, and tribal law enforcement and prosecutors to consider potential federal prosecution for new cases involving a defendant who: (a) was arrested in possession of a firearm; (b) is believed to have used a firearm in committing a crime of violence or drug trafficking crime prosecutable in federal court; or (c) is suspected of actively committing violent crime(s) in the community on behalf of a criminal organization.
- **Enforcing the Background Check System.** United States Attorneys, in

---

*Public document originally published as U.S. Department of Justice, "Project Guardian and Project Safe Neighborhoods," https://www.justice.gov/archives/ag/about-project-guardian (May 26, 2021).

consultation with the Special Agent in Charge of the Bureau of Alcohol, Tobacco, Firearms and Explosives (ATF) in their district, will create new, or review existing, guidelines for intake and prosecution of federal cases involving false statements (including lie-and-try, lie-and-buy, and straw purchasers) made during the acquisition or attempted acquisition of firearms from Federal Firearms Licensees. Particular emphasis is placed on individuals convicted of violent felonies or misdemeanor crimes of domestic violence, individuals subject to protective orders, and individuals who are fugitives where the underlying offense is a felony or misdemeanor crime of domestic violence; individuals suspected of involvement in criminal organizations or of providing firearms to criminal organizations; and individuals involved in repeat denials.

- **Improved Information Sharing.** On a regular basis, and as often as practicable given current technical limitations, ATF will provide to state law enforcement fusion centers a report listing individuals for whom the National Instant Criminal Background Check System (NICS) has issued denials, including the basis for the denial, so that state and local law enforcement can take appropriate steps under their laws.

- **Coordinated Response to Mental Health Denials.** Each United States Attorney will ensure that whenever there is federal case information regarding individuals who are prohibited from possessing a firearm under the mental health prohibition, such information continues to be entered timely and accurately into the United States Attorneys' Offices' case-management system for prompt submission to NICS. ATF should engage in additional outreach to state and local law enforcement on how to use this denial information to better assure public safety. Additionally, United States Attorneys will consult with relevant district stakeholders to assess feasibility of adopting disruption of early engagement programs to address mental-health-prohibited individuals who attempt to acquire a firearm. United States Attorneys should consider, when appropriate, recommending court-ordered mental health treatment for any sentences issued to individuals prohibited based on mental health.

- **Crime Gun Intelligence Coordination.** Federal, state, local, and tribal prosecutors and law enforcement will work together to ensure effective use of the ATF's Crime Gun Intelligence Centers (CGICs), and all related resources, to maximize the use of modern intelligence tools and technology. These tools can greatly enhance the speed and effectiveness in identifying trigger-pullers and finding their guns, but the success depends in large part on state, local, and tribal law enforcement partners sharing ballistic evidence and firearm recovery data with the ATF. Federal law enforcement represents only about 15 percent of all law enforcement resources nationwide. Therefore, partnerships with state, local, and tribal law enforcement and the communities they serve are critical to addressing gun crime. The Department recognizes that sharing information with our state, local, and tribal law enforcement partners at every level will enhance public safety, and provide a greater depth of resources available to address gun crime on a national level.

Project Safe Neighborhoods (PSN) is a nationwide commitment to reduce gun and gang crime in America by networking existing local programs that target these issues and providing these programs with additional tools necessary to be successful. Project

Safe Neighborhoods has operated as the U.S. Department of Justice's primary initiative focused on the reduction of gun crime and gang-related violence since May of 2001.

Since its inception, approximately $2 billion has been committed to this initiative. This funding is being used to hire new federal and state prosecutors, support investigators, provide training, distribute gun lock safety kits, deter juvenile gun crime, and develop and promote community outreach efforts as well as to support other gun and gang violence reduction strategies.

Building upon successful proven programs of the past, such as Boston's Ceasefire Project, Richmond's Project Exile, and the Ten-City Strategic Approaches to Community Safety Initiative (SACSI), PSN is a nationwide, community-based effort that combines prevention and deterrence strategies with increased federal prosecution of serious offenders. When it was initiated, PSN focused on federal firearms offenders, and was expanded in 2006 to include violent street gangs. The current PSN strategy focuses on both the eradication of illegal firearms and the interdiction of violent gang activity.

There are five core components to the PSN strategy: strategic planning, partnerships, training, outreach and accountability. Initially, PSN was designed to increase partnerships among federal, state, and local law enforcement agencies through the formation of a local gun crime enforcement task force. Additional partnerships were established with local governments, social service providers, and community groups to increase resources for prevention efforts, as well as to increase the legitimacy of law enforcement interventions.

The Eastern District of California is committed to PSN as part of its larger anti-violent crime strategy and is actively involved in task forces and prosecutions throughout the district.

Operation Relentless Pursuit

Today, December 18, 2019, Attorney General William P. Barr announced the launch of Operation Relentless Pursuit, an initiative aimed at combating violent crime in seven of America's most violent cities through a surge in federal resources.

Joined at a press conference in Detroit, Michigan, by Bureau of Alcohol, Tobacco, Firearms and Explosives (ATF) Acting Director Regina Lombardo, Drug Enforcement Administration (DEA) Acting Administrator Uttam Dhillon, FBI Director Christopher A. Wray, and U.S. Marshals Service Director Donald W. Washington, Attorney General Barr pledged to intensify federal law enforcement resources into Albuquerque, Baltimore, Cleveland, Detroit, Kansas City, Memphis, and Milwaukee—seven American cities with violent crime levels several times the national average.

"Americans deserve to live in safety," said Attorney General William P. Barr. "And while nationwide violent crime rates are down, many cities continue to see levels of extraordinary violence. Operation Relentless Pursuit seeks to ensure that no American city is excluded from the peace and security felt by the majority of Americans, while also supporting those who serve and protect in these communities with the resources, training, and equipment they need to stay safe."

"The men and women of ATF are deeply committed to and focused on reducing crime gun violence in our communities," said ATF Acting Director Regina Lombardo. "We are proud that our efforts have significantly contributed to the historic reductions in violence that our nation has realized in recent years. Operation Relentless Pursuit combines the resources of ATF, DEA, FBI, and U.S. Marshals to support our state and local law enforcement partners in those cities that—regrettably—continue to be plagued by rates of violent crime that are simply too high. Through Relentless Pursuit, we pledge to hold accountable the trigger-pullers, firearm traffickers, violent criminals and those who supply them the guns to terrorize our communities. ATF will aggressively utilize every available tool, including our crime gun enforcement teams, National Integrated Ballistic Information Network and firearms tracing to identify, investigate and support the prosecution of the most violent firearm offenders."

"Drug traffickers—including cartels and street gangs—will stop at nothing to turn a profit, often using violence and intimidation to expand their reach," said DEA Acting Administrator Uttam Dhillon. "This targeted surge of resources will further strengthen our ability to work with our federal, state, and local partners to pursue the worst offenders and make our communities safer."

"The FBI remains committed to providing our specialized expertise and resources to assist our federal, state and local partners fighting violent crime," said FBI Director Christopher A. Wray. "We are here today to reaffirm our dedication to reducing violent crime in the cities selected for Operation Relentless Pursuit to combat the threats that arise from gangs and criminal enterprises that drive violence in the communities we are sworn to protect."

"The U.S. Marshals Service is proud of the integral role we play in supporting Attorney General Barr's strong leadership and commitment to combating violent crime and enhancing public safety throughout our nation," said U.S. Marshals Service Director Donald W. Washington. "We will continue to work with our local, state, and federal partners to make communities safer by addressing violent crime at its core and taking the worst of the worst fugitives and other felons off the streets."

The operation will involve increasing the number of federal law enforcement officers to the selected cities, as well as bulking up federal task forces through collaborative efforts with state and local law enforcement partners. The surge in federal agents will be complemented by a financial commitment of up to $71 million in federal grant funding that can be used to hire new officers, pay overtime and benefits, finance federally deputized task force officers, and provide mission-critical equipment and technology.

8. The Bureau and Law Enforcement*

U.S. Bureau of Alcohol, Tobacco, Firearms and Explosives

ATF recognizes the role that firearms play in violent crimes and pursues an integrated regulatory and enforcement strategy. Investigative priorities focus on armed violent offenders and career criminals, narcotics traffickers, narco-terrorists, violent gangs, and domestic and international arms traffickers. Sections 924€ and € of Title 18 of the United States Code provide mandatory and enhanced sentencing guidelines for armed career criminals and narcotics traffickers as well as other dangerous armed criminals.

ATF uses these statutes to target, investigate and recommend prosecution of these offenders to reduce the level of violent crime and to enhance public safety. ATF also strives to increase State and local awareness of available Federal prosecution under these statutes. To curb the illegal use of firearms and enforce the Federal firearms laws, ATF issues firearms licenses and conducts firearms licensee qualification and compliance inspections. In addition to aiding the enforcement of Federal requirements for gun purchases, compliance inspections of existing licensees focus on assisting law enforcement to identify and apprehend criminals who illegally purchase firearms.

The inspections also help improve the likelihood that crime gun traces will be successful, since inspectors educate licensees in proper record keeping and business practices.

Tools and Services for Law Enforcement

National Tracing Center

What is Firearms Tracing? Firearms tracing is the systematic tracking of the movement of a firearms recovered by law enforcement officials from its first sale by the manufacturer or importer through the distribution chain (wholesaler/retailer) to the first retail purchaser. Comprehensive firearms tracing is the routine tracing of every crime gun recovered within a geographic area or specific law enforcement jurisdiction.

National Integrated Ballistic Information Network (NIBIN)

NIBIN Program—How it Works? The NIBIN Program automates ballistics evaluations and provides actionable investigative leads in a timely manner. NIBIN is the only

*Public document originally published as U.S. Bureau of Alcohol, Tobacco, Firearms and Explosives, "The Bureau and Law Enforcement," https://www.atf.gov/firearms (2021).

interstate automated ballistic imaging network in operation in the United States and is available to most major population centers in the United States. Prior to the NIBIN Program, firearms examiners performed this process manually which was extremely labor intensive. To use NIBIN, firearms examiners or technicians enter cartridge casing evidence into the Integrated Ballistic Identification System. These images are correlated against the database. Law enforcement can search against evidence from their jurisdiction, neighboring ones, and others across the country. This program is one investigative tool accessed by law enforcement that allows each of us to share information and cooperation easily making all of us more effective in closing cases.

Firearms and Ammunition Technology

The Firearms and Ammunition Technology Division (FATD) provides expert technical support to ATF, other Federal agencies, State and local law enforcement, the firearms industry, Congress, and the general public. This Division is responsible for technical determinations concerning types of firearms approved for importation into the United States and for rendering opinions regarding the classification of suspected illegal firearms and newly designed firearms. Further, FATD provides the U.S. Department of Justice, State prosecutors' offices, district attorneys' offices, and military courts with expert firearms testimony on the identification and origin of firearms and other matters relating to firearms and the firearms industry. The Division maintains an extensive firearms reference collection, as well as technical firearms reference files and library and firearms databases.

Firearms Related Training for Law Enforcement

The National Firearms Examiner Academy provides training for apprentice/ entry level firearm and toolmark examiners from Federal, state and local law enforcement agencies. The Academy curriculum is composed of the fundamentals of firearms and toolmark examinations and serves as a basis for the trainee, under supervision, to develop into a qualified firearm and toolmark examiner.

Apply for a License

Once you have decided to make an application for a Federal Firearms License (commonly referred to as an "FFL"), send the completed application to the ATF post office box listed on the application form, Application for License (FFL)—ATF Form 7/7CR. The application must be accompanied by the proper application fee, which you can pay by check, credit card or money order (we do not accept cash).

First review and background check. Once the application fee is processed, the Federal Firearms Licensing Center (FFLC) will enter your application information into its database and commence a full review of your application. For all license types, except type 03, required supporting materials, including fingerprint card(s) and photograph(s) will also be reviewed.

As required by law, the FFLC will then conduct an electronic background check on all the Responsible Persons you have identified on your application. ATF defines a Responsible Person (RP) as a sole proprietor, partner, or anyone having the power to direct the management, policies, and practices of the business or activity as it pertains to firearms. In a corporation this includes corporate officers, shareholders, board members, or any other employee with the legal authority described above. All responsible persons must complete their own Part B—Responsible Person Questionnaire of the ATF Form 7/7CR.

For all license types, except type 03 (onsite inspections are not required for Collector of Curio and Relics FFLs), the FFLC will then send the applications to the nearest ATF field office having responsibility for the area in which the business is located.

Interview and final review. The field office supervisor will issue an assignment to an Industry Operations Investigator (IOI) who will conduct an in-person interview with you. The IOI will discuss federal, state and local requirements with you, and go over your application with you to ensure the information is correct and current.

The IOI will then prepare a report of his/her interview, the inspection and make a recommendation to either issue you the license or deny the application. Some reasons for denial may include failure to comply with State or local law (such as zoning ordinances), evidence of previous willful violations of the Gun Control Act, or falsification of the application.

The field office supervisor will also review the report and then submit his/her recommendation to the FFLC.

Assuming that all background checks have been completed and your business address and proposed business operations are in compliance with state and local law, the FFLC will complete the application processing and issue you the license. This process will take approximately 60 days from the receipt of a properly completed application.

How to Renew a Federal Firearms License (FFL)

Under § 478.45, Renewal of License, if a licensee intends to continue the business or activity described on a license issued under this part during any portion of the ensuing year, the licensee shall, unless otherwise notified in writing by the Chief, FFLC, execute and file with ATF prior to the expiration of the license an application for a license renewal, ATF Form 8 Part II, in accordance with the instructions on the form, and the required fee. In the event the licensee does not timely file an ATF Form 8 Part II, the licensee must file an ATF Form 7 as required by § 478.44, and obtain the required license before continuing business. A renewal application will automatically be mailed by ATF to the "mailing address" on the license approximately 90 days prior to the expiration of the license. If the application is not received 30 days prior to the expiration date, the licensee should contact the FFLC.

When you have sent your Federal Firearms License (FFL) Renewal Application, ATF Form 8 Part II, to ATF prior to the expiration of your federal firearms license and the application form has been postmarked before the expiration date, you may request a Letter of Authorization (LOA) from the Federal Firearms Licensing Center (FFLC) to facilitate and carry on your business operations while your renewal application is in a pending status. The LOA provides evidence to your distributors that you may continue your business operations under your current license until ATF has completed the processing of your renewal application, even if the time needed by ATF to process the application extends beyond the expiration date of the current license. The LOA will state that operations may continue under the existing license for a period of up to six months. If the FFLC does not complete processing of the application within the six-month period specified in the LOA, you may request the FFLC to extend the LOA. You may also provide copies of the LOA to your suppliers.

9. NIBIN, CGICs, and eTrace*

U.S. Bureau of Alcohol, Tobacco, Firearms and Explosives

In 1997, ATF established the National Integrated Ballistic Information Network (NIBIN) to provide local, state, tribal and federal law enforcement partners with an automated ballistic imaging network. This technology is vital to any violent crime reduction strategy because it enables investigators to match ballistics evidence with other cases across the nation. This process also helps reveal previously hidden connections between violent crimes in different states and jurisdictions.

NIBIN is only used for criminal investigations and does not capture or store ballistic information acquired at the point of manufacture, importation, or sale. NIBIN is the only national network that allows for the capture and comparison of ballistic evidence to aid in solving and preventing violent crimes involving firearms. NIBIN and eTrace are two key tools that ATF's Crime Gun Intelligence Centers (CGIC) use to identify violent shooters and their sources of crime guns.

The Numbers

- 4.5 million pieces of ballistic evidence are currently stores in NIBIN.
- 307,000 NIBIN leads were generated and over 132,000 NIBIN hits were confirmed during its 24-year history.
- 472,948 pieces of evidence were acquired and 104,206 NIBIN leads were generated by 237 NIBIN locations in fiscal year 2020.

How NIBIN Works

NIBIN technology compares images of submitted ballistic evidence from shooting scenes and recovered firearms and produces a list of possible similar results. Trained NIBIN technicians then conduct a correlation review of these results, identifying NIBIN leads or potential links or associations from the same firearm. A NIBIN lead is an unconfirmed, potential association between two or more pieces of firearm ballistic evidence and is based on a correlation review of the digital images in the NIBIN database.

---

*Public document originally published as U.S. Bureau of Alcohol, Tobacco, Firearms and Explosives, "NIBIN, CGICs, and eTrace," https://www.atf.gov/resource-center/fact-sheet/fact-sheet-national-integrated-ballistic-information-network (September 2021).

When needed for court or other purposes, a firearms examiner will conduct a microscopic examination of the actual physical evidence to confirm a NIBIN lead as a hit. A NIBIN hit occurs when two or more firearms ballistic evidence acquisitions are identified as a confirmed match by a firearms examiner. The data is then compiled into intelligence reports that are used for investigations and court cases.

Partnering with Law Enforcement

NIBIN relies on the close coordination of its partner law enforcement agencies at the local, state, federal, tribal and territorial levels to compile their data and share intelligence about violent crimes. NIBIN's success depends on four critical steps:

- Comprehensive Collection and Entry: Partner agencies must collect and submit all evidence suitable for entry into NIBIN, regardless of the crime. Evidence includes cartridge cases recovered from crime scenes, as well as test fires from recovered crime guns.
- Timely Turnaround: Violent crime investigations can rapidly go cold, so the goal is to enter the evidence into the network as quickly as possible to identify potential NIBIN leads for investigators.
- Investigative Follow-Up and Prosecution: Linking otherwise unassociated crimes gives investigators a better chance to identify and arrest shooters before they reoffend.
- Feedback Loop: Without feedback, NIBIN partners cannot know how their efforts are making the community safer, which is necessary for sustained success.

Combating Violent Crime

Before NIBIN was created, law enforcement agencies did not have access to technology that allowed them to research, identify and cross-reference firearms ballistic data in one online system. Since its launch, the technology behind NIBIN has provided participating law enforcement agencies with an automated method to share, research, identify and cross-reference firearms ballistic data across a nationwide network. ATF maintains and operates NIBIN's infrastructure at no charge to law enforcement partners.

Along with eTrace, NIBIN is a critical part of ATF's Crime Gun Intelligence Center (CGIC) operations, which directly support the Department of Justice's Operation Relentless Pursuit and Project Guardian. CGICs are multiagency law enforcement collaborations focused on stopping gun crimes by collecting, analyzing, and distributing intelligence reports about crime guns, mass shootings, and major incidents across jurisdictions.

Crime Gun Intelligence Centers (CGICs)

ATF launched its Crime Gun Intelligence Centers (CGICs) in July 2016 as an interagency collaboration designed to collect, analyze and distribute intelligence data about crime guns, mass shootings, and major incidents across multiple jurisdictions. CGICs provide investigative leads and support to crime gun intelligence initiatives across the United States and beyond.

CGICs use vital tools such as the National Integrated Ballistic Information Network (NIBIN) to support their mission. Analysts use NIBIN to collect and compare digital scans of guns and cartridge casings found at crime scenes across the country. Law enforcement officials use the potential matches or "leads" that NIBIN generates to identify links between shootings and other firearms-related cases in different jurisdictions.

ATF CGICs take a preventative approach to violent crime by targeting and prosecuting the sources of crime guns. Their key tool in this effort is eTrace, a secure, web-based law enforcement network run by ATF's National Tracing Center. The system assists the NTC and other law enforcement agencies during their comprehensive traces of recovered crime guns from manufacturing to the last legal purchase. Investigators use this data to uncover patterns of firearms trafficking, identify illegal and "straw" firearms purchasers, and develop leads to recover firearms used in violent crimes.

CGICs are staffed by ATF special agents, industry operations investigators, other law enforcement agencies, forensics experts, intelligence specialists and prosecutors focused on stopping violent gun crimes. These close partnerships allow CGICs to provide actionable intelligence that is specific to local communities, resulting in more communication, investigative leads, and prosecutions.

The Numbers

- 25 CGICs are strategically located across the nation to analyze criminal intelligence and support interagency responses to violent crimes.
- 116,233 investigative leads were generated by 242 NIBIN locations in fiscal year (FY) 2020.
- 490,800 crime guns were traced back to their origins by the National Tracing Center in FY 2020.

Combating Violent Crime

CGICs disrupt the shooting cycle by identifying and prosecuting shooters and their sources of crime guns. These continued efforts directly support the Department of Justice's Operation Relentless Pursuit and Project Guardian initiatives.

eTrace: Internet-Based Firearms Tracing and Analysis

eTrace is a web-based application that tracks the purchase and/or use history of firearms used in violent crimes. The system, available in both English and Spanish, is key in generating investigative leads to help solve violent crimes across the country. These leads help law enforcement agencies quickly identify potential firearm traffickers and suspects in criminal investigations. Firearms tracing through eTrace provides for the systematic tracking of a recovered firearm from the original manufacturer or importer, through the subsequent distribution chain (wholesaler/retailer) in order to identify an unlicensed purchaser.

The data in eTrace comes from local, state, federal, and international law enforcement agencies. Authorized users can search eTrace data fields such as agency name, gun serial number, type of crime, recovery date and names of people involved. In addition, participating law enforcement agencies can opt to share firearms trace data with all other eTrace users in their state. eTrace thus allows its users to detect patterns of violent crime across jurisdictions.

The Numbers

- 490,800 firearms trace requests were processed by the National Tracing Center in fiscal year 2020.
- 8,177 law enforcement agencies use eTrace in their investigations, including agencies from 49 agencies from 46 foreign countries.

How eTrace Makes a Difference

When firearms are found at a crime scene, it is critical for investigators to quickly track down the origin of the weapons and any possible suspects. eTrace serves as a one-stop shop for comparing firearms data across multiple jurisdictions, helping agencies close cases faster. The benefits of eTrace include:

- Robust statistical reports that readily generate new investigative leads
- Faster processing of firearms trace requests
- Targeted trace data relevant to a specific state or local jurisdiction
- Real-time data verification and trace status updates

eTrace is part of the broader ATF mission to catch violent offenders and criminal suppliers, and get their firearms off the street. ATF is constantly looking to leverage technology like eTrace to streamline the investigative process.

Combating Violent Crime

eTrace is the primary investigatory tool of ATF's National Tracing Center (NTC). ATF is the sole federal agency authorized to trace firearms, however ATF is only authorized to trace firearms for law enforcement agencies involved in a bona fide criminal investigations. ATF provides the eTrace application free of charge to authorized law enforcement agencies.

The eTrace system allows law enforcement agencies to conduct comprehensive traces of recovered crime guns and establish potential leads in their investigations. The system also provides an information platform that allows agencies to develop long-term strategies on how best to reduce firearms-related crime, firearms trafficking and violence in their communities.

10. Five Federal Policies on Guns You've Never Heard Of*

Suevon Lee

U.S. gun policy is set by both state and federal law. We previously published an explainer on the ways states have eased gun restrictions. But federal policy, too, has become more gun friendly in recent years—and we're not just talking about the 2008 Supreme Court ruling that struck down the handgun ban in Washington, D.C., and held that people have a right to keep guns in their homes.

Here, we outline five federal policies relating to guns you may not have known about:

1. A federal firearms trace database is off-limits to the public.

How often do federally licensed gun dealers sell guns that are then used in crimes? It's hard to know, because for nearly a decade such gun trace data has been hidden from the public. Even local law enforcement had been, until recently, barred from accessing the database for anything but narrow investigations.

Under the Gun Control Act of 1968, licensed dealers are required to record certain information about a buyer and the gun's serial number at the point of sale. When a gun is recovered from a crime scene, local law enforcement agencies can request The Bureau of Alcohol, Tobacco, Firearms and Explosives to trace the firearm's origins. The retrieved information is compiled into a crime gun trace database maintained by ATF. A tool to catch criminals, the database in the early 2000s became a political flashpoint, as the Washington Post details. Outside research tying seized guns to a small handful of dealers spurred the federal government to impose tougher sanctions and inspections on gun retailers and manufacturers.

But those sanctions sparked a backlash: Since 2003, the Tiahrt Amendments, so named after the former Kansas Republican congressman who introduced the measures, have concealed the database from the public. Prior to 2010, local police could access the database only to investigate an individual crime but not to look for signs of broader criminal activity.

Despite the relaxing of some restrictions, parts of the original Tiahrt Amendment remain in place. The ATF can't require gun dealers to conduct an inventory to account for lost or stolen guns; records of customer background checks must be destroyed within

*This story was originally published by ProPublica as Suevon Lee, "Five Federal Policies on Guns You've Never Heard Of," https://www.propublica.org/article/five-federal-policies-on-guns-you-never-heard-of (January 7, 2013). Reprinted with permission of the publisher.

24 hours if they are clean enough to allow the sale; and trace data can't be used in state civil lawsuits or in an effort to suspend or revoke a gun dealer's license.

> 2. The military can't impose additional regulations on service members who own guns.

Following the November 2009 shooting at Fort Hood military base in Texas that killed 13 people and wounded more than two dozen others, the Department of Defense proposed guidelines that included, among other things, a new policy around private firearms. (The semiautomatic pistol used by accused gunman Army psychiatrist Maj. Nidal Malik Hasan was purchased at a store off-base.)

Consideration of tighter gun regulations, such as the registering of non-military guns, sparked at least one new piece of federal legislation.

Less than a year after the shooting, U.S. Sen. Jim Inhofe, R–Okla., introduced a bill prohibiting new regulations on Defense Department personnel's private guns. It also prohibited commanders from inquiring into private gun ownership. At the time, Inhofe stated that the measure would "prevent current and potential Second Amendment violations for those serving and employed by the Department of Defense."

There has been a recent revision: In the 2013 National Defense Authorization Act recently passed by Congress, a new provision does allow military commanders to ask about private firearms if there is reason to believe a service member is at high risk of committing suicide.

"It codifies the ability of military commanders to have a conversation with someone they feel is suicidal. This is all about conversation, not confiscation," said John Madigan, senior director of public policy at The American Foundation for Suicide Prevention, which pushed for the measure.

> 3. You can carry a gun inside a national park or check a gun when riding Amtrak.

In 2009, Congress passed a measure, tucked into a larger credit card reform bill, to allow visitors to national parks and wildlife refuges to carry a loaded firearm. (Previously, the guns had to be locked, unloaded and stowed away.) Under the amendment, which took effect February 2010, visitors can carry firearms only in those parks located in states that permit concealed guns in their own state parks. Although the U.S. Department of the Interior had lifted the 25-year ban the year before the law passed, a federal judge had blocked implementation after gun control groups objected.

Also in 2009, Congress voted to allow customers riding Amtrak to check guns and ammunition in their luggage. (Though airlines have a similar policy, the federally subsidized national rail service barred guns in any luggage, checked or carry-on, after the 9/11 terrorist attacks.) In a statement shortly before the measure took effect, its sponsor, Republican Sen. Roger Wicker of Mississippi, said it would provide "hunters, sportsmen, and gun owners with more choices for traveling."

> 4. The gun industry is shielded from many lawsuits involving criminal misuse of guns.

In 2005, Congress enacted a law that immunizes gun dealers and manufacturers from liability for injuries resulting in the "criminal or unlawful misuse" of a firearm. The law authorized dismissal of any applicable pending lawsuits and prohibited future claims.

During floor debate, the bill's primary sponsor, former Idaho Republican Sen. Larry Craig, said the measure wouldn't provide the gun industry with blanket immunity, just prohibit "one extremely narrow category of lawsuits: lawsuits that attempt to force the gun industry to pay for the crimes of third parties over whom they have no control."

Indeed, the 2005 law provides for certain exceptions, including cases in which a gun dealer or manufacturer is aware the firearm will be used to a commit a crime and the suit is brought by the victim directly harmed. The law also allows suits based on a manufacturing or design defect, but not for lacking certain safety features.

Under the law, it would be much harder to obtain a settlement of the kind that families of the victims in the Washington-area sniper shootings of 2002 received. In 2004, those families won a $2.5 million settlement from the manufacturer of the Bushmaster XM-15 assault rifle used in the shootings and from the licensed Tacoma, Washington, store from where the gun was stolen.

"The law has not stopped gun litigation, but it has created an obstacle for litigation," said Jonathan E. Lowy, director of the Legal Action Project at The Brady Center to Prevent Gun Violence, which filed the lawsuit, alleging that the defendants' negligence allowed the snipers to obtain the firearm. "Today, you would almost certainly face motions to dismiss by the dealer and manufacturer, and there is a significant number of judges who would dismiss the case," he said.

5. Congress has removed federal funding for firearms-related research.

Funding used to be set aside for the Centers for Disease Control and Prevention to research the impact of gun ownership—but that was taken away in the mid–90s.

The New York Times explains that as the CDC became "increasingly assertive about the importance of studying gun-related injuries and deaths as a public health phenomenon," the National Rifle Association assailed its findings as politically skewed and lobbied to defund research.

One study commissioned by the CDC's National Center for Injury Prevention and Control found that the risks of keeping a gun in the home outweigh the benefits: "A gun kept in the home is far more likely to be involved in the death of a family member of the household than it is to be used to kill in self-defense," its authors wrote in 1993.

In 1996, an amendment proposed by then-Arkansas Republican Congressman Jay Dickey removed $2.6 million from the center's budget, the same amount earmarked for firearms research. When funding to CDC was later restored, legislation included the directive that "none of the funds made available for injury prevention and control at the Centers for Disease Control and Prevention may be used to advocate or promote gun control." Critics charge that language had a chilling effect on CDC's support for gun-related research.

The CDC Injury Center today collects data generally on homicides, suicides and injuries in homes, schools and communities. But when it comes to firearms-specific research, "I never heard the money was replaced," said Dr. David Satcher, the former U.S. Surgeon General who served as CDC's director from 1993 to 1998 and now leads The Satcher Health Leadership Institute at Morehouse School of Medicine.

"I don't think this (1993) study was saying the government should take guns away from people. I think it was saying people should know what happens when you have a gun," Satcher told ProPublica. "A major benefit of that kind of research is, it keeps informing and updating people: What do we know about gun violence? What do we know about the benefits of owning a gun? I think those are the kinds of questions we need to ask in public health."

Correction: This story has been corrected to note that the Bureau of Alcohol, Tobacco, Firearms and Explosives collects trace data only for guns involved in a criminal investigation. A previous version of the story incorrectly stated that the ATF maintains a general database of guns purchased from licensed dealers.

11. Extreme Risk Protection Order Model Legislation*

U.S. DEPARTMENT OF JUSTICE

Commentary: Research has shown that states can save lives by authorizing courts to issue extreme risk protection orders (ERPOs) that temporarily prevent a person in crisis from accessing firearms. This model legislation provides a framework for states to consider as they determine whether and how to craft laws allowing law enforcement, concerned family members, or others to seek these orders and to intervene before warning signs turn into tragedy. The model draws on a significant number of similar laws adopted across the country. Orders of this nature may be sought in some jurisdictions, for example, by family members or others concerned that an individual who is suicidal or otherwise in crisis will use a firearm to seriously injure or kill himself or herself or another person.

The model legislation is designed to identify the main features (and varying specifics) of existing ERPO statutes that have been adopted in a number of states. These existing statutes may be of two types—"warrant" statutes that authorize courts to issue orders permitting law enforcement to search for and seize the firearms of dangerous individuals, and "order" statutes that authorize courts to issue temporary orders prohibiting dangerous individuals from possessing or acquiring firearms.

The "warrant" statutes provide an immediate basis for law enforcement to seek court orders temporarily preventing individuals in crisis from accessing or possessing guns. However, standing alone, these warrants do not provide an ongoing prohibition against such persons' possession or acquisition of firearms, and do not provide a basis for entering those persons into the National Instant Criminal Background Check System and corresponding state firearm background check systems as individuals prohibited from possessing firearms.

The "order" statutes provide for ongoing prohibitions of firearms possession and acquisition, and a basis for entering dangerous individuals into the background check systems as ineligible to possess firearms. However, their design may require a law enforcement officer to initially present the order to the dangerous person and ask him or her to surrender his or her firearms. If the person does not comply, and the firearms are not in plain view during the encounter, a second step may be required in which the

*Public document originally published as U.S. Department of Justice, "Extreme Risk Protection Order Model Legislation," https://www.justice.gov/doj/reducing-gun-violence/commentary-extreme-risk-protection-order-model-legislation#model (June 7, 2021).

law enforcement officer goes back to court and secures a search warrant to look for and seize the subject's firearms. The delay may inadvertently give the subject advance notice and time to hide the firearms—or potentially time to use them to seriously injure or kill someone before the police can return with a search warrant.

This model legislation combines both approaches. It includes language that would authorize the judicial issuance of no-firearms orders for dangerous individuals and the concurrent issuance of search warrants to search for and seize their firearms. It further provides that, in qualifying emergency circumstances, the subject may be served with the order concurrently with or after the search is carried out. The process would be overseen by a court to ensure the protection of the individual's rights. Legislation authorizing ERPOs would supplement, not replace, existing laws authorizing the issuance of protection orders to prevent intimate partner violence. This legislation similarly would not displace existing state laws on involuntary commitments.

ERPO laws are likely to be more effective when their implementation is adequately funded and supported by a broad array of affected stakeholders. Law enforcement, health care providers, community leaders, victim advocates, and others may not only help shape the appropriate scope of a state's particular legislation, but also be critical to ensuring that people in the community are aware of the process for petitioning for an ERPO. Similarly, law enforcement should receive adequate training on ERPO laws, including on issues, for example, like filing a petition and executing an ERPO, implicit bias, de-escalation techniques, and crisis intervention.

The Department is not endorsing any particular formulation of an ERPO statute, and the model is not intended to provide a comprehensive scheme that could be adopted wholesale. Rather, this model statute draws from the state laws already in existence; identifies key provisions that may be important to help ensure fair, effective, and safe implementation for such a law; and identifies options for states to consider. In drafting its own legislation, each state must account for its own policy, legal, constitutional, administrative, and operational considerations and requirements. States may also wish to review any proposed federal legislation that would create incentives for establishing particular forms of ERPO laws.

Sec. 1. Extreme Risk Protection Orders

(a) DEFINITIONS.—

(1) "Petitioner" means:

(A) A law enforcement officer or agency, including an attorney for the state;

(B) A member of the family of the respondent, which shall be understood to mean a parent, spouse, child, or sibling of the respondent;

(C) A member of the household of the respondent;

(D) A dating or intimate partner of the respondent;

(E) A health care provider [as defined by state law] who has provided health services to the respondent;

(F) An official of a school or school system in which the respondent is enrolled or has been enrolled within the preceding [six months/one year/two years/other appropriate time period specified by state law]; or

(G) [Any other appropriate persons specified by state law.]

(2) "Respondent" means the person against whom an order under Section 2 or 3 has been sought or granted.

(b) TYPES OF ORDERS.—The petitioner may apply for an emergency ex parte order as provided in Section 2 or an order following a hearing as provided in Section 3.

Sec. 2. Emergency Ex Parte Order

(a) BASIS FOR ORDER.—The court shall issue an emergency ex parte extreme risk protection order upon submission of an application by a petitioner, supported by an affidavit or sworn oral statement of the petitioner or other witness, that provides specific facts establishing probable cause that the respondent's possession or receipt of a firearm will pose a [significant danger/extreme risk/other appropriate standard established by state law] of personal injury or death to the respondent or another person. The court shall take up and decide such an application on the day it is submitted, or if review and decision of the application on the same day is not feasible, then as quickly as possible but in no case later than [appropriate time period specified by state law].

(b) CONTENT OF ORDER.—An order issued under this section shall—

(1) prohibit the respondent from possessing, using, purchasing, manufacturing, or otherwise receiving a firearm;

(2) order the respondent to provisionally surrender any firearms in his or her possession or control, and any license or permit allowing the respondent to possess or acquire a firearm, to any law enforcement officer presenting the order or to a law enforcement agency as directed by the officer or the order; and

(3) inform the respondent of the time and place of the hearing under Section 3 to determine whether he or she will be subject to a continuing prohibition on possessing and acquiring firearms.

(c) SEARCH AND SEIZURE.—

(1) If the application and its supporting affidavit or statement establish probable cause that the respondent has access to a firearm, on his or her person or in an identified place, the court shall concurrently issue a warrant authorizing a law enforcement agency to search the person of the respondent and any such place for firearms and to seize any firearm therein to which the respondent would have access.

(2) The court may subsequently issue additional search warrants of this nature based on probable cause that the respondent has retained, acquired, or gained access to firearm while an order under this section remains in effect.

(3) If the owner of a firearm seized pursuant to this subsection is a person other than the respondent, the owner may secure the return of the firearm as provided in Section 3(c)(3)

(d) TIME FOR SERVICE AND SEARCHES.—The responsible law enforcement agency shall serve the order on the respondent, and carry out any search authorized under subsection (c)(1), [promptly/immediately/within other appropriate time period specified by state law] following issuance of the order. If a search is authorized under subsection (c)(1), the agency may serve the order on the respondent concurrently with or after the execution of the search.

Sec. 3. Order After Hearing

(a) ORDER AFTER HEARING.—Upon application for an extreme risk protection order, supported by an affidavit or sworn oral statement of the petitioner or other witness that provides specific facts giving rise to the concern about the [significant danger/ extreme risk/other appropriate standard established by state law] described in Section 2, the court may issue an order under this section, which shall be effective for a period of up to [one year/other appropriate time period specified by state law], after a hearing. An order issued under this section shall—

(1) prohibit the respondent from possessing, using, purchasing, or otherwise receiving a firearm; and

(2) order the respondent to surrender any firearm in his or her possession or control, and any license or permit allowing the respondent to possess or acquire a firearm, to any law enforcement officer presenting the order or to a law enforcement agency as directed by the officer or the order.

(b) BASIS FOR ORDER.—The court shall issue such an order based on [a preponderance of the evidence/other appropriate standard specified by state law] that the respondent's possession or receipt of a firearm will pose a [significant danger/extreme risk/other appropriate standard specified by state law] of personal injury or death to the respondent or another person. In determining the satisfaction of this requirement, the court shall consider all relevant facts and circumstances after reviewing the petitioner's application and conducting the hearing described in Section 2(d). The court may order a psychological evaluation of the respondent, including voluntary or involuntary commitment of the respondent for purposes of such an evaluation, to the extent authorized by other law.

(c) SEARCH AND SEIZURE.—

(1) If the evidence presented at the hearing establishes probable cause that the respondent has access to a firearm, on his or her person or in an identified place, the court shall concurrently issue a warrant authorizing a law enforcement agency to search the person of the respondent and any such place for firearms and to seize any firearm therein to which the respondent would have access.

(2) The court may subsequently issue additional search warrants of this nature based on probable cause that the respondent has retained, acquired, or gained access to a firearm while an order under this section remains in effect.

(3) If the owner of a firearm seized pursuant to this subsection is a person other than the respondent, the owner may secure the prompt return of the firearm by providing an affidavit to the law enforcement agency affirming his or her ownership of the firearm and providing assurance that he or she will safeguard the firearm against access by the respondent. The law enforcement agency shall return the firearm to the owner upon its confirmation, including by a check of the National Instant Criminal Background Check System and the applicable state firearm background check system, that the owner is not legally disqualified from possessing or receiving the firearm.

(4) [Any provisions under state law permitting the transfer of seized firearms to a person not prohibited from possessing them.]

(d) TIME FOR HEARINGS AND SERVICE.—

(1) A hearing under this section shall be held within [appropriate time period specified by state law] days of the filing of the application, or within [appropriate time period specified by state law] days of the issuance of an emergency ex parte order under

Section 2, if such an order is issued. The responsible law enforcement agency shall serve notice of the hearing on the respondent [promptly/immediately/within 72 hours/within an appropriate time period specified by state law] after the filing of the application or issuance of an emergency ex parte order, but notice may be provided by publication or mailing if the respondent cannot be personally served within the specified period. The respondent shall be entitled to one continuance of up to [appropriate time period specified by state law] days on request, and the court may thereafter grant an additional continuance or continuances for good cause. Any emergency ex parte order under Section 2 shall remain in effect until the hearing is held. The court may temporarily extend the emergency order at the hearing, pending a decision on a final order.

(2) The responsible law enforcement agency shall serve an order issued under this section on the respondent, and carry out any search authorized under subsection (c)(1), [promptly/immediately/within an appropriate time period specified by state law] following issuance of the order. If a search is authorized under subsection (c)(1), the agency may serve the order on the respondent concurrently with or after the execution of the search.

(e) TERMINATION AND RENEWAL OF ORDERS.—

(1) A respondent may file a motion to terminate an order under Section 3 one time during the effective period of that order. The respondent shall have the burden of proving, by the same standard of proof required for issuance of such an order, that he or she does not pose a [significant danger/extreme risk/other appropriate standard specified by state law] of personal injury or death to himself or herself or another.

(2) The petitioner may seek renewals of an order under this section for an additional [six months/one year/other appropriate time period specified by state law] at any time preceding its expiration. Renewals after the initial order shall be granted subject to the same standards and requirements as an initial order. The preceding order shall remain in effect until the renewal hearing is held and the court grants or denies a renewed order.

(3) If the respondent fails to appear at, or cannot be personally served in relation to, any hearing or renewal hearing under this section, the default does not affect the court's authority to issue an order or entitle the respondent to challenge the order prior to its expiration. The order will lapse after [the period established in Section 3(a)] if no eligible petitioner seeks its renewal.

Sec. 4. Into Background Check Systems

The court shall forward any order issued under Section 2 or 3 to an appropriate law enforcement agency on the day it is issued. Upon receipt of an order under Section 3, the law enforcement agency shall make the order available to the National Instant Criminal Background Check System and any state system used to identify persons who are prohibited from possessing firearms.

Sec. 5. Penalties for Violations

The following persons shall be subject to [appropriate criminal penalties specified by state law]:

(1) FILER OF FALSE OR HARASSING APPLICATION.—Any person filing an application under Section 2 or 3 containing information that he or she knows to be materially false, or for the purpose of harassing the respondent.

(2) RESPONDENT NOT COMPLYING WITH ORDER.—Any person who knowingly violates an order under Section 2 or 3, including by possessing or acquiring a firearm in violation of the order or failing to surrender a firearm as required by the order.

(3) PROVIDER OF PROHIBITED ACCESS TO RESPONDENT.—Any person who knowingly provides the subject of an order under Section 2 or 3 access to a firearm, in violation of an assurance the person has provided in an affidavit under Section 2(c)(3) or 3(c)(3) that he or she will safeguard the firearm against access by the respondent.

12. Definition of "Frame or Receiver" and Identification of Firearms[*]

U.S. Bureau of Alcohol, Tobacco, Firearms and Explosives

On May 7, 2021, the Attorney General signed ATF proposed rule 2021R-05, Definition of "Frame or Receiver" and Identification of Firearms. The goal of the proposed rule is to ensure the proper marking, recordkeeping, and traceability of all firearms manufactured, imported, acquired and disposed by federal firearms licensees.

Summary of Proposed Rule 2021R-05

ATF's proposed rule, *Definition of "Frame or Receiver" and Identification of Firearms*, would:

- Provide new definitions of "firearm frame or receiver" and "frame or receiver" Amend the definition of:
    - ◊ <open>"firearm" to clarify when a firearm parts kit is considered a "firearm," and
    - ◊ "gunsmith" to clarify the meaning of that term and to explain that gunsmiths may be licensed solely to mark firearms for unlicensed persons.
        - ◊ Provide definitions for:
        - ◊ "complete weapon,"
        - ◊ "complete muffler or silencer device,"
        - ◊ "privately made firearm (PMF)," and
        - ◊ "readily" for purposes of clarity given advancements in firearms technology.
- Provide a definition of "importer's or manufacturer's serial number"
- Provide a deadline for marking firearms manufactured.
- Clarify marking requirements for firearm mufflers and silencers.
- Amend the format for records of manufacture/acquisition and disposition by manufacturers and importers.
- Amend the time period records must be retained at the licensed premises.

---

[*]Public document originally published as U.S. Bureau of Alcohol, Tobacco, Firearms and Explosives, "Definition of 'Frame or Receiver' and Identification of Firearms," https://www.atf.gov/rules-and-regulations/-definition-frame-or-receiver (May 7, 2021).

Proposed New Definition of Firearm "Frame or Receiver"

Under the proposed rule, a "**frame or receiver**" is any externally visible housing or holding structure for one or more fire control components. A "**fire control component**" is one necessary for the firearm to initiate, complete, or continue the firing sequence, including, but not limited to, any of the following: hammer, bolt, bolt carrier, breech-block, cylinder, trigger mechanism, firing pin, striker, or slide rails.

Any firearm part falling within the new definition that is identified with a serial number must be presumed, absent an official determination by ATF or other reliable evidence to the contrary, to be a frame or receiver.

More than one externally visible part may house or hold a fire control component on a particular firearm, such as with a split or modular frame or receiver. Under these circumstances, ATF may determine whether a specific part or parts of the weapon is the frame or receiver, which may include an internal frame or chassis at least partially exposed to the exterior to allow identification.

The proposed rule maintains current classifications and marking requirements of firearm frames or receivers, except that licensed manufacturers and importers must mark on new designs or configurations either: their name (or recognized abbreviation), and city and state (or recognized abbreviation) where they maintain their place of business; or their name (or recognized abbreviation) and their abbreviated FFL number, on each part defined as a frame or receiver, along with the serial number.

The proposed rule includes examples of types and models firearms and identifies the frame or receiver. Most examples also include an illustration identifying the frame or receiver. It also explains when a partially complete, disassembled, or inoperable frame or receiver is considered a "frame or receiver," and explains that a destroyed frame or receiver is not considered a "frame or receiver."

Firearm Parts Kits

The proposed rule explains that when a partially complete **frame or receiver parts kit** has reached a stage in manufacture where it may readily be completed, assembled, converted, or restored to a functional state, it is a "frame or receiver" that must be marked.

Weapon parts kits with partially complete frames or receivers and containing the necessary parts such that they may readily be completed, assembled, converted, or restored to expel a projectile by the action of an explosive are "firearms" for which each frame or receiver of the weapon would need to be marked.

A weapon, including a weapon parts kit, in which each frame or receiver of the weapon or within such kit is destroyed is not considered a "firearm."

Licensing of Dealer/Gunsmiths

Under the proposed rule, dealers/gunsmiths can mark firearms for the maker or owner of a **privately made firearm (PMF)** and may be licensed to engage solely in that business.

Dealer/gunsmiths are not authorized to perform repair, modify, embellish, refurbish, or install parts in or on firearms (frames, receivers, or otherwise) for or on behalf of a licensed importer or licensed manufacturer because those firearms are for sale or distribution. A license as a Type 07 manufacturer would be required.

Marking Requirements for Firearms Other Than PMFs

Under the proposed rule, licensed manufacturers and importers must identify each part defined as a frame or receiver (or specific part[s] determined by ATF) of each firearm they manufacture or import with a serial number, licensee's name (or recognized abbreviation) where they maintain their place of business; or their name (or recognized abbreviation) and abbreviated federal firearms license number as a prefix, followed by a hyphen, and then followed by a number as a suffix (e.g., "12345678-[number]").

Each part defined as a frame or receiver, machinegun, or firearm muffler or firearm silencer that is not a component part of a complete weapon or device at the time it is sold, shipped, or otherwise disposed of by the licensee must be identified with a serial number and all additional identifying information, except that the model designation and caliber or gauge may be omitted if that information is unknown at the time the part is identified.

Licensees must mark complete weapons, or frames or receivers disposed of separately, as the case may be, no later than seven days following the date of completion of the active manufacturing process or prior to disposition, whichever is sooner.

Marking and Recordkeeping Requirements for PMFs

Under the proposed rule, a "**privately made firearm**" (PMF) is a firearm, including a frame or receiver, assembled or otherwise produced by a person other than a licensed manufacturer, and without a serial number or other identifying markings placed by a licensed manufacturer at the time the firearm was produced. The term does not include an NFA registered firearm, or one made before October 22, 1968 (unless remanufactured after that date).

Licensees must:

- Properly mark each PMF acquired before the effective date of the rule within 60 days after the rule becomes final, or before the date of disposition (including to a personal collection), whichever is sooner.
- Properly mark previously acquired PMFs themselves or may arrange to have another licensee mark the firearm on their behalf. PMFs currently in inventory that a licensee chooses not to mark may also be destroyed or voluntarily turned-in to law enforcement within the 60-day period.
- Once the rule becomes final, and unless already marked by another licensee, properly mark each PMF within seven days following the date of receipt or other acquisition (including from a personal collection), or before the date of disposition (including to a personal collection), whichever is sooner.
- Mark PMFs acquired after the rule becomes effective themselves or under their direct supervision by another licensee with the supervising licensee's information.

- Mark PMFs with the same serial number on each frame or receiver of a weapon that begins with the FFL's abbreviated license number (first three and last five digits) as a prefix followed by a hyphen on any "privately made firearm" (as defined) that the licensee acquired (e.g., "12345678-[number]").
- Record PMFs in their acquisition and disposition records, whether or not kept overnight, and update their acquisition entries with information marked on PMFs.

Licensees may refuse to accept PMFs or arrange for private individuals to have them marked by another licensee before accepting them, provided they are properly marked in accordance with this proposed rule.

Marking, Registration, and Transfer Requirements for Silencers

Under the proposed rule, a "frame or receiver" of a firearm muffler or silencer device is defined as a housing or holding structure for one or more essential internal components of the device, including, but not limited to, baffles, baffling material, or expansion chamber.

Manufacturers and makers of complete muffler or silencer devices need only mark each part (or specific part[s] previously determined by ATF) of the device defined as a "frame or receiver" under this rule. However, individual muffler or silencer parts must be marked if they are disposed of separately from a complete device unless transferred by qualified manufacturers to other qualified licensees for the manufacture or repair of complete devices.

A qualified manufacturer may:

- Transfer a silencer part to another qualified manufacturer without immediately identifying or registering such part provided that, upon receipt, it is actively used to manufacture a complete muffler or silencer device.
- Transfer a replacement silencer part other than a frame or receiver to a qualified manufacturer or dealer without identifying or registering such part provided that, upon receipt, it is actively used to repair a complete muffler or silencer device that was previously identified and registered in accordance with this part.

Persons may temporarily convey a lawfully possessed NFA firearm, including a silencer, to a qualified manufacturer or dealer for the sole purpose of repair, identification, evaluation, research, testing, or calibration, and return to the same lawful possessor without additional identification or registration.

Records of Acquisition and Disposition

Under the proposed rule, records of manufacture/importation/acquisition and disposition by manufacturers and importers must be consolidated into one book similar to dealers, and the format containing the applicable columns is specified as part of the regulation.

The proposed rule specifies required information for duplicate entries in licensees' acquisition and disposition books so there are no open entries (i.e., bound books must be "closed out").

Record Retention

Under the proposed rule, all licensees must retain forms, including ATF Forms 4473, and acquisition and disposition records until the business or licensed activity is discontinued.

Paper forms and records over 20 years of age may be stored in a separate warehouse, which is considered part of the licensed premises and subject to inspection. Paper acquisition and disposition records stored separately are those that do not contain any open disposition entries and with no dispositions recorded within 20 years.

13. Factoring Criteria for Firearms with Attached "Stabilizing Braces"*

U.S. DEPARTMENT OF JUSTICE

Background

The Attorney General is responsible for enforcing the GCA, as amended, and the NFA, as amended.[1] This includes the authority to promulgate regulations necessary to enforce the provisions of the GCA and NFA. See 18 U.S.C. 926(a); 26 U.S.C. 7801(a)(2)(A)(ii), 7805(a). The Attorney General has delegated the responsibility for administering and enforcing the GCA and NFA to the Director of ATF, subject to the direction of the Attorney General and the Deputy Attorney General. See 28 CFR 0.130(a)(1)-(2). Accordingly, the Attorney General and ATF have promulgated regulations implementing both the GCA and the NFA. See 27 CFR parts 478, 479. The ATF Director delegated the authority to classify firearms pursuant to the GCA and NFA to ATF's Firearms Technology Criminal Branch ("FTCB") and the Firearms Technology Industry Services Branch ("FTISB"), within the Firearms and Ammunition Technology Division ("FATD"), Office of Enforcement Programs and Services ("EPS").[2] FATD supports the firearms industry and the general public by, among other things, responding to technical inquiries and by testing and evaluating firearms voluntarily submitted to ATF for classification under the GCA or NFA. There is no requirement that the firearms industry or the public submit firearms to ATF for evaluation of the firearm's proper classification under Federal law.

The statutory definitions of "firearm" under the GCA and the NFA are different.[3] In 1934, Congress passed the NFA in order to regulate certain Start Printed Page 30827 "gangster" type weapons.[4] These weapons were viewed as especially dangerous and unusual, and, as a result, are subject to taxes and are required to be registered with ATF.[5] See 26 U.S.C. 5811, 5821, 5841, 5845. The Supreme Court in District of Columbia v. Heller, 554 U.S. 570 (2008), recognized these additional constraints as consistent with the Second Amendment. "We also recognize another important limitation on the right to keep and carry arms." [United States v. Miller, 307 U.S. 174 (1939)], said, as we have explained, that the sorts of weapons protected were those "in common use at the time." See 307 U.S., at 179, 59 S. Ct. 816. We think that limitation is fairly supported by the historical tradition of prohibiting the carrying of "dangerous and unusual weapons." Id. at 627.

---

*Public document originally published as U.S. Department of Justice, "Factoring Criteria for Firearms with Attached 'Stabilizing Braces,'" https://www.federalregister.gov/documents/2021/06/10/2021-12176/factoring-criteria-for-firearms-with-attached-stabilizing-braces (June 10, 2021).

As a result of the different definitions in the GCA and NFA, classification of a weapon as a "firearm" under the GCA or the NFA affects how it is regulated under Federal law. For instance, a weapon classified as a "firearm" under only the GCA is subject to interstate controls, but is not subject to making or transfer taxes, and need not be registered in the National Firearms Registration and Transfer Record ("NFRTR") as required by the NFA. See 18 U.S.C. 922(a)(1); 26 U.S.C. 5812, 5822, 5841, 5845. In contrast, weapons classified as NFA firearms are generally regulated under both statutes. This includes rifles having a barrel or barrels less than 16 inches in length (also known as "short-barreled rifles") and shotguns having a barrel or barrels less than 18 inches in length (also known as "short-barreled shotguns."). Under the NFA and implementing regulations, the term "rifle" is defined to mean "a weapon designed or redesigned, made or remade, and intended to be fired from the shoulder and designed or redesigned and made or remade to use the energy of the explosive in a fixed cartridge to fire only a single projectile through a rifled bore for each single pull of the trigger and shall include any such weapon which may be readily restored to fire a fixed cartridge." See 26 U.S.C. 5845(c); 27 CFR 479.11. In addition to the NFA requirements, the GCA also imposes specific restrictions on the transportation, sale, and delivery of "short-barreled rifles" and "short-barreled shotguns." See 18 U.S.C. 922(a)(4), (b)(4). Therefore, FATD's classifications of a particular firearm allow industry members to plan, develop, and distribute products in compliance with the law, thereby reducing their risk of incurring criminal or civil penalties, or the potential for costly corrective actions, including a possible recall by the manufacturer.

Generally, when FATD evaluates a submitted firearm sample, it examines its overall configuration, physical characteristics, and objective design features that are relevant under the statutory definitions of the GCA and NFA, and any other information that directly affects the classification of a particular firearm configuration as presented by that sample. The numerous configurations, materials, and designs of modern firearms require thorough examination and consideration to ensure proper classification. Even though firearms may have a similar appearance (i.e., shape, size, etc.), an ATF classification of a firearm pertains only to the particular sample submitted because of the vast variations in submissions, the application of different relevant statutes and judicial interpretations of these statutes, the manufacturer's or maker's stated intent,[6] and the objective design features supporting or undercutting that stated intent that may be legally and technically significant.

In recent years, some manufacturers have produced and sold devices ("stabilizing braces") designed to be attached to large or heavy pistols and that are marketed to help a shooter "stabilize" his or her arm to support single-handed firing. The first individual to submit a forearm brace to determine if it changed the classification of a "pistol" advised ATF that "the AR15 pistol is very difficult to control with the one-handed precision stance due to the forward weight of the weapon and the recoil of the 5.56, 7.62 or 7.62[sic] x39 NATO caliber rounds."[7] There, the submitter explained that the intent of the brace was to facilitate one-handed firing of the AR-15 pistol for those with limited strength or mobility due to a disability, and to reduce bruising to the forearm when firing with one hand. According to this individual, the brace concept was inspired by the needs of combat veterans with disabilities who still enjoy recreational shooting but could not reliably control heavy pistols without assistance. However, whereas some accessories marketed as "stabilizing braces" may make it easier for a person to fire a weapon with one hand

and would not result in a determination that the firearm with the attached brace is a "rifle," there are other accessories also marketed as "stabilizing braces" that may be attached to a weapon platform for the purpose of circumventing the GCA and NFA prohibitions on the sale, delivery, transportation, or unregistered possession and taxation of "short-barreled rifles." As described below, the addition of an accessory that is Start Printed Page 30828 marketed as a "stabilizing brace" to a pistol does not guarantee that the resulting firearm will still be classified as a pistol. Indeed, classifying a firearm based on a limited or singular characteristic (i.e., the marketing label of the manufacturer that the item is a "stabilizing brace"), "has the potential to be significantly overinclusive or underinclusive." [8]

Because short-barreled rifles are among the firearms considered unusual and dangerous, subjecting them to regulation under the NFA, it is especially important that such weapons be properly classified. Indeed, firearms with "stabilizing braces" have been used in at least two mass shootings, with the shooters in both instances reportedly shouldering the "brace" as a stock, demonstrating the efficacy as "short-barreled" rifles of firearms equipped with such "braces." [9]

The GCA and NFA regulate "firearms" and, with limited exceptions, do not regulate individual components. Accordingly, ATF does not classify unregulated components or accessories alone under the GCA and NFA. [10] However, components or accessories, when attached to a firearm, can affect the classification of a firearm because: (1) A component's or an accessory's likely use may be relevant in assessing the manufacturer's or maker's purported intent with respect to the design of a firearm; and (2) the design of a component or an accessory may result in a firearm falling within a particular statutory definition. Examples include: (1) The attachment of a forward secondary grip [11] to a "pistol," where the resulting firearm would no longer be designed to be held and fired with a single hand; and (2) a wallet holster [12] where the handgun can be fired while inserted, thus changing the classification of these handguns into an "any other weapon." See 26 U.S.C. 5845(e). A "stabilizing brace," of which there are several variations, is yet another example of a component or an accessory that may change the classification of the firearm to which it is attached.

ATF's longstanding and publicly known position is that a firearm does not evade classification under the NFA merely because the firearm is configured with a device marketed as a "stabilizing brace" or "arm brace." [13] When a purported "stabilizing brace" and an attached weapon's objective design features indicate that the firearm is actually designed and intended to be fired from the shoulder, such weapon may fall within the scope of the NFA, requiring registration and payment of tax. Accordingly, ATF must evaluate on a case-by-case basis whether a particular firearm configured with a "stabilizing brace" bears the objective features of a firearm designed and intended to be fired from the shoulder and is thus subject to the NFA. The use of a purported "stabilizing brace" cannot be a tool to circumvent the NFA (or the GCA) and the prohibition on the unregistered possession of "short-barreled rifles."

As the purpose of the NFA is "to regulate certain weapons likely to be used for criminal purposes," United States v. Thompson/Center Arms Co., 504 U.S. 505, 517 (1992), ATF cannot ignore the design features of a firearm that place it within the scope of the NFA's regulation. This is the case even when a manufacturer characterizes or markets a firearm accessory in a manner that suggests a use that does not correspond to its objective design. The characterization of an accessory by the manufacturer, including assertions in advertising, is not dispositive. If ATF's evaluation of a submitted sample demonstrates that the objective design features of the firearm, as configured, do not support the manufacturer's purported intent and, in fact, suggest an altogether different intent, ATF will classify the firearm based on the objective design features, as Federal law requires. See Sig Sauer, Inc. v. Brandon, 826 F.3d 598, 601–02 (1st Cir. 2016).

It is estimated that manufacturers of stabilizing braces have sold 3 million stabilizing braces since 2013. ATF has observed that the development and production of rifled barrel weapons with "stabilizing braces" has become more prevalent in the firearms industry and that, consequently, requests for classifications for this kind of firearm design have also increased. ATF has classified several firearms equipped with "stabilizing braces" and the objective features used to make these classifications have been described in letters to the industry as well as in criminal cases. However, ATF has received criticism for not more widely publishing the criteria and for not publishing a definitive approach in the application of that criteria. Therefore, to aid the firearms industry and public in understanding the criteria that FATD considers when evaluating firearm samples that are submitted with an attached "stabilizing brace" or similar component or accessory, ATF proposes a worksheet to be entitled Factoring Criteria for Rifled Barrel Weapons with Accessories [14] commonly referred to as "Stabilizing Braces," ATF Worksheet 4999 ("Worksheet 4999"). The purpose of this worksheet is to allow individuals or members of the firearms industry to evaluate whether a weapon incorporating a "stabilizing brace" that they intend to submit to FATD or offer for sale will be considered a "short-barreled rifle" or "firearm" under the GCA and NFA. FATD will use the criteria within ATF Worksheet 4999 and resulting point value when evaluating and classifying a submitted firearm.

These criteria and worksheet do not apply to firearms with a smooth bore that use shotgun ammunition. These types of firearms, commonly referred to as "pistol grip shotguns," were never designed to be fired from one hand (e.g., Mossberg Shockwave, Remington Tac-Start Printed Page 3082914). ATF has always classified these weapons as GCA "firearms," not shotguns or pistols, as they do not incorporate a stock, like a shotgun, and are not designed to be fired from one hand, like a pistol. Thus, the addition of a "stabilizing brace" does not assist with single-handed firing, but rather redesigns the firearm to provide surface area for firing from the shoulder.

Application of ATF Worksheet 4999

Similar to the Factoring Criteria for Weapons, ATF Form 4590 ("Form 4590"), which is used for the importation of pistols and revolvers, the proposed ATF Worksheet 4999 has a point system assigning a weighted value to various characteristics of the fully assembled firearm as configured when submitted for classification. A firearm that accumulates less than 4 points in Section II (Accessory Characteristics), and less than 4 points in Section III (Configuration of Weapon), will generally be determined not to be designed to be fired from the shoulder, unless there is evidence that the manufacturer or maker expressly intended to design the weapon to be fired from the shoulder. A firearm that accumulates 4 points or more in Section II or Section III will be determined to be designed and intended to be fired from the shoulder.

As a preliminary factor when evaluating a submitted sample, certain prerequisites (i.e., weapon weight and overall length) will be applied to determine if the firearm will even be considered as a possible pistol or immediately determined to be a rifle, as defined by the applicable statutes. As discussed, "stabilizing braces" were originally marketed as intended to assist persons with disabilities and others lacking sufficient grip strength to control heavier pistols. Therefore, attaching a "stabilizing brace" to a typical pistol, where no assistance is necessary, or attaching one to a firearm so heavy or difficult to control that one-handed shooting is impractical or inaccurate, regardless of the manufacturer's stated intent, will change the design of the firearm into a rifle intended to be fired from the shoulder. Indeed, the purported "stabilizing brace" would have no design function other than to facilitate the firing of the weapon from the shoulder.

On the proposed Worksheet 4999, objective design characteristics or features that are common to rifles, features associated with shoulder stocks, and those features limiting the ability to use the "stabilizing brace" as an actual brace are assigned point values. These point values range from 0 to 4 points based upon the degree of the indicator, explained as follows:

- 1 point: Minor Indicator (the weapon could be fired from the shoulder)
- 2 points: Moderate Indicator (the weapon may be designed and intended to be fired from the shoulder)
- 3 points: Strong Indicator (the weapon is likely designed and intended to be fired from the shoulder)
- 4 points: Decisive Indicator (the weapon is designed and intended to be fired from the shoulder)

As in ATF Form 4590, the point values associated with particular features or designs are based upon their relative importance in classifying the firearm under the law. In this case, design factors that are more likely to demonstrate a manufacturer's or maker's intent to produce a "short-barreled rifle" and market it as a "braced pistol" accrue more points than those that reveal less evidence. There are certain inherent features that may support a design as a "stabilizing brace" and also a shoulder stock. For example, a large amount of surface area on the rear of a purported "stabilizing brace" may indicate that it is designed to be fired from the shoulder and facilitate its use as a shoulder stock. However, that characteristic may also be the result of incorporating substantial stabilizing support that envelopes the shooter's arm (e.g., the original SB15 "stabilizing brace"), allowing one-handed firing of a large pistol. These complexities cannot serve merely to exempt all firearms with purported "stabilizing braces" from classification as "rifles." Indeed, the statutory definitions of "rifle" in the GCA and NFA describe that type of weapon as one "intended to be fired from the shoulder." See 18 U.S.C. 921(a)(7); 26 U.S.C. 5845(c). The ATF Worksheet 4999 is necessary to enforce the law consistently, considering the diversity of firearm designs and configurations.

As stated above, if the total point value of the firearm submitted is equal to or greater than 4—in either Section II or III—then the firearm, with the attached "stabilizing brace," will be determined to be "designed or redesigned, made or remade, and intended to be fired from the shoulder," or a "rifle" under the GCA and NFA. The firearm will be classified as a "short-barreled rifle" under the GCA and NFA, and as an NFA "firearm," if the attached barrel is also less than 16 inches. The ATF Worksheet 4999 will provide the public and the firearms industry with a detailed methodology for ensuring legal compliance.

By using ATF Worksheet 4999, ATF is ensuring uniform consideration and application of these criteria when evaluating firearm samples with attached "stabilizing braces." ATF also notes that some makers or manufacturers have received a classification of a "stabilizing brace" without it being attached to a firearm or may have received a classification for a firearm that would be considered a NFA firearm under these criteria. Therefore, any maker or manufacturer who has received a classification prior to the effective date of the rule is encouraged to resubmit the firearm with the attached "stabilizing brace" to ensure that the prior classification is consistent with this new rule and to avoid any possible criminal or tax penalties for the continued manufacture, transfer, or possession of a NFA firearm. As iterated above, FATD's classifications allow industry members to plan and develop products that comply with the law, and thereby reduce their risk of incurring criminal or civil penalties, or the need for corrective actions, including a recall by the manufacturer. ATF recognizes that these factors may affect industry members and members of the public, as they may manufacture or already own firearms with a "stabilizing brace" attached. ATF wants to assist affected persons and industry members and provides the additional information in this proposed rule to aid them in complying with Federal laws and regulations.

For Section III, see: https://www.federalregister.gov/documents/2021/06/10/2021-12176/factoring-criteria-for-firearms-with-att.

NOTES

1. NFA provisions still refer to the "Secretary of the Treasury." However, the Homeland Security Act of 2002, Public Law 107-296, 116 Stat. 2135, transferred the functions of ATF from the Department of the Treasury to the Department of Justice, under the general authority of the Attorney General. 26 U.S.C. 7801(a)(2); 28 U.S.C. 599A(c)(1). Thus, for ease of reference, this notice of proposed rulemaking refers to the Attorney General throughout.

2. Delegation of Authorities within the Bureau of Alcohol, Tobacco, Firearms and Explosives, Delegation Order 1100.168C (Nov. 5, 2018).

3. 18 U.S.C. 921(a)(3) (GCA definition of firearm); 26 U.S.C. 5845(a) (NFA definition of firearm).

4. Congress chose to regulate these firearms by taxing them. Therefore, the NFA is part of the Internal Revenue Code.

5. Courts have recognized the dangerousness and uniqueness of NFA firearms and that possession of unregistered firearms poses a danger to the community. United States v. Jennings, 195 F.3d 795, 799 (5th Cir. 1999) (Congress determined that the unregistered possession of the particular firearms regulated under the NFA should be outlawed because of "the virtual inevitability that such possession will result in violence"); see United States v. Cox, 906 F.3d 1170 (10th Cir. 2018) ("[T]he historical tradition of prohibiting the carrying of dangerous and unusual weapons" supported limiting the Second Amendment's protection to weapons "in common use at the time" of ratification. (quoting District of Columbia v. Heller, 554 U.S. 570, 626-27 (2008)); United States v. Marzzarella, 614 F.3d 85, 95 (3rd Cir. 2010) (explaining that a long gun with a shortened barrel is both dangerous and unusual, because "its concealability fosters its use in illicit activity," and "because of its heightened capability to cause damage"); United States v. Amos, 501 F.3d 524, 531 (6th Cir. 2007) (McKeague, J., dissenting) ("[A] sawed-off shotgun can be concealed under a large shirt or coat. . . . [T]he combination of low, somewhat indiscriminate accuracy, large destructive power, and the ability to conceal . . . makes a sawed-off shotgun useful for only violence against another person, rather than, for example, against sport game."); Bezet v. United States, 276 F. Supp. 3d 576, 611-12 (E.D. La. 2017), aff'd, 714 F. App'x. 336 (5th Cir. 2017) ("Prior to the enactment of the NFA, Congress recognized that the country struggled to control the violence wrought by 'gangsters, racketeers, and professional criminals.' . . . Similarly to the GCA, the NFA was adopted by Congress to establish a nationwide system to regulate the sale, transfer, license, and manufacturing of certain 'dangerous weapons' such as 'machine guns, sawed-off shotguns, sawed-off rifles, and other firearms, other than pistols and revolvers, which may be concealed on the persons, and silencers.' . . . [T]he NFA targets 'certain weapons likely to be used for criminal purposes.'"); United States v. Gonzalez, No. 2:10-cr-00967, 2011 WL 5288727, at *5 (D. Utah Nov. 2, 2011) ("Congress specifically found that 'short-barreled rifles are primarily weapons of war and have no appropriate sporting use or use for personal protection'" [quoting S. Rep. No. 90-1501, at 28 (1968)]).

6. See Sig Sauer, Inc. v. Brandon, 826 F.3d 598 (1st Cir. 2016) (noting that, in the firearms classification context, it is appropriate for ATF to consider "a part's design features . . . as part of the inquiry into" the intended use of that part). The court noted that "[s]uch an objective approach to ferreting out a party's intent is a very familiar one in the law. See, e.g., United States v. Siciliano, 578 F.3d 61, 77 (1st Cir. 2009) (noting that objective evidence is useful to `buttress or rebut direct testimony as to intent'); cf. Washington v. Davis, 426 U.S. 229, 253, 96 S. Ct. 2040, 48 L. Ed. 2d 597 (1976) (Stevens, J., concurring) (`Frequently the most probative evidence of intent will be objective evidence of what actually happened rather than evidence describing the subjective state of mind of the actor.'); United States v. Gaw, 817 F.3d 1 (1st Cir. 2016) ("[T]he law is long since settled that the prosecution may prove its case without direct evidence of a defendant's guilty knowledge so long as the array of circumstantial evidence possesses sufficient persuasive power." [quoting United States v. O'Brien, 14 F.3d 703, 706 (1st Cir. 1994)])."

7. Classification request from NST Global LLC (Nov. 8, 2012).

8. Innovator Enters., Inc. v. Jones, 28 F. Supp. 3d 14, 25 (D.D.C. 2014).

9. See, e.g., Cameron Knight, "Dayton shooter used a modified gun that may have exploited a legal loophole," *USA Today* (published Aug. 5, 2019, updated Aug. 6, 2019) https://www.usatoday.com/story/news/nation/2019/08/05/dayton-shooter-used-gun-may-have-exploited-legal-loophole/1927566001/ (the firearm used in a shooting killing 9 people and wounding 14 had a "pistol brace" used to "skirt" regulation of short-barrel rifles); Melissa Macaya et al., "10 killed in Colorado grocery store shooting," *CNN* (updated Mar. 23, 2021), https://www.cnn.com/us/live-news/boulder-colorado-shooting-3-23-21/h_0c662370eefaeff05eac3ef8d5f29e94 (reporting that the firearm used in a shooting that killed 10 was an AR-15 pistol with an "arm brace").

10. ATF does, however, make these types of classifications under the Arms Export Control Act ("AECA"), 22 U.S.C. 2778, with respect to the permanent importation of "defense articles."

11. See U.S. v. Black, 739 F.3d 931, 934-36 (6th Cir. 2014).

12. See FFL Newsletter, August 1997, at 5-6 (https://www.atf.gov/firearms/docs/newsletter/federal-firearms-licensees-newsletter-%E2%80%93-august-1997/download).

13. See ATF, Open Letter on the Redesign of "Stabilizing Braces," (Jan. 16, 2015); and a letter to industry counsel clarifying the 2015 Open Letter, Letter for Mark Barnes, Counsel to SB Tactical, LLC, from Marvin G. Richardson, Assistant Director, ATF Enforcement Programs & Services, 90000:GM, 5000, Re: Reversal of ATF Open Letter on the Redesign of "Stabilizing Braces" (Mar. 21, 2017) (made widely available to the public on various websites, for example, see https://johnpierceesq.com/wp-content/uploads/2017/03/ATF-Letter-March-21-2017.pdf and https://www.sigsauer.com/wp-content/uploads/2017/04/atf-letter-march-21-2017.pdf).

14. As used in this rule and worksheet, the term "accessory" is intended as a general term to describe the marketing of items commonly known as "stabilizing braces" and does not affect any ATF determinations whether such items when attached to a handgun are, in fact, "accessories" not necessary for the operation of the handgun, but which enhance its usefulness or effectiveness, or whether they are component parts necessary to properly operate a weapon, such as a rifle. Furthermore, use of that term does not affect any determinations whether such items are "defense articles" under the Arms Export Control Act. Please direct all inquiries as to possible liability for the firearms and ammunition excise tax, 26 U.S.C. 4181-82, to the United States Department of Treasury, Alcohol and Tobacco Tax and Trade Bureau ("TTB").

14. Republicans Say No to CDC Gun Violence Research*

Lois Beckett

After the Sandy Hook school shooting, Rep. Jack Kingston (R-GA) was one of a few congressional Republicans who expressed a willingness to reconsider the need for gun control laws.

"Put guns on the table, also put video games on the table, put mental health on the table," he said less than a week after the Newtown shootings. He told a local TV station that he wanted to see more research done to understand mass shootings. "Let's let the data lead rather than our political opinions."

For nearly 20 years, Congress has pushed the Centers for Disease Control and Prevention (CDC) to steer clear of firearms violence research. As chairman of the appropriations subcommittee that traditionally sets CDC funding, Kingston has been in a position to change that. Soon after Sandy Hook, Kingston said he had spoken to the head of the agency. "I think we can find some common ground," Kingston said.

More than a year later, as Kingston competes in a crowded Republican primary race for a U.S. Senate seat, the congressman is no longer talking about common ground.

In a statement to ProPublica, Kingston said he would oppose a proposal from President Obama for $10 million in CDC gun research funding. "The President's request to fund propaganda for his gun-grabbing initiatives through the CDC will not be included in the FY2015 appropriations bill," Kingston said.

Rep. Steve Womack (R-AR), the vice chairman of the subcommittee, also "supports the long-standing prohibition of gun control advocacy or promotion funding," his spokeswoman said.

CDC's current funding for gun violence prevention research remains at $0.

As gun violence spiked in the early 1990s, the CDC ramped up its funding of firearms violence research. Then, in 1996, it backed off under pressure from Congress and the National Rifle Association. Funding for firearms injury prevention activities dropped from more than $2.7 million in 1995 to barely $100,000 by 2012, according to CDC figures.

After the Sandy Hook shootings, Obama issued a presidential memorandum "directing the Centers for Disease Control to research the causes and prevention of gun violence."

---

*This story was originally published by ProPublica as Lois Beckett, "Republicans Say No to CDC Gun Violence Research," https://www.propublica.org/article/republicans-say-no-to-cdc-gun-violence-research (April 21, 2014). Reprinted with permission of the publisher.

Following Obama's instructions, the authoritative Institute of Medicine put together a report on priorities for research on reducing gun violence. Among the questions that need answers, according to the report: Do background checks—the most popular and prominent gun control policy proposal—actually reduce gun violence? How often do Americans successfully use guns to protect themselves each year? And—a question that Kingston himself had raised repeatedly—what is the relationship between violence in video games and other media and "real-life" violence?

Dr. Mark Rosenberg, who led the CDC's gun violence research in the 1990s, said that the National Rifle Association and other opponents of funding have often fueled a misconception: that Americans can be for guns or for gun research, but not both.

"The researchers at CDC are committed to two goals: one goal is preventing firearm injuries. The second goal is to preserve the rights of legitimate gun owners. They have been totally misportrayed," Rosenberg said.

A long list of associations that represent medical professionals—including the American Medical Association, the American Psychological Association and the American Academy of Pediatrics—signed a letter last year urging Congress to fund gun violence prevention research.

"If all we wanted to do was protect the rights of legitimate gun owners, we wouldn't pass any legislation, and if we just wanted to reduce firearm injuries and death, we might say, 'Take all guns out of civilian hands,'" Rosenberg said. "The trick is, we want to do both at the same time, and that requires research."

The NRA did not respond to a request for comment. Last year, the NRA's director of public affairs, Andrew Arulanandam, told CNN that more government gun research is not needed.

"What works to reduce gun violence is to make sure that criminals are prosecuted and those who have been found to be a danger to themselves or others don't have access to firearms," Arulanandam said. "Not to carry out more studies."

Kingston has touted his A+ rating from the NRA. But in his opponents in the Senate primary race are also running on their gun-rights records. (One of them recently made headlines with an AR-15 assault rifle giveaway.)

The CDC is not the only source of federally funded research on gun violence. In response to Obama's push for more research, the National Institutes of Health (NIH), which invests $30 billion in medical research each year, put out a call for new research projects on gun violence prevention last fall. While the first submission deadline has passed, it's not yet clear how many projects will be funded, or how much money NIH will devote to the effort. An NIH spokeswoman said there is no set funding amount.

Congress also approved Obama's request for additional CDC funding last year to broaden the reach of the National Violent Death Reporting System (NVDRS), a detailed database of the circumstances surrounding all kinds of violent deaths, including gun deaths. Obama has asked for $23 million this year, to expand the data collection to all 50 states and Washington, D.C.

A CDC spokeswoman said that while the agency "does not receive any dedicated funding for firearm related injury prevention research," Congress does fund "research on a variety of related topics, including youth violence, child maltreatment, domestic violence, and sexual violence."

"We remain committed to treating gun violence as the public health issue it is, which is why we need the best researchers in this country working on this topic," a White House spokesperson said in a statement.

Sen. Tom Harkin (D-IA), chair of the Senate appropriations subcommittee that oversees CDC funding, successfully pushed for more NVDRS funding last year. He told ProPublica in a statement that investing in gun violence research is a "critical need," but that it has to be balanced "with many competing priorities."

Other Democrats in the Senate and House—including Sen. Edward Markey (D-MA) and Rep. Carolyn Maloney (D-NY)—have continued to push for more funding.

• B. State Safety Regulations •

15. More States Are Allowing Guns on College Campuses*

NEAL H. HUTCHENS *and* KERRY B. MELEAR

A community college instructor in Texas recently started off the academic year by wearing a bulletproof vest and army helmet to class. He did this to protest a law that, starting this August, authorizes individuals to carry concealed handguns at public community colleges in Texas. In 2016, the same law had already allowed guns at four-year institutions.

Texas and 10 other states now have laws permitting concealed carry of guns at colleges and universities. So far in 2017, campus carry bills have been introduced in at least 16 other states.

As scholars of higher education law, we have both been following campus carry legislation quite closely. Kerry published an analysis of campus carry laws and policies and Neal has worked with an advocacy group that opposes guns on campus.

While state laws and campus policies vary widely across the U.S., our view is that colleges and universities should not be forced to allow guns on their campuses—particularly in a political climate that has seen violence at dozens of colleges across the country.

Why Do People Want Guns on Campus?

One key argument in favor of campus carry laws comes from the idea that arming students and faculty will protect the community in the case of a violent incident, such as the deadly mass shooting at Virginia Tech University in 2007.

This campaign is also part of a larger effort—led by the National Rifle Association—to expand rights for individuals to carry guns in public places, including at colleges and universities.

In 2004, such sentiments helped propel Utah to become the first state to allow guns

*Originally published as Neal H. Hutchens and Kerry B. Melear, "More States Are Allowing Guns on College Campuses," *The Conversation*, https://theconversation.com/more-states-are-allowing-guns-on-college-campuses-81791 (August 17, 2017). Reprinted with permission of the publisher.

on campus. Utah Republican State Sen. Michael Waddoups explained his support of the law: "If government can't protect you, you should have the right to protect yourself."

Since Utah passed its law, other states have followed, with legislative interest picking up notably in the last five years. In May of 2017, Georgia joined the ranks as the 11th state to allow some form of concealed carry-on public campuses.

Overview of State Laws

Though Arkansas, Colorado, Georgia, Idaho, Kansas, Mississippi, Oregon, Tennessee, Texas, Utah, and Wisconsin all have campus carry laws, there are important differences among them.

For some states, firearms are regularly permitted. Public colleges and universities in Utah and Arkansas must allow any individual with an appropriate permit to carry a concealed gun on campus, including inside campus buildings. In Tennessee, full-time employees, but not students, may carry concealed weapons.

A handful of states have given schools some measure of autonomy. In Wisconsin and Kansas, public institutions may choose to prohibit guns in specific buildings, but guns must be allowed elsewhere on campus. In Kansas, such an action requires the school to put in place certain security measures, like metal detectors and armed security guards in the buildings where guns have been banned.

Meanwhile, some states are quite specific when it comes to one area of campus: sporting events. Earlier this year, Arkansas passed its campus carry law, which was quickly amended to prohibit guns at athletic contests. Georgia also doesn't allow guns at college sporting events, but the law does allow concealed handguns at tailgating.

What about the other 39 states?

Individual colleges and universities have discretion in 23 states to decide whether guns are allowed on their campus. Among these, public institutions in Ohio can set their own policies when it comes to guns in campus areas and buildings, but firearms are allowed by law to be in locked cars in parking areas.

The final 16 states prohibit outright the concealed carrying of guns at any college or university.

Research Doesn't Support Campus Carry

From our perspective—and based on an emerging body of research—allowing individuals to carry guns on campus is not an effective way to prevent mass shootings and, in fact, may be more likely to lead to violent outcomes.

Recent research by scholars at Johns Hopkins University discusses how guns on campus may allow suicidal individuals easier access to firearms. They note this is especially troubling since younger people, highly represented on college campuses, can be more susceptible to suicidal behavior that results in death or hospitalization. Indeed, suicide is the second-leading cause of death among college-aged individuals.

In general, gun deaths are more likely connected to personal disputes or domestic violence than mass shootings. The researchers at Johns Hopkins suggests that trend is true on college campuses as well, with gun incidents more likely to involve interpersonal conflict than a random shooting event.

While not focused specifically on campus gun laws, another new study determined that states with concealed carry laws have experienced increases in violent crime.

We believe that, rather than an effective deterrent to violence, guns on campus are more likely to put people at risk.

What Do Colleges Think?

The prevailing sentiments at many schools across the U.S. seem to suggest that institutions of higher learning likely don't view campus carry as enhancing safety.

While public colleges and universities in Texas must allow firearms to be carried, private institutions have the option of adopting campus carry under the state's law. Yet, so far, only one private university in the state has done so.

What's more, several universities in campus carry states have sought to challenge state laws. While ultimately unsuccessful, public institutions in Utah and Colorado engaged in lawsuits in an effort to keep guns off their campuses.

A Better Approach

Dozens of recent incidents at colleges across the country have shown that campuses are currently epicenters of protest and unrest. The recent violence prompted by white nationalist gatherings at and near the University of Virginia highlighted this in a disturbing fashion.

In short, it's not unreasonable to expect university administrators to be concerned that permitting guns on their campuses could lead to violence, cause fear in their community, and interfere with their educational mission.

These are the same administrators who can limit educational and civic activities that they feel are potentially dangerous (like making campus venues unavailable for certain events). But in 11 states, administrators aren't able to make these decisions when it comes to faculty and students carrying concealed weapons.

We believe that guns on campus should be prohibited outright—as they are in many states. However, if states insist on maintaining campus carry laws, institutions should at least be given the legal discretion to design appropriate policies for their unique campus contexts.

16. Mass Shootings Do Little to Change State Gun Laws*

JOAQUIN SAPIEN

Following the mass shooting in Connecticut, the Obama administration and law-makers around the country have promised to re-examine gun control in America.

ProPublica decided to take a look at what's happened legislatively in states where some of the worst shootings in recent U.S. history have occurred to see what effect, if any, those events had on gun laws.

We found that while legislators in Virginia, Alabama, Arizona, New York, Texas, and Colorado sometimes contemplated tightening rules after rampage shootings, few measures gained passage. In fact, several states have made it easier to buy more guns and take them to more places.

Here's a rundown of what's happened in each of those states:

Virginia: After 23-year-old Virginia Tech student Seung Hui Cho killed 32 students and faculty members at the university in April 2007, then-Gov. Tim Kaine assigned a blue-ribbon task force to examine gun policies in the state. The task force made dozens of recommendations that, among other things, suggested that the state intensify background checks for gun purchasers, and ban firearm possession on college campuses. None of the recommendations became law.

The most significant change in Virginia came two weeks after the shooting when Kaine signed an executive order requiring the names of all people involuntarily committed to mental health facilities to be provided to a federal database called the National Instant Criminal Background Check System, or NICS. Licensed gun dealers are supposed to check the database before they sell anyone a gun.

President George W. Bush subsequently signed federal legislation requiring all states to submit their mental health records to NICS, but to gain the support of the NRA, Congress agreed to two concessions. It made changes to the way the government defined who was "mentally defective," excluding people, for example, who had been "fully released or discharged" from mandatory treatment. The law also gave mentally ill people an avenue for restoring their gun rights if they could prove to a court that they had been rehabilitated. After the law passed, the NRA pushed state lawmakers to limit roadblocks for people applying to regain their rights.

---

*This story was originally published by ProPublica as Joaquin Sapien, "Mass Shootings Do Little to Change State Gun Laws," https://www.propublica.org/article/mass-shootings-do-little-to-change-state-gun-laws (January 3, 2013). Reprinted with permission of the publisher.

Virginia is particularly open to restoring peoples' gun rights. A 2011 *New York Times* investigation found that the restoration process in the state allowed some people to regain access to guns simply by writing a letter to the state. Others were permitted to carry guns just weeks or months after being hospitalized for psychiatric treatment.

This past year the Virginia state legislature repealed a law that had barred people from buying more than one handgun per month—a law put in place because so many guns purchased in Virginia were later used in crimes committed in states with more restrictions.

The legislature also has made several changes to its gun permitting process. In March, the state eliminated municipalities' ability to require fingerprints as part of a concealed weapon permit application. The state used to require gun owners to undergo training with a certified instructor in order to get permits, but in 2009 it adopted a law allowing people to take an hour-long online test instead. Since Virginia adopted the law, the number of concealed handgun permits the state has issued increased dramatically and many of the permits were issued to people who live in other states where Virginia permits are accepted.

In 2010, Virginia became one of five states to allow permit holders to carry concealed and loaded weapons into bars and restaurants.

Alabama: In Alabama, gun control advocates have won two small legislative victories since March 2009, when 28-year-old sausage plant worker Michael McLendon went on a three-town shooting spree, killing 10 people.

In 2011, the state made it illegal for people to buy weapons for someone else who doesn't have permission to carry one or to provide false information about their identity to a licensed gun dealer. The law was intended to help crack down on gun trafficking. (According to data compiled by non-profit Mayors Against Illegal Guns, the state had the fifth highest rate of crime gun exports in 2009.)

After Florida teen Trayvon Martin was shot and killed by neighborhood watch volunteer George Zimmerman in February 2012, the Alabama state legislature made a slight revision to its version of a law known as the "castle doctrine," which is meant to allow property owners to protect their homes against intruders. Alabama changed its law so that a shooter would only be entitled to civil immunity for shooting a trespasser if the property owner reacted "reasonably."

Arizona: After former U.S. Rep. Gabrielle Giffords, D–Ariz., was shot in the head in a hail of bullets that killed six and wounded 13, a bill was introduced in the state legislature to limit gun magazines to 10 bullets, but the bill failed in the face of pressure from the gun lobby. A similar bill was proposed in Connecticut last year; it didn't pass either.

In March 2012, Arizona Gov. Jan Brewer signed a bill with the opposite effect, forbidding the Arizona Game and Fish Commission from limiting magazine capacity for any gun approved for hunting.

According to rankings assembled by the Law Center to Prevent Gun Violence, Arizona, is "49th out of 50—having enacted some of the weakest gun violence prevention laws in the country."

Arizona doesn't require a license to carry a concealed firearm in public, nor does it limit the number of firearms that someone can buy at once.

New York: After a mass shooting at an immigration services center in Binghamton, New York, where 13 people were killed and four were wounded, the state assembly entertained several bills on gun control. None passed. One bill would have given police more control over records related to firearm sales. Another would have banned 50-caliber weapons and allowed people to turn them into the state in exchange for fair market value.

Perhaps the most controversial bill in the package would have required the use of a technology called microstamping on all bullets sold in the state.

Using this technology, a serial number could be stamped on bullet casings so they could be traced back to a particular gun. The gun industry argued that the technology would be too expensive and was still unproven. Some gun manufacturers were so upset by it that they threatened to leave the state. The bill passed the Assembly in June, but the Senate did not vote on it.

In January 2012, the legislature repealed a law that previously required handgun manufacturers and dealers to share information about bullet casings and ballistics with the state. Critics of the law said the database used to maintain the information cost too much and didn't help police.

Texas: There's been no effort to tighten gun control in Texas since Army Maj. Nidal Hasan, 39, killed 13 and wounded 32 at a military processing center at Fort Hood in 2009.

In 2011, legislators passed two bills that gave gun carriers greater freedom to take their weapons to more places. One bill restricted employers from prohibiting guns from vehicles in parking areas and another allowed foster parents to carry handguns while transporting their foster children, as long as they are licensed carriers.

Colorado: Colorado's state legislature has not convened since Aurora graduate student James Eagan Holmes, 24, killed 12 and wounded 58 in a movie theater in July. At the time, Colorado Gov. John Hickenlooper suggested that families of victims needed time to grieve before a discussion on gun control could begin in the state.

After the Connecticut shooting, Hickenlooper said that "the time is right" for the state to consider stronger gun control legislation. He has introduced a measure to strengthen background checks for gun buyers.

17. New Public Database Reveals Striking Differences in How Guns Are Regulated from State to State*

MICHAEL SIEGEL *and* MOLLY PAHN

From 2014 to 2015, the United States experienced its largest annual increase in firearm deaths over the past 35 years, a 7.8 percent upturn in a single year. In 45 of the 50 states the rate of overall deaths from firearms increased and the firearm homicide rate rose in every state except West Virginia.

What did Congress do to confront this problem? Only four bills addressing firearm violence made it out of committee during the 2015–2016 congressional session. Not one was enacted.

Because of inaction on the part of the federal government, it is up to each individual state to develop its own policies to reduce gun violence. To evaluate the effectiveness of these laws, researchers and policymakers need a way to track differences in state firearm legislation over an extended time period. Previously, there was no such resource.

We have just released a new public database that tracks a wide range of firearm laws across all 50 states for the past 27 years.

For the first time, long-term trends in the enactment of gun safety laws can be compared between states. We found striking disparities between states in both the number of firearm laws and the rate of adoption of these laws over time.

Fewer Limits for Gun Owners

Our database includes 133 different measures intended to reduce gun violence, noting the presence or absence of each in all 50 states from 1991 to the present.

Five states currently have fewer than five of these 133 possible firearm law provisions in place, while two states have 100 or more. Between 1991 and 2016, one state enacted 62 of the firearm law provisions, while 16 states actually repealed more provisions than they enacted.

States are increasingly enacting laws that allow people to shoot other people as a

---

*Originally published as Michael Siegel and Molly Pahn, "New Public Database Reveals Striking Differences in How Guns Are Regulated from State to State," *The Conversation*, https://theconversation.com/new-public-database-reveals-striking-differences-in-how-guns-are-regulated-from-state-to-state-78015 (May 23, 2017). Reprinted with permission of the publisher.

first resort in public, instead of retreating when threatened. If a person perceives a threat of serious bodily harm, so-called "stand your ground" laws allow them to fire their gun with immunity from prosecution, as long as they are in a place they have a legal right to be. Between 2004 and 2017, 24 states enacted a "stand your ground" law.

States are also increasingly loosening the requirements for carrying concealed weapons. Today, there are 12 states that allow people to carry a concealed weapon without any permit or license. This year alone, three states have already enacted laws that eliminate required permits for carrying concealed weapons.

More Laws Are Being Enacted to Protect the Gun Industry

States are also increasingly enacting laws that protect the gun industry from potential liability. These laws prevent citizens who are injured by firearms from suing gun manufacturers for damages resulting from the misuse of their products. They also stop local governments from filing lawsuits against gun manufacturers.

No other consumer product manufacturer enjoys such broad immunity. A similar law at the federal level resulted in the dismissal of a lawsuit against gun manufacturers brought by the families of children killed in the Newtown tragedy in Connecticut.

While only seven states had such a law in 1991, 33 states now have a gun industry immunity law.

In 1998, the Federal Bureau of Investigation implemented a federal background check system for gun purchases from licensed dealers. Since then, only eight states have closed a loophole in this law by requiring universal background checks for all firearm purchases in their state, even those from unlicensed sellers. This "gun show loophole" allows any adult to purchase a gun without being subject to a background check merely by purchasing from a private seller, rather than a licensed dealer.

Today, adults in 37 states can legally purchase a firearm from a private seller without being required to undergo a background check.

There is, however, one area of gun regulation that most of the states, even those with very few other gun safety laws, are progressively pursuing: laws that prohibit domestic violence offenders from possessing firearms. In 1991, only three states had enacted laws that prohibit gun possession by people convicted of misdemeanor crimes of domestic violence. Today, 28 states have such laws in place.

In a similar shift, in 1991, not a single state prohibited firearm possession by people subject to permanent domestic violence-related restraining orders. Today, 27 states have this provision.

Why Our Database Matters

By examining trends in firearm legislation, rather than just looking at a single snapshot in time, we can discover patterns in firearm law adoption. These patterns may reflect changes in social norms or specific lobbying campaigns by special interest groups.

For example, the surge in "stand your ground" laws was not a coincidence, but the result of a concerted National Rifle Association lobbying campaign. Florida's 2005 law—the second to be adopted, after Utah's in 1994—was crafted by former NRA president Marion Hammer. These laws were pushed by the American Legislative Exchange Council (ALEC), of which the NRA was a member. An NRA official co-chaired an ALEC committee that drafted a model law, which was then introduced in states throughout the country.

More than anything else, this database is intended to help researchers evaluate the effectiveness of different state-level approaches to reducing gun violence. By examining the relationship between changes in these laws over time and changes in firearm mortality, researchers may be able to identify which policies are effective and which are not.

In our view, legislators must balance the protection of the constitutional right to possess a firearm for self-defense with the responsibility to reduce firearm-related injury and death. To do this, they need to distinguish policies that effectively reduce firearm violence from those that are ineffective and therefore superfluous. Reliable longitudinal data can help them find ways to mitigate the impact that gun violence has on the lives of thousands of Americans each year.

18. California Firearms Laws Summary[*]

Cɪᴀʟɪꜰᴏʀɴɪᴀ Oꜰꜰɪᴄᴇ ᴏꜰ ᴛʜᴇ Aᴛᴛᴏʀɴᴇʏ Gᴇɴᴇʀᴀʟ

Introduction

As the owner of a firearm, it is your responsibility to understand and comply with all federal, state and local laws regarding firearms ownership. Many of the laws described below pertain to the possession, use and storage of firearms in the home and merit careful review. The California Firearms Laws Summary 2016 provides a general summary of California laws that govern common possession and use of firearms by persons other than law enforcement officers or members of the armed forces. It is not designed to provide individual guidance for specific situations, nor does it address federal or local laws. The legality of any specific act of possession or use will ultimately be determined by applicable federal and state statutory and case law. Persons having specific questions are encouraged to seek legal advice from an attorney, or consult their local law enforcement agency, local prosecutor or law library. The California Department of Justice (DOJ) and all other public entities are immune from any liability arising from the drafting, publication, dissemination, or reliance upon this information.

Persons Ineligible to Possess Firearms

The following persons are prohibited from possessing firearms (Pen. Code, §§ 29800–29825, 29900; Welf. & Inst. Code, §§ 8100, 8103):

Lifetime Prohibitions

- Any person convicted of any felony or any offense enumerated in Penal Code section 29905.
- Any person convicted of an offense enumerated in Penal Code section 23515.
- Any person with two or more convictions for violating Penal Code section 417, subdivision (a)(2).
- Any person adjudicated to be a mentally disordered sex offender. (Welf. & Inst. Code, § 8103, subd. [a][1].)

---

[*]Public document originally published as California Office of the Attorney General, "California Firearms Laws Summary," https://oag.ca.gov/firearms (2021).

- Any person found by a court to be mentally incompetent to stand trial or not guilty by reason of insanity of any crime, unless the court has made a finding of restoration of competence or sanity. (Welf. & Inst. Code, § 8103, subds. [b][1], [c][1], and [d][1].)

10-Year Prohibitions

- Any person convicted of a misdemeanor violation of the following: Penal Code sections 71, 76, 136.5, 140, 148, subdivision (d), 171b, 171c, 171d, 186.28, 240, 241, 242, 243, 244.5, 245, 245.5, 246, 246.3, 247, 273.5, 273.6, 417, 417.1, 417.2, 417.6, 422, 626.9, 646.9, 830.95, subdivision (a), 17500, 17510, subdivision (a), 25300, 25800, 27510, 27590, subdivision (c), 30315, or 32625, and Welfare and Institutions Code sections 871.5, 1001.5, 8100, 8101, or 8103.

5-Year Prohibitions

- Any person taken into custody as a danger to self or others, assessed, and admitted to a mental health facility under Welfare and Institutions Code sections 5150, 5151, 5152; or certified under Welfare and Institutions Code sections 5250, 5260, 5270.15. Persons certified under Welfare and Institutions Code sections 5250, 5260, or 5270.15 may be subject to a lifetime prohibition pursuant to federal law.

Juvenile Prohibitions

- Juveniles adjudged wards of the juvenile court are prohibited until they reach age 30 if they committed an offense listed in Welfare and Institutions Code section 707, subdivision (b). (Pen. Code, § 29820.)

Miscellaneous Prohibitions

- Any person denied firearm possession as a condition of probation pursuant to Penal Code section 29900, subdivision (c).
- Any person charged with a felony offense, pending resolution of the matter. (18 U.S.C. § 922[g].)
- Any person while he or she is either a voluntary patient in a mental health facility or under a gravely disabled conservatorship (due to a mental disorder or impairment by chronic alcoholism) and if he or she is found
- to be a danger to self or others. (Welf. & Inst. Code, § 8103, subd. [e].)
- Any person addicted to the use of narcotics. (Pen. Code, § 29800, subd. [a] .)
- Any person who communicates a threat (against any reasonably identifiable victim) to a licensed psychotherapist which is subsequently reported to law enforcement, is prohibited for six months. (Welf . & Inst. Code, § 8100, subd. [b].)
- Any person who is subject to a protective order as defined in Family Code section 6218 or Penal Code section 136.2, or a temporary restraining order issued pursuant to Code of Civil Procedure sections 527.6 or 527.8.

Personal Firearms Eligibility Check

Any person may obtain from the DOJ a determination as to whether he or she is eligible to possess firearms (review of California records only). The personal firearms eligibility check application form and instructions are on the DOJ website at http://oag. ca.gov/firearms/forms. The cost for such an eligibility check is $20. (Pen. Code, § 30105.)

Sales and Transfers of Firearms

In California, only licensed California firearms dealers who possess a valid Certificate of Eligibility (COE) are authorized to engage in retail sales of firearms. These retail sales require the purchaser to provide personal identifier information for the Dealer Record of Sale (DROS) document that the firearms dealer must submit to the DOJ. There is a mandatory 10-day waiting period before the firearms dealer can deliver the firearm to the purchaser. During this 10-day waiting period, the DOJ conducts a firearms eligibility background check to ensure the purchaser is not prohibited from lawfully possessing firearms. Although there are exceptions, generally all firearms purchasers must be at least 18 years of age to purchase a long gun (rifle or shotgun) and 21 years of age to purchase a handgun (pistol or revolver). Additionally, purchasers must be California residents with a valid driver's license or identification card issued by the California Department of Motor Vehicles.

Generally, it is illegal for any person who is not a California licensed firearms dealer (private party) to sell or transfer a firearm to another non-licensed person (private party) unless the sale or transfer is completed through a licensed California firearms dealer. A "Private Party Transfer" (PPT) can be conducted at any licensed California firearms dealership. The buyer and seller must complete the required DROS document in person at the licensed firearms dealership and deliver the firearm to the dealer who will retain possession of the firearm during the mandatory 10-day waiting period. In addition to the applicable state fees, the firearms dealer may charge a fee not to exceed $10 per firearm for conducting the PPT.

The infrequent transfer of firearms between immediate family members is exempt from the law requiring PPTs to be conducted through a licensed firearms dealer. For purposes of this exemption, "immediate family member" means parent and child, and grandparent and grandchild but does not include brothers or sisters. (Pen. Code, § 16720.) The transferee must also comply with the Firearm Safety Certificate requirement described below, prior to taking possession of the firearm. Within 30 days of the transfer, the transferee must also submit a report of the transaction to the DOJ. Download the form (Report of Operation of Law or Intra-Familial Firearm Transaction BOF 4544A) from the DOJ website at http://oag.ca.gov/firearms/forms or complete and submit the form electronically via the internet at https://CFARS.doj.ca.gov.

The reclaiming of a pawned firearm is subject to the DROS and 10-day waiting period requirements.

Specific statutory requirements relating to sales and transfers of firearms follow:

Proof-of-Residency Requirement

To purchase a handgun in California, you must present documentation indicating that you are a California resident. Acceptable documentation includes a utility bill from within the last three months, a residential lease, a property deed or military permanent duty station orders indicating assignment within California.

The address provided on the proof-of-residency document must match either the address on the DROS or the address on the purchaser's California driver's license or identification card. (Pen. Code, § 26845.)

Firearm Safety Certificate Requirement

To purchase or acquire a firearm, you must have a valid Firearm Safety Certificate (FSC). To obtain an FSC, you must score at least 75 percent on an objective written test pertaining to firearms laws and safety requirements. The test is administered by DOJ Certified Instructors, who are often located at firearms dealerships. An FSC is valid for five years. You may be charged up to $25 for an FSC. Firearms being returned to their owners, such as pawn returns, are exempt from this requirement.

In the event of a lost, stolen or destroyed FSC, the issuing DOJ Certified Instructor will issue a replacement FSC for a fee of $5. You must present proof of identity to receive a replacement FSC. (Pen. Code, §§ 31610–31670.)

Safe Handling Demonstration Requirement

Prior to taking delivery of a firearm, you must successfully perform a safe handling demonstration with the firearm being purchased or acquired. Safe handling demonstrations must be performed in the presence of a DOJ Certified Instructor sometime between the date the DROS is submitted to the DOJ and the delivery of the firearm, and are generally performed at the firearms dealership. The purchaser, firearms dealer and DOJ Certified Instructor must sign an affidavit stating the safe handling demonstration was completed. The steps required to complete the safe handling demonstration are described in the Appendix. Pawn returns and intra-familial transfers are not subject to the safe handling demonstration requirement. (Pen. Code, § 26850.)

Firearms Safety Device Requirement

All firearms (long guns and handguns) purchased in California must be accompanied with a firearms safety device (FSD) that has passed required safety and functionality tests and is listed on the DOJ's official roster of DOJ-approved firearm safety devices. The current roster of certified FSDs is available on the DOJ website at http://oag.ca.gov/firearms/fsdcertlist. The FSD requirement also can be satisfied if the purchaser signs an affidavit declaring ownership of either a DOJ-approved lock box or a gun safe capable of accommodating the firearm being purchased. Pawn returns and intra-familial transfers are not subject to the FSD requirement. (Pen. Code, §§ 23635–23690.)

Roster of Handguns Certified for Sale in California

No handgun may be sold by a firearms dealer to the public unless it is of a make and model that has passed required safety and functionality tests and is listed on the DOJ's official roster of handguns certified for sale in California. The current roster of handguns certified for sale in California is on the DOJ website at http://certguns.doj.

ca.gov/. PPTs, intrafamilial transfers, and pawn/consignment returns are exempt from this requirement. (Pen. Code, § 32000.)

One-Handgun-per-30-Days Limit

No person shall make an application to purchase more than one handgun within any 30-days period. Exemptions to the one-handgun-per-30-days limit include pawn returns, intra-familial transfers and private party transfers. (Pen. Code, § 27540.)

Prohibited Firearms Transfers and Straw Purchases

What Is a Straw Purchase?

A straw purchase is buying a firearm for someone who is prohibited by law from possessing one, or buying a firearm for someone who does not want his or her name associated with the transaction.

It is a violation of California law for a person who is not licensed as a California firearms dealer to transfer a firearm to another unlicensed person, without conducting such a transfer through a licensed firearms dealer. (Pen. Code, § 27545.) Such a transfer may be punished as a felony. (Pen. Code, § 27590.)

Furthermore, it is a violation of federal law to either (1) make a false or fictitious statement on an application to purchase a firearm about a material fact, such as the identity of the person who ultimately will acquire the firearm (commonly known as "lying and buying") (18 U.S.C. 922[a][6]), or (2) knowingly transfer a firearm to a person who is prohibited by federal law from possessing and purchasing it . (18 U.S.C. 922[d].) Such transfers are punishable under federal law by a $250,000 fine and 10 years in federal prison. (18 U.S.C. 924[a][2].)

Things to Remember About Prohibited Firearms Transfers and Straw Purchases

- An illegal firearm purchase (straw purchase) is a federal crime.
- An illegal firearm purchase can bring a felony conviction sentence of 10 years in jail and a fine of up to $250,000.
- Buying a gun and giving it to someone who is prohibited from owning one is a state and federal crime.
- Never buy a gun for someone who is prohibited by law or unable to do so.

Reporting Requirements for New California Residents

New California residents must report their ownership of firearms to the DOJ or sell/transfer them in accordance with California law, within 60 days of bringing the firearm into the state. Persons who want to keep their firearms must submit a New Resident Firearm Ownership Report (BOF 4010A), along with a $19 fee, to the DOJ. Forms are available at licensed firearms dealers, the Department of Motor Vehicles or on-line at the DOJ website at http://oag.ca.gov/firearms/forms. Forms may also be completed and submitted electronically via the internet at https://CFARS.doj.ca.gov (Pen. Code, § 27560.)

Shipment of Firearms

Long guns may be mailed through the U.S. Postal Service, as well as most private parcel delivery services or common carriers. Handguns may not be sent through the U.S. Postal Service. A common or contract carrier must be used for shipment of handguns. However, pursuant to federal law, non-licensees may ship handguns only to persons who hold a valid Federal Firearms License (FFL).

Both in-state and out-of-state FFL holders are required to obtain approval (e.g., a unique verification number) from the California DOJ prior to shipping firearms to any California FFL. (Pen. Code, § 27555.)

Carrying Firearms Aboard Common Carriers

Federal and state laws generally prohibit a person from carrying any firearm or ammunition aboard any commercial passenger airplane. Similar restrictions may apply to other common carriers such as trains, ships and buses. Persons who need to carry firearms or ammunition on a common carrier should always consult the carrier in advance to determine conditions under which firearms may be transported.

Firearms in the Home, Business or at the Campsite

Unless otherwise unlawful, any person over the age of 18 who is not prohibited from possessing firearms may have a loaded or unloaded firearm at his or her place of residence, temporary residence, campsite or on private property owned or lawfully possessed by the person. Any person engaged in lawful business (including nonprofit organizations) or any officer, employee or agent authorized for lawful purposes connected with the business may have a loaded firearm within the place of business if that person is over 18 years of age and not otherwise prohibited from possessing firearms. (Pen. Code, §§ 25605, 26035.)

Note: If a person's place of business, residence, temporary residence, campsite or private property is located within an area where possession of a firearm is prohibited by local or federal laws, such laws would prevail.

Transportation of Firearms

Handguns

California Penal Code section 25400 does not prohibit a citizen of the United States over 18 years of age who is in lawful possession of a handgun, and who resides or is temporarily in California, from transporting the handgun by motor vehicle provided it is unloaded and stored in a locked container. (Pen. Code, § 25610.)

The term "locked container" means a secure container which is fully enclosed and locked by a padlock, key lock, combination lock, or similar locking device. This includes the trunk of a motor vehicle, but does not include the utility or glove compartment. (Pen. Code, § 16850.)

Rifles and Shotguns

Nonconcealable firearms (rifles and shotguns) are not generally covered within the provisions of California Penal Code section 25400 and therefore are not required to be transported in a locked container. However, as with any firearm, nonconcealable firearms must be unloaded while they are being transported. A rifle or shotgun that is defined as an assault weapon pursuant to Penal Code section 30510 or 30515 must be transported in accordance with Penal Code section 25610.

Registered Assault Weapons and .50 BMG Rifles

Registered assault weapons and registered .50 BMG rifles may be transported only between specified locations and must be unloaded and in a locked container when transported. (Pen. Code, § 30945, subd. [g].)

The term "locked container" means a secure container which is fully enclosed and locked by a padlock, key lock, combination lock, or similar locking device. This includes the trunk of a motor vehicle, but does not include the utility or glove compartment. (Pen. Code, § 16850.)

Use of Lethal Force in Self-Defense

The question of whether use of lethal force is justified in self-defense cannot be reduced to a simple list of factors. This section is based on the instructions generally given to the jury in a criminal case where self-defense is claimed and illustrates the general rules regarding the use of lethal force in self-defense.

Permissible Use of Lethal Force in Defense of Life and Body

The killing of one person by another may be justifiable when necessary to resist the attempt to commit a forcible and life-threatening crime, provided that a reasonable person in the same or similar situation would believe that (a) the person killed intended to commit a forcible and life-threatening crime; (b) there was imminent danger of such crime being accomplished; and (c) the person acted under the belief that such force was necessary to save himself or herself or another from death or a forcible and life-threatening crime . Murder, mayhem, rape and robbery are examples of forcible and life-threatening crimes. (Pen. Code, § 197.)

Self-Defense Against Assault

It is lawful for a person being assaulted to defend themselves from attack if he or she has reasonable grounds for believing, and does in fact believe, that he or she will suffer bodily injury. In doing so, he or she may use such force, up to deadly force, as a reasonable person in the same or similar circumstances would believe necessary to prevent great bodily injury or death. An assault with fists does not justify use of a deadly weapon in self-defense unless the person being assaulted believes, and a reasonable person in the same or similar circumstances would also believe, that the assault is likely to inflict great bodily injury.

It is lawful for a person who has grounds for believing, and does in fact believe, that great bodily injury is about to be inflicted upon another to protect the victim from attack. In so doing, the person may use such force as reasonably necessary to prevent the injury. Deadly force is only considered reasonable to prevent great bodily injury or death.

Note: The use of excessive force to counter an assault may result in civil or criminal penalties.

Limitations on the Use of Force in Self-Defense

The right of self-defense ceases when there is no further danger from an assailant. Thus, where a person attacked under circumstances initially justifying self-defense renders the attacker incapable of inflicting further injuries, the law of self-defense ceases and no further force may be used . Furthermore, a person may only use the amount of force, up to deadly force, as a reasonable person in the same or similar circumstances would believe necessary to prevent imminent injury. It is important to note the use of excessive force to counter an assault may result in civil or criminal penalties.

The right of self-defense is not initially available to a person who assaults another. However, if such a person attempts to stop further combat and clearly informs the adversary of his or her desire for peace but the opponent nevertheless continues the fight, the right of self-defense returns and is the same as the right of any other person being assaulted.

Protecting One's Home

A person may defend his or her home against anyone who attempts to enter in a violent manner intending violence to any person in the home. The amount of force that may be used in resisting such entry is limited to that which would appear necessary to a reasonable person in the same or similar circumstances to resist the violent entry. One is not bound to retreat, even though a retreat might safely be made. One may resist force with force, increasing it in proportion to the intruder's persistence and violence, if the circumstances apparent to the occupant would cause a reasonable person in the same or similar situation to fear for his or her safety.

The occupant may use a firearm when resisting the intruder's attempt to commit a forcible and life-threatening crime against anyone in the home provided that a reasonable person in the same or similar situation would believe that (a) the intruder intends to commit a forcible and life-threatening crime; (b) there is imminent danger of such crime being accomplished; and (c) the occupant acts under the belief that use of a firearm is necessary to save himself or herself or another from death or great bodily injury . Murder, mayhem, rape, and robbery are examples of forcible and life-threatening crimes.

Any person using force intended or likely to cause death or great bodily injury within his or her residence shall be presumed to have held a reasonable fear of imminent peril of death or great bodily injury to self, family, or a member of the household when that force is used against another person, not a member of the family or household, who unlawfully and forcibly enters or has unlawfully and forcibly entered the residence and the person using the force knew or had reason to believe that an unlawful and forcible entry had occurred . Great bodily injury means a significant or substantial physical injury. (Pen. Code, § 198.5.)

NOTE: If the presumption is rebutted by contrary evidence, the occupant may be criminally liable for an unlawful assault or homicide.

Defense of Property

The lawful occupant of real property has the right to request a trespasser to leave the premises. If the trespasser does not do so within a reasonable time, the occupant may use force to eject the trespasser. The amount of force that may be used to eject a trespasser is limited to that which a reasonable person would believe to be necessary under the same or similar circumstances.

Carrying a Concealed Weapon Without a License

It is illegal for any person to carry a handgun concealed upon his or her person or concealed in a vehicle without a license issued pursuant to Penal Code section 26150. (Pen. Code, § 25400.) A firearm locked in a motor vehicle's trunk or in a locked container carried in the vehicle other than in the utility or glove compartment is not considered concealed within the meaning of the Penal Code section 25400; neither is a firearm carried within a locked container directly to or from a motor vehicle for any lawful purpose. (Pen. Code, § 25610.)

The prohibition from carrying a concealed handgun does not apply to licensed hunters or fishermen while engaged in hunting or fishing, or while going to or returning from the hunting expedition. (Pen. Code, § 25640.) Notwithstanding this exception for hunters or fishermen, these individuals may not carry or transport loaded firearms when going to or from the expedition. The unloaded firearms should be transported in the trunk of the vehicle or in a locked container other than the utility or glove compartment. (Pen. Code, § 25610.)

There are also occupational exceptions to the prohibition from carrying a concealed weapon, including authorized employees while engaged in specified activities. (Pen. Code, §§ 25630, 25640.)

Loaded Firearms in Public

It is illegal to carry a loaded firearm on one's person or in a vehicle while in any public place, on any public street, or in any place where it is unlawful to discharge a firearm. (Pen. Code, § 25850, subd. [a].)

It is illegal for the driver of any motor vehicle, or the owner of any motor vehicle irrespective of whether the owner is occupying the vehicle to knowingly permit any person to carry a loaded firearm into the vehicle in violation of Penal Code section 25850, or Fish and Game Code section 2006. (Pen. Code, § 26100.)

A firearm is deemed loaded when there is a live cartridge or shell in, or attached in any manner to, the firearm, including, but not limited to, the firing chamber, magazine, or clip thereof attached to the firearm. A muzzle-loading firearm is deemed loaded when it is capped or primed and has a powder charge and ball or shot in the barrel or cylinder. (Pen. Code, § 16840.)

In order to determine whether a firearm is loaded, peace officers are authorized to examine any firearm carried by anyone on his or her person or in a vehicle while in any public place, on any public street or in any prohibited area of an unincorporated territory. Refusal to allow a peace officer to inspect a firearm pursuant to these provisions is, in itself, grounds for arrest. (Pen. Code, § 25850, subd. [b].)

The prohibition from carrying a loaded firearm in public does not apply to any person while hunting in an area where possession and hunting is otherwise lawful or while practice shooting at target ranges. (Pen. Code, §§ 26005, 26040.) There are also occupational exceptions to the prohibition from carrying a loaded firearm in public, including authorized employees while engaged in specified activities. (Pen. Code, §§ 26015, 26030.)

Note: Peace officers and honorably retired peace officers having properly endorsed identification certificates may carry a concealed weapon at any time. Otherwise, these exemptions apply only when the firearm is carried within the scope of the exempted conduct, such as hunting or target shooting, or within the course and scope of assigned duties, such as an armored vehicle guard trans porting money for his employer. A person who carries a loaded firearm outside the limits of the applicable exemption is in violation of the law, notwithstanding his or her possession of an occupational license or firearms training certificate. (Pen. Code, § 12031 [b].)

Openly Carrying an Unloaded Handgun

It is generally illegal for any person to carry upon his or her person or in a vehicle, an exposed and unloaded handgun while in or on:

- A public place or public street in an incorporated city or city and county; or
- A public street in a prohibited area of an unincorporated city or city and county (Pen. Code, § 26350.)

It is also illegal for the driver or owner of a motor vehicle to allow a person to bring an open and exposed unloaded handgun into a motor vehicle in specified public areas. (Pen. Code, § 17512.)

Punishment for Carrying Unregistered Handgun

Any person who commits the crime of carrying a concealed handgun while having both the handgun and ammunition for that handgun on his/her person or in his/ her vehicle may be subject to a felony enhancement if the handgun is not on file (registered) in the DOJ's Automated Firearms System. (Pen. Code, § 25400, subd. [c].)

Any person who commits the crime of carrying a loaded handgun on his/her person in a prohibited place may be guilty of a felony if the handgun is not on file (registered) in the DOJ's Automated Firearms System. (Pen. Code, § 25850, subd. [c].)

Miscellaneous Prohibited Acts

Obliteration or Alteration of Firearm Identification

It is illegal for any person to obliterate or alter the identification marks placed on any firearm including the make, model, serial number or any distinguishing mark lawfully assigned by the owner or by the DOJ. (Pen. Code, § 23900.)

It is illegal for any person to buy, sell or possess a firearm knowing its identification has been obliterated or altered. (Pen. Code, § 23920.)

Unauthorized Possession of a Firearm on School Grounds

It is illegal for any unauthorized person to possess or bring a firearm upon the grounds of, or into, any public school, including the campuses of the University of California, California State University campuses, California community colleges, any private school (kindergarten through 12th grade) or private university or college. (Pen. Code, § 626 .9.)

Unauthorized Possession of a Firearm in a Courtroom, the State Capitol, etc.

It is illegal for any unauthorized person to bring or possess any firearm within a courtroom, courthouse, court building or at any meeting required to be open to the public. (Pen. Code, § 171b.)

It is illegal for any unauthorized person to bring or possess a loaded firearm within (including upon the grounds of) the State Capitol, any legislative office, any office of the Governor or other constitutional officer, any Senate or Assembly hearing room, the Governor's Mansion or any other residence of the Governor or the residence of any constitutional officer or any Member of the Legislature. For these purposes, a firearm shall be deemed loaded whenever both the firearm and its unexpended ammunition are in the immediate possession of the same person. (Pen. Code, §§ 171c, 171d, 171e.)

Drawing or Exhibiting a Firearm

If another person is present, it is illegal for any person, except in self-defense, to draw or exhibit a loaded or unloaded firearm in a rude, angry or threatening manner or in any manner use a firearm in a fight or quarrel. (Pen. Code, § 417.)

Threatening Acts with a Firearm on a Public Street or Highway

It is illegal for any person to draw or exhibit a loaded or unloaded firearm in a threatening manner against an occupant of a motor vehicle which is on a public street or highway in such a way that would cause a reasonable person apprehension or fear of bodily harm. (Pen. Code, § 417.3.)

Discharge of a Firearm in a Grossly Negligent Manner

It is illegal for any person to willfully discharge a firearm in a grossly negligent manner which could result in injury or death to a person. (Pen. Code, § 246.3.)

Discharge of a Firearm at an Inhabited/Occupied Dwelling, Building, Vehicle, Aircraft

It is illegal for any person to maliciously and willfully discharge a firearm at an inhabited dwelling, house, occupied building, occupied motor vehicle, occupied aircraft, inhabited house car or inhabited camper. (Pen. Code, § 246.)

Discharge of a Firearm at an Unoccupied Aircraft, Motor Vehicle, or Uninhabited Building or Dwelling

It is illegal for any person to willfully and maliciously discharge a firearm at an unoccupied aircraft. It is illegal for any person to discharge a firearm at an unoccupied motor vehicle, building or dwelling. This does not apply to an abandoned vehicle, an unoccupied motor vehicle or uninhabited building or dwelling with permission of the owner and if otherwise lawful. (Pen. Code, § 247.)

Discharge of a Firearm from a Motor Vehicle

It is illegal for any person to willfully and maliciously discharge a firearm from a motor vehicle. A driver or owner of a vehicle who allows any person to discharge a firearm from the vehicle may be punished by up to three years imprisonment in state prison. (Pen. Code, § 26100.)

Criminal Storage

"Criminal storage of firearm of the first degree"—Keeping any loaded firearm within any premises that are under your custody or control and you know or reasonably should know that a child (any person under 18) is likely to gain access to the firearm without the permission of the child's parent or legal guardian and the child obtains access to the firearm and thereby causes death or great bodily injury to himself, herself, or any other person. (Pen. Code, § 25100, subd. [a].)

"Criminal storage of firearm of the second degree"—Keeping any loaded firearm within any premises that are under your custody or control and you know or reasonably should know that a child (any person under 18) is likely to gain access to the firearm without the permission of the child's parent or legal guardian and the child obtains access to the firearm and thereby causes injury, other than great bodily injury, to himself, herself, or any other person, or carries the firearm either to a public place or in violation of Penal Code section 417. (Pen. Code, § 25100, subd. [b].)

Neither of the criminal storage offenses (first degree, second degree) shall apply whenever the firearm is kept in a locked container or locked with a locking device that has rendered the firearm inoperable. (Pen. Code, § 25105.)

Sales, Transfers and Loans of Firearms to Minors

Generally, it is illegal to sell, loan or transfer any firearm to a person under 18 years of age, or to sell a handgun to a person under 21 years of age. (Pen. Code, § 27505.)

Possession of a Handgun or Live Ammunition by Minors

It is unlawful for a minor to possess a handgun unless one of the following circumstances exist:

- The minor is accompanied by his or her parent or legal guardian and the minor is actively engaged in a lawful recreational sporting, ranching or hunting activity, or a motion picture, television or other entertainment event;
- The minor is accompanied by a responsible adult and has prior written consent of his or her parent or legal guardian and is involved in one of the activities cited above; or
- The minor is at least 16 years of age, has prior written consent of his or her parent or legal guardian, and the minor is involved in one of the activities cited above. (Pen. Code, §§ 29610, 29615.)

It is unlawful for a minor to possess live ammunition unless one of the following circumstances exist:

- The minor has the written consent of a parent or legal guardian to possess live ammunition;
- The minor is accompanied by a parent or legal guardian; or
- The minor is actively engaged in, or is going to or from, a lawful, recreational sport, including, competitive shooting, or agricultural, ranching, or hunting activity . (Pen. Code, §§ 29650, 29655.)

New Firearms/Weapons Laws

AB 892 (Stats. 2015, ch. 203)—Purchase of State-Issued Handgun by Spouse/ Domestic Partner of Peace Officer Killed in the Line of Duty
- Provides an exception to the Unsafe Handgun Act allowing the spouse/ domestic partner of a peace officer killed in the line of duty to purchase their spouse/domestic partner's service weapon. (Pen. Code, § 32000.)

AB 950 (Stats. 2015, ch. 205)—Gun Violence Restraining Orders

- Allows a person who is subject to a gun violence restraining order to transfer his or her firearms or ammunition to a licensed firearms dealer for the duration of the prohibition. If the firearms or ammunition have been surrendered to a law enforcement agency, the bill would entitle the owner to have them transferred to a licensed firearms dealer. (Pen. Code, §§ 29830.)
- Extends to ammunition, current authority for a city or county to impose a charge relating to the seizure, impounding, storage, or release of a firearm. (Pen. Code, § 33880.)

AB 1014 (Stats. 2014, ch. 872)—Gun Violence Restraining Orders

- Beginning June 1, 2016, authorizes courts to issue gun violence restraining orders, ex parte gun violence restraining orders, and temporary emergency gun violence restraining orders if the subject of the petition poses a significant danger of personal injury to himself, herself, or another by having in his or her custody or control, owning, purchasing, possessing, or receiving a firearm and that the order is necessary to prevent personal injury to himself, herself, or another, as specified. (Pen. Code, §§ 18100 18205.)
- Beginning June 1, 2016, makes it a misdemeanor to own or possess a firearm or ammunition with the knowledge that he or she is prohibited from doing so by a gun violence restraining order. (Pen. Code, § 18205.)
- Beginning June 1, 2016, makes it a misdemeanor to file a petition for a gun violence restraining order with the intent to harass or knowing the information in the petition to be false. (Pen. Code, § 18200.)

AB 1134 (Stats. 2015, ch. 785)—Licenses to Carry Concealed Handguns

- Authorizes the sheriff of a county to enter into an agreement with the chief or other head of a municipal police department of a city for the chief or other head of a municipal police department to process all applications for licenses to carry a concealed handgun, renewals of those licenses, and amendments of those licenses, for that city's residents. (Pen. Code, § 26150.)

AB 2220 (Stats. 2014, ch. 423)—Private Patrol Operators

- Beginning July 1, 2016, establishes procedures allowing a Private Patrol Operator (PPO) business entity to be the registered owner of a firearm.
- Beginning July 1, 2016, allows a security guard to be assigned a firearm by the PPO and for a firearm custodian to be designated by the PPO. (Pen. Code, §§ 16970, 31000, 32650.)
- SB 199 (Stats. 2014, ch. 915)—BB Devices and Imitation Firearms
- Beginning January 1, 2016, amends the definitions of a "BB device" and an "imitation firearm." (Pen. Code, §§ 16250, 16700.)

SB 707 (Stats. 2015, ch. 766)—Gun-free School Zones

- Recasts Gun-Free School Zone Act provisions relating to a person holding a valid license to carry a concealed firearm to allow that person to carry a firearm in an area that is within 1,000 feet of, but not on the grounds of, a public or private school providing instruction in kindergarten or grades 1 to 12, inclusive. (Pen. Code, § 626.9.)
- Creates an exemption from the Gun-Free School Zone Act for certain appointed peace officers authorized to carry a firearm by their appointing agency, and for certain retired reserve peace officers authorized to carry a concealed or loaded firearm. (Pen. Code, § 626.9.)
- Deletes the exemption that allows a person holding a valid license to carry a concealed firearm to bring or possess a firearm on the campus of a university or college. (Pen. Code, § 30310.)
- Deletes the exemption that allows a person to carry ammunition or reloaded

ammunition onto school grounds if the person is licensed to carry a concealed firearm. (Pen. Code, § 30310.)

- Creates a new exemption authorizing a person to carry ammunition or reloaded ammunition onto school grounds if it is in a motor vehicle at all times and is within a locked container or within the locked trunk of the vehicle. (Pen. Code, § 30310.)

19. Becoming a DOJ Certified Instructor*

California Department of Justice

Effective January 1, 2015, all DOJ Certified Instructor applicants are required to have a valid Certificate of Eligibility (COE) and must obtain a COE prior to submitting an application as a DOJ Certified Instructor.

The Certificate of Eligibility instructions and application is available at Certificate of Eligibility Please note that COEs must be renewed annually. The COE processing time is approximately 4–8 weeks.

Once you have obtained your COE number from the Bureau of Firearms, you can apply to become a DOJ Certified Instructor by completing a Firearm Safety Certificate (FSC) Program DOJ Certified Instructor application (form BOF 037) available at https://oag.ca.gov/firearms/forms or apply online through the FSC Certified Instructor Firearm Certification System at https://fcs.doj.ca.gov/login-form. Please note that a DOJ Certified Instructor's certification is valid for five years provided he or she maintains a valid COE. The processing time for manual applications is up to four weeks and online applications is 3–4 business days.

To renew DOJ Certified Instructor certification a FSC Program DOJ Certified Instructor application (form BOF 037) available at https://oag.ca.gov/firearms/forms must be submitted with the renewal box checked or renewing online through the FSC Certified Instructor Firearm Certification System at https://fcs.doj.ca.gov/login-form and accepting the Conditions of Use.

Firearm Safety Certificate Program

Effective January 1, 2015, the Handgun Safety Certificate program was replaced with the Firearm Safety Certificate (FSC) program. Under the FSC program, requirements that previously applied to handguns only now apply to all firearms (handguns and long guns), unless exempt. A list of exemptions is available on this website.

A valid Handgun Safety Certificate can still be used to purchase/acquire handguns only until it expires. For long gun purchases/acquisitions made January 1, 2015, and thereafter, an FSC will be required. Once an FSC is obtained, it can be used for both handgun and long gun purchases/acquisitions.

FSCs are acquired by taking and passing a written test on firearm safety, generally

---

*Public document originally published as California Department of Justice, "Becoming a DOJ Certified Instructor," https://oag.ca.gov/firearms/fscinfo (2021).

at participating firearms dealerships and private firearms training facilities. A Firearm Safety Certificate Study Guide to help individuals prepare for the FSC test is available for viewing/downloading from this website. A Firearm Safety webinar is also available for viewing or download on the Videos page.

The firearm safety demonstration protocols and DOJ Certified Instructor standards have been established and implemented by DOJ. An explanation of the firearm safety demonstration can be found starting on page 12 of the Firearm Safety Certificate Study Guide.

Specified Training Organizations in Firearms Safety

Organizations Specified by Penal Code section 31635, subdivision (b) as providing Acceptable Firearms Safety Training.

Penal Code section 31635, subdivision (b), authorizes Department of Justice to certify individuals possessing a training certificate from an organization enumerated under this subdivision to be a DOJ Certified Instructor.

The training organizations specified under Penal Code section 31635, subdivision (b) are:

- Department of Consumer Affairs, State of California-Firearm Training Instructor.
- Director of Civilian Marksmanship, Instructor or Rangemaster.
- Federal Government, Certified Rangemaster or Firearm Instructor.
- Federal Law Enforcement Training Center, Firearm Instructor Training Program or Rangemaster.
- United States Military, Military Occupational Specialty (MOS) as marksmanship or firearms instructor. Assignment as Range Officer or Safety Officer is not sufficient.
- National Rifle Association-Certified Instructor, Law Enforcement Instructor, Rangemaster, or Training Counselor.
- Commission on Peace Officer Standards and Training (POST), State of California-Firearm Instructor or Rangemaster.
- Authorization from a State of California accredited school to teach a firearm training course.

Comparable Training in Firearms Safety

Entities Recognized by DOJ as Providing Comparable Firearm Safety Training to Those Entities Specified by Penal Code section 31635, subdivision (b).

Penal Code section 31635, subdivision (b) authorizes the California Department of Justice (DOJ) to recognize entities which provide firearms safety training comparable to the entities specified within that subdivision. Individuals possessing a Certificate of Completion from any of the entities so recognized by DOJ may apply to be a DOJ Certified Instructor.

The entities recognized by DOJ as providing firearms safety training comparable to the entities specified by Penal Code section 31635, subdivision (b) are:

2nd Amendment Sports, Bakersfield, (661) 323-4512
29 Outdoor Gear, American Canyon, (510) 376-0303
Baptist Security Training, Vacaville, (707) 386-2689
Basic Gun Safety, Huntington Beach, (714) 864-0203
BullsEye Tactical Firearms Training, Castella, (530) 235-0721
Burton Lewis Agency, LLC, Elk Grove, (916) 834-9728
Cal Guns Training, Ventura, (805) 765-1486
California Firearms Safety School, San Francisco & Monterey, (415) 816-0099
CCW USA Firearms Training, Santee, (619) 871-9834
Coast Tactical Training, Orange, (562) 583-1790
Darrell's Shooting Sports, San Juan Capistrano, (949) 599-4148
Defensive Accuracy, Lodi, (408) 687-3791
Dobbs Firearm Training, Suisun City, (888) 486-0250
Double Tap Training, Granada Hills, (818) 363-1777
Down Range Indoor Training Center, Chico, (530) 896-1992
Fast Response Security, Inc., California City, (661) 775-5650
Firearms Training Associates, Yorba Linda, (714) 701-9918
Firearms Training Institute, San Jose, (408) 506-1884
First Priority Security Consulting LLC, Tracy, (510) 736-4333
Five Star Firearms and Training, Truckee, (530) 587-5239
Friedman Handgun Training, Pleasant Hill, (925) 818-6642
FSC Instructor Training Course, Alameda or Mariposa Counties, (510) 552-4742
Geoffrey D Peabody, Placerville, (916) 644-0991
Greenhorn Outfitter, LLC, Bakersfield, (661) 319-5426
The Gun Range San Diego, San Diego, (858) 573-1911
The Gun School, Tulare, Kings, Monterey, San Luis Obispo and Santa Barbara, (559) 936-9909
Gun World, Burbank, (818) 238-9071
Hammer Stryke Self-Reliance Training, Inc, (209) 614-1718
High Caliber Tactical, Fresno, (559) 903-7547
Hillside Range, Los Banos, (209) 704-1708
I Can Defend, Ramona, (760) 789-0987
JLPFI—John Lewis Professional Firearms Instruction, Fresno, (559) 349-3833
John Albert Holder, Redwood Valley, (707) 489-3380
Kings Gun Center LLC, Hanford, (559) 585-2000
KIT Group, LLC, Santa Ana, (714) 721-9233
Liberty Firearms Training, Sacramento, (916) 870-1854
Lock n Load Concealed Carry Training, Shingle Springs, (916) 705-2258
Marshall Security Training Academy, Los Angeles, (323) 660-0636
Martin B. Retting Inc., Culver City, (310) 837-2412
Modern Warrior Gunsmithing, Los Angeles, (818) 930-5289
NorCal Med Tac, Aptos, (831) 970-0440
Oro Jewelry and Loan, Oroville, (530) 533-3336
OSOS Security Services Training Facility, Mill Valley, (415) 519-3549
Pacific Outfitters, Eureka, (707) 443-6328
Powers Security Training, Bakersfield, (661) 871-7273
Practical Firearms Training, LLC, French Camp, (925) 487-4390

Premier Tactical Training, Fresno, (559) 779-7742
Prestigious Investigative Firearms Training Facility, Upland, (909) 303-3153
The Range, Grass Valley, (530) 273-4440
Range Master, San Luis Obispo, (805) 545-0322
Ray Walters, Modesto, (209) 613-5994
Richard E Haase Calaboose II, Sacramento, (916) 332-2207
Rosengarten Firearm Training, Ripon, (209) 610-1425
Rynearson Safety Training, Redding, (530) 524-3288
Safe Firearms Education, San Jose, (408) 348-7966
Safe Gun Handling Course, Elk Grove, (916) 714-4867
Safe Insight LLC, Lynnwood, Washington, (417) 233-1444
Safety and Firearm Training Center, Granite Bay, (916) 825-1384
Safety Firearm Training, Ukiah, (707) 489-3380
Scott R. James II Firearm Sales & Training, Visalia, (559) 352-6982
Seale Enterprises, Olivehurst, (530) 632-4101
SEC Unarmed Private Independent Security Service, Calexico, (760) 357-0412
Shoot Safe, Huntington Beach, (714) 625-1507
Shoot Safe Learning, Torrance, (310) 464-0855
Shooter's Paradise, LLC, Yuba City, (530) 673-4100
ShootSoCal Firearms Training, Buena Park, (818) 359-7056
Showket Training, Novato, (415) 497-1983
Southern Shooting Supply, Tehachapi, (661) 823-1223
Triple Threat Solutions, Bakersfield, (661) 374-1180
Valley Defense Consulting, Inc., Modesto, (209) 552-5728
Valley Gun, Inc., Bakersfield, (661) 352-9468
Wade Roberts Firearms Training, Tulare, (559) 303-2848
William M E McLaren, Oceanside, (858) 337-7876

20. Firearms and Toolmarks*

Utah Department of Public Safety

Part of the Department of Public Safety's Forensics Services, the Firearm and Toolmarks section conducts a wide variety of examinations ranging from function testing of firearms to serial number restoration to fracture matching. The most commonly requested examination, incorrectly referred to as ballistics tefsting, is determining whether ammunition components were fired from a particular firearm.

Using valid scientific procedures, the Firearm and Toolmark section conducts safety and function testing on firearms, analyzes fired ammunition components to determine general rifling characteristics, compare fired and unfired ammunition components to determine if they were fired by a specific firearm, restore serial numbers that have been obscured or obliterated, conduct distance determinations to estimate muzzle to target distance, conduct ejection pattern tests, reconstruct shooting scenes, determine if a specific tool made a certain toolmark, and conduct fracture match examinations. The Firearm and Toolmarks section conducts several trainings throughout the year, and testifies in court to the results of examinations.

The Firearms and Tool Mark section is broken down into several sub-disciplines: Firearms Examination, NIBIN, Toolmark Analysis, Serial Number Restoration, Distance Determination, and Shooting Reconstruction.

Firearms Examinations

A firearms comparison, incorrectly referred to as a ballistics examination, is the most commonly requested and involves determining whether or not evidence from a scene (such as cartridges, fired bullets or cartridge cases) was fired from a specific firearm. Case work includes determining what kind of firearm is involved, if it is functional, if any alterations were made to the firearm, and if it is safe to fire—making test fires. Those test fires are then compared to evidence found at a crime scene using a comparison microscope. Even if no firearm is recovered, the fired and unfired ammunition components can still be examined to determine manufacturer, how many firearms were involved, as well as give investigators a list of possible weapons that could have fired those components.

---

*Public document originally published as Utah Department of Public Safety, "Firearms and Toolmarks," https://forensicservices.utah.gov/testing-services/firearms-and-toolmarks/.

National Integrated Ballistic Information Network (NIBIN)

The National Integrated Ballistic Information Network (NIBIN) is a database system that captures, stores, and correlates digital images of fired cartridge cases recovered from crime scenes and test-fired firearms. NIBIN searches for other cartridge cases with similar tool marks, creating a list of possible associations. This correlation process can result in leads or hits that have tactical and strategic uses for law enforcement. NIBIN also helps law enforcement analyze and understand patterns of gun crime, including gun sharing and trafficking. The NIBIN program has proven successful at linking crimes and identifying shooters. For example, in 2019 there were 74 groups of NIBIN hits which linked over 180 cases and led to actionable intelligence for law enforcement.

How NIBIN Works

The National Integrated Ballistic Information Network (NIBIN) is a database that allows for known (test fires) and unknown (evidence) cartridge cases to be imaged and searched against other images in the database. As new images are entered, NIBIN continues to search against previous entries. The default search are for Utah includes all of Utah's entries, along with entries in neighboring states like Colorado or Nevada. Manual searches can be conducted against any other NIBIN site in the U.S. upon request. These searches, analyzed by an algorithm, result in a list of possible associations that are examined by trained NIBIN Technicians or Firearms Examiners located at the UBFS or the ATF's NIBIN National Correlation Training Center (NNCTC).

A Lead Notification is issued if a possible association is found using the NIBIN system software. As this evidence has not been examined microscopically by a Firearms Examiner, a Lead Notification cannot be used for court purposes.

A complete examination of all related evidence, resulting in a Crime Lab report, is necessary if the case goes to trial. As of September 20, 2021, all new NIBIN entries will be correlated by the NNCTC. The NNCTC will be responsible for disseminating their results. For questions related to NIBIN, contact NIBIN Program Administrator Jennifer Gelston (jgelston@utah.gov) or the Firearms Section at (801) 816-3810.

Toolmark Analysis

This analysis involves tedious microscopic examinations and empirical testing to determine if a mark found at a scene was made by a specific tool. These examinations can be challenging due to the various ways a tool can be held, applied, and used. Examinations range from bolt cutters used to cut locks, tires stabbed with knives, or wire cutters used to cut copper pipe. While often encountered in property crimes, these marks can also be found in other cases such as homicides (i.e., knife marks on bone or cartilage).

Serial Number Restoration

Serial numbers are unique identifiers applied to an item such as a firearm, electronic equipment, or vehicles. Serial numbers can include letters, numbers, and special characters. The Gun Control Act of 1968 requires all imported and newly manufactured firearms to have a unique identifier on the frame or receiver of the firearm. Destroying, or attempting to destroy, serial numbers is a federal crime. While the presence alone of an obliterated number can be documented and used for prosecution, restoring the number allows for tracing the history of the item. Restoration can be accomplished using methods ranging from polishing to chemical etching.

Distance Determinations

When a firearm is discharged, a projectile exits the barrel along with residues including burnt, partially burnt, and unburnt powder particles. Estimating the distance between the muzzle of a firearm and a target is based on the pattern of these residues left behind on the target surface. Target surfaces can include skin, clothing, and vehicles. The size and density of the residue pattern varies with distance and can be compared to test patterns made with the same firearm, the same or similar ammunition, and a similar target substrate. Along with a visual examination, surfaces can be treated chemically to reveal patterns left behind by nitrates and lead.

Distance determinations can also be performed with shotguns by analyzing the spread of the projectiles over a distance.

Results of distance determinations are usually reported as a range, such as "greater than 6 inches but less than 15 inches." This is a result of the numerous variables involved in the testing including the ammunition lot, target surface composition, weather, intervening objects, etc.

Shooting Reconstructions

Reconstructing a crime scene involving discharged firearms can assist in determining the most likely scenario. The information derived from a reconstruction can assist in defining a sequence of events, determining the number and/or sequence of shots, as well as ruling out/in possible scenarios.

At the scene, bullet impacts and trajectories can be determined and measured. Reports, photographs, diagrams, etc., are all important. At the lab, firearms examinations are necessary to determine which firearm fired which bullet, cartridge case, etc. Distance determinations can also apply, as well as ejection pattern analysis.

No two reconstructions are alike—some may require more experimentation than others. In general though, reconstructions can help explain what happened and make sense of a scene, as well as rule out what could NOT have happened.

Along with conducting reconstructions, the Firearm and Tool Mark Section teaches a 3-day Introduction to Firearms and Shooting Scene Reconstruction class that helps agencies to not only understand how to approach a shooting scene but also what can be helpful in reconstructions. The class includes the following topics:

- Introduction to firearms examinations and what the UBFS Firearm and Tool Mark Section can do for you.
- Hands on familiarity with various firearms and ammunition

- Bullet impacts, ricochets, and trajectories
- Live demonstrations of shotgun projectile dispersions
- Live demonstrations using vehicles to examine differences between calibers, gauge, projectile style, direct impacts, ricochets, etc.

21. Weapons and Schools*

Washington Office of Superintendent of Public Instruction

School safety and security is increased by limiting the availability of weapons and potential weapons on school grounds. Both state and federal law regulate the possession of firearms and other dangerous weapons at school and near schools.

State and federal law require each public school district and each approved private school to report to OSPI all known incidents involving the possession of weapons on school premises, transportation systems, or in areas of facilities while being used exclusively by public or private schools. In addition, public school districts are required by Title IV (Safe and Drug-Free Schools) and by Title X (Unsafe School Choice Option) of the Elementary Secondary Education Act (ESEA) to report the number of suspensions and expulsions for specific types of student behaviors.

Firearms on School Grounds

RCW 28A.600.420 pertaining to firearms on school grounds follow the federal GFSA, but also require the expulsion of a student found in possession of a firearm anywhere on school grounds, on school transportation, or at school-sponsored events. This does not apply to students who possess firearms under the authority of a school district, such as for a demonstration, rifle competition, or firearms safety course. Superintendents may modify firearm expulsions on a case-by-case basis.

RCW 9.41.280 makes possession of firearms and other dangerous weapons on school grounds a gross misdemeanor with certain exceptions. Prohibited dangerous weapons include items such as butterfly knives, switchblade knives, daggers, martial arts weapons including nun-chu-ka sticks and throwing stars, metal knuckles, air guns, and stun guns or Taser devices. Possession of these items under state law is generally grounds for expulsion.

Look-Alike Weapons

There have been a number of recent cases where students have faced serious disciplinary action for possessing AirSoft and other look-alike weapons on campus. In many

*Public document originally published as Washington Office of Superintendent of Public Instruction, "Weapons and Schools," https://www.k12.wa.us/student-success/health-safety/school-safety-center/school-safety-resource-library/weapons-and-schools (2020).

cases, these simulated weapons may meet the definition of a dangerous weapon because they expel a projectile. Students may also face discipline under the provisions of RCW 28A.600.420 if they act with malice and display an item that appears to be a firearm, even if the item is not in fact dangerous.

Exemptions

Exemptions to state and federal prohibitions on possession of firearms are made for persons who are licensed by the state to carry a concealed pistol. The GFSZA provides an allowance for licensed persons to possess firearms within 1000 feet of a school, and state law allows those licensed to carry a concealed pistol to possess a firearm on school grounds while picking up or dropping off a student. State law prohibits loaded firearms inside school facilities except for security and law enforcement.

Knives

Except as provided under RCW 9.41.280, state law does not prohibit the possession of common pocket knives or other sharp tools on school grounds. However, school policies and rules do typically prohibit students from possessing knives on school grounds or at school events. Local ordinances may also prohibit minors from possessing knives—either on or off of school grounds.

Protective Spray Devices

Under RCW 9.91.160, students age 14 years and older may legally possess personal protective spray devices (such as Mace and pepper spray) if that student has parent permission. Schools or other units of government may not prohibit the possession of personal protection spray devices, if the student is at least 14 years of age with parent permission, or of any person age 18 or older.

Definitions for Weapons Reporting

An incident results in the removal of one or more students from their regular school setting for at least an entire school day. A single incident may result in the suspension or expulsion of more than one student. An incident that does not remove a student for the entire school day is outside the scope of this report. However, an incident in which a student possessed or brought a firearm to school should be counted even if the expulsion was modified or no penalty was imposed.

Handgun includes all incidents when a student is known to have possessed a handgun on school grounds or school transportation, whether or not the handgun was intended to be used as a weapon.

Rifle/Shotgun includes all incidents when a student is known to have possessed a rifle or shotgun on school grounds or school transportation, whether or not the firearm was intended to be used as a weapon.

Other firearm includes incidents in which one or more students possessed or brought another type of firearm not named above, including zip guns, starter guns, and flare guns to school. As defined by the Gun Free Schools Act, other firearms include:

(1) any weapon (including a starter gun) which will or is designed to or may readily be converted to expel a projectile by the action of any explosive;

(2) the frame or receiver of any weapon described above;

(3) any firearm muffler or firearm silencer;

(4) any destructive device, which includes:

(a) any explosive, incendiary, or poison gas (such as: bomb, grenade, rocket having a propellant charge of more than four ounces, missile having an explosive or incendiary charge of more than one quarter ounce, mine, or similar device).

(b) any weapon which will, or which may be readily converted to, expel a projectile by the action of an explosive or other propellant, and which has any barrel with a bore of more than one-half inch in diameter.

(c) any combination or parts either designed or intended for use in converting any device into any destructive device described in the two immediately preceding examples, and from which a destructive device may be readily assembled.

Knife includes incidents where a student possessed a knife or dagger on school grounds, whether or not the item was used as a weapon or intended as a weapon.

Other weapon includes incidents in which one or more students possessed or brought anything used as a weapon that is not classified as a handgun, rifle/shotgun, knife/dagger, or other firearm to schools. Examples include chains, pipes, razor blades or similar instruments with sharp cutting edges; ice picks, pointed instruments (pencils, pens); nun-cha-ka sticks; brass knuckles; stars; billy clubs; tear gas guns; electrical weapons (stun guns); BB or pellet guns; and explosives or propellants.

22. Clashes in the Capital

Public Opinion on Virginia's New Gun Legislation*

CENTER FOR PUBLIC POLICY AT VCU'S WILDER SCHOOL

On January 20, Richmond, Virginia, held its breath. This day, also known as, "Lobby Day," brought more than 20,000 people to the state capital in a rally against gun legislation proposed in the latest session by the Democratic legislators, who now hold the majority in both Virginia's House and Senate (in addition to the office of the governor). With their induction, many Democrat legislators vowed to bring about progressive gun policies, including a limit on handgun purchases, the establishment of background checks and the allowance of local governments to ban guns in parks and public buildings.

The proposed bills emerging from the newly flipped state legislature have caused the gun debate in Virginia to escalate. Pro-gun rights advocates like those who participated in the Lobby Day rally fear that the establishment of the proposed bills will infringe upon their second amendment rights. On the other side of the aisle, pro-gun-control advocates fear that violence will emerge from a lack of gun restrictions. In 2019, a mass shooting at a government building only two hours from the site of the rally resulted in the deaths of 12 people. The proposed bills, they believe, will prevent further mass shootings from occurring and taking more lives.

To gain a better understanding of public opinion in Virginia on the proposed gun legislation, the Center for Public Policy at Virginia Commonwealth University's L. Douglas Wilder School of Government and Public Affairs included questions on the topic in the Winter 2010–2020 Wilder School Commonwealth Poll. The poll was a representative sample of 818 adults, and had a margin of error of +/- 4.80 percentage points.

Two of the gun-related questions explored in the poll were:

Which of the following statements comes closest to your overall view of gun laws in this country?

1. Gun laws should be MORE strict than they are today.
2. Gun laws are about right.
3. Gun laws should be LESS strict than they are today.

Please indicate whether you would favor or oppose the following proposals about gun policy. Do you feel that way strongly or somewhat?

---

*Originally published as The Center for Public Policy at VCU's Wilder School, "Clashes in the Capital: Public Opinion on Virginia's New Gun Legislation," 22, *PA Times*, https://patimes.org/clashes-in-the-capital-public-opinion-on-virginias-new-gun-legislation/ (January 27, 2020). Reprinted with permission of the publisher.

     1. Preventing people with mental illnesses from purchasing guns.

     2. Banning assault-style weapons.

     3. Banning high-capacity ammunition magazines that hold more than 10 rounds.

     4. 4.Making private gun sales and sales at gun shows subject to background checks.

A majority (53%) of participants responded that gun laws should be stricter today. Three-in-10 said laws were about right, and only 17 percent thought that laws should be less strict.

In addition, significant number of Virginians supported the implementation of background checks (74% strongly favored, 9% somewhat favored) and the limitation of purchasing ability for individuals with a mental illness (70% strongly favored, 14% somewhat favored). While not as significant as the first two, the majority of Virginians said they supported the banning of both assault-style (47% strongly favored, 10% somewhat favored) and high-capacity guns (42% strongly favored, 14% somewhat favored). Despite the large number of people who attended the rally to oppose the proposed gun legislation, the data indicate that the majority of Virginians support the new legislation.

This polarized public opinion, as well as mass demonstrations such as the rally, presents a clear dilemma as legislators and Governor Ralph Northam consider the strong opinions of their constituents. Following the rally, Northam released a statement saying:

"Thousands of people came to Richmond to make their voices heard. Today showed that when people disagree, they can do so peacefully. The issues before us evoke strong emotions, and progress is often difficult. I will continue to listen to the voices of Virginians, and I will continue to do everything in my power to keep our Commonwealth safe."

At the time this article was written several bills have passed in Virginia's Senate and will thus move on to the House, including the "Red flag," law (which allows law enforcement to remove the firearms of those deemed to be a risk to themselves or others), a bill limiting handgun purchases to one per month, a bill mandating universal background checks and a bill that allows localities to establish gun-free zones. However, the 22,000 protestors that stood on the Virginia Capital, many of whom travelled from outside states, are a clear indication that pro-gun activists will continue fighting such legislation. Whether common ground is possible with such a polarized issue remains unclear; however, having a data-driven understanding of the public's opinion on this topic is valuable for legislators. Creating legislation based on the majority's beliefs rather than the group with the loudest voices will further bolster the backbone of our democratic system by amplifying the true voices of the people.

23. "Red Flag" Gun Laws Get Another Look After Indiana, Colorado Shootings*

CHRISTIE ASCHWANDEN

On New Year's Eve 2017, sheriff's deputies in the Denver suburb of Highlands Ranch responded to a domestic disturbance. Before the night was over, four officers had been shot and Douglas County Sheriff's Deputy Zackari Parrish III was dead.

The gunman was a 37-year-old man with a history of psychotic episodes whose family had previously tried to take his guns away but found themselves without legal recourse to do so.

"We tried every legal avenue we could to not only protect him, but to protect the community," said Douglas County Sheriff Tony Spurlock. At that time, however, there was nothing more they could do.

That changed with the passage of the Deputy Zackari Parrish III Violence Prevention Act, a "red flag" law that took effect in January 2020. It gives judges the ability to issue "extreme risk protection orders" allowing law enforcement to seize firearms from people deemed dangerous to themselves or others.

Colorado is among the most recent of 19 states to have enacted red flag laws. Connecticut was first, in 1999. Since then, the data has been mixed on whether the laws have prevented suicides and inconclusive on their power to curb mass shootings. The Connecticut law did not prevent the 2012 mass shooting at Sandy Hook Elementary School in Newtown, for instance, though proponents usually point to the laws as one tool for preventing shootings, not one that's 100 percent effective.

But law enforcement officials who support the laws say they have clearly saved lives. A study published in 2019 looked at 21 cases in California in which extreme risk protection orders were granted from 2016 to 2018, and found that as of August 2019 none of the subjects of these orders had committed a murder or suicide, though it's impossible to prove the orders prevented such outcomes.

The red flag law hadn't been invoked in Colorado, the site of some of the nation's most infamous mass shootings, when a gunman killed 10 people in a Boulder grocery store in March.

In Indiana, where a former FedEx employee shot and killed eight people at an Indianapolis facility before killing himself in April, prosecutors did not seek a court hearing

*Originally published as Christie Aschwanden, "'Red Flag' Gun Laws Get Another Look After Indiana, Colorado Shootings," *Kaiser Health News*, April 26, 2021. Reprinted with permission of the publisher. *Kaiser Health News* is a nonprofit news service covering health issues. It is an editorially independent program of the Kaiser Family Foundation that is not affiliated with Kaiser Permanente.

under that state's red flag law last year after the suspect's mother reported to police that her son was suicidal.

Mass shootings may grab the most attention, but they are too rare to measure whether red flag laws help prevent them, said Rosanna Smart, an economist who studies gun violence at the Rand Corp.

The suspect arrested and charged with murder and attempted murder in the Boulder shooting had a history of violent outbursts dating back three years or longer, so it is hard to assess, while facts of the case are still being gathered, whether the red flag law could have been applied to him.

In 2018 the man pleaded guilty to third-degree assault after punching a fellow student at his suburban Denver high school in an attack the victim called unprovoked. He also was kicked off the school's wrestling team after making threats of violence.

Police seized a shotgun from the Indianapolis shooting suspect after his mother reported in 2020 that she was worried her son, then 18, was considering "suicide by cop," or deliberately provoking a lethal response by officers. An Indiana prosecutor told The Associated Press that authorities did not seek a hearing under the red flag law because they worried they would have to return the shotgun to him if they lost in court.

Most gun deaths in the U.S. are suicides, and Smart said about two-thirds of red flag cases regard somebody as at risk for self-harm.

Last April, Smart and her colleagues published a review of research on the effects of red flag laws and found "very inconclusive" evidence that they're effective as a means to reduce overall firearm suicide or homicide rates.

"I wouldn't say it's strongly one way or another," Smart said.

Research by Aaron Kivisto, a psychologist at the University of Indianapolis, used a method called "synthetic control" to calculate that 10 years after the enactment of Indiana's 2005 red flag law there was a 7.5 percent reduction in suicides compared with what would have been expected without the law, and the drop was driven exclusively by reductions in firearm suicides.

In Connecticut, the results were more of a "mixed bag," Kivisto said. Initially, the effect was "negligible," but the Connecticut law wasn't used much until after the Virginia Tech shooting in 2007, in which a student killed 32 people and wounded 17. After that shooting, seizures in Connecticut rose fivefold and Kivisto's group did then see a reduction in firearm suicides in the state, but they also found that those reductions were largely offset by increases in non-gun suicides. Still, taking all the studies together, Kivisto said, "The biggest takeaway is that the evidence supporting red flag laws as one means of reducing suicide appears to be consistently supported."

Colorado's suicide rates are among the highest in the nation, but it's too soon to know yet whether the state's red flag law has made a difference, especially given how unusual 2020 was in so many other ways.

From January 1, 2020, to March 26, 2021, Colorado tallied 141 red flag cases. Extreme risk orders were granted under the law in 28 of the state's 64 counties, including some of the more than 35 counties whose sheriffs or county leaders opposed the law and declared themselves "Second Amendment sanctuaries," where the law would not be enforced, said state Rep. Tom Sullivan, a Democrat. Sullivan, one of the bill's sponsors, has been a gun control advocate since his 27-year-old son, Alex, was among the 12 killed by a gunman in the 2012 Aurora movie theater shooting.

Where the red flag law has been used in Colorado, "it's clearly saved those individuals' lives. Those people are still alive, and their family members are still alive, and they're not in custody for homicide," Douglas County Sheriff Spurlock said. "I do think it keeps my officers safer, and it keeps our community safer."

But the law still has numerous opponents. Weld County Sheriff Steve Reams counters that situations like the one last fall in which an extreme risk protection order was approved for a 28-year-old man making plans to assassinate state Attorney General Phil Weiser should be dealt with using criminal charges, rather than a red flag law.

"Red flag, to me, doesn't look like a primary way of dealing with a potentially criminal situation," said Reams, who called Sheriff Spurlock a good friend with whom he's repeatedly debated the issue.

As for people at risk of self-harm, Reams said he'd rather have better ways to get them mental health treatment than take their guns away.

Opponents of red flag laws say they're unconstitutional, but a challenge to Colorado's law on constitutional grounds filed by the group Rocky Mountain Gun Owners and several Republican lawmakers was dismissed by a state District Court judge in Denver last spring.

Some opposition to Colorado's law focuses on the execution, rather than the intent. Dave Kopel, an adjunct law professor at the University of Denver and an analyst with the Libertarian-leaning Cato Institute, has testified in favor of red flag laws in the Colorado legislature but is critical of the current law for what he says are weaknesses in due process.

"The accuser never has to appear in court or be cross-examined," he said, and that means the judge may hear only one side of the case. "My view, as a constitutional law professor, is that you should write the law with strong due process protections at the start."

But Spurlock, a Republican, said there is more due process in implementing Colorado's red flag law than there is in police obtaining a search warrant. He said he supports gun rights but does not support allowing possession by felons or people who are a danger to themselves or others.

"That's why I supported the red flag. And I will continue to do so. I know for a fact that it saves lives, and it's not harming anyone," he said.

24. Summary of State and Federal Machine Gun Laws*

Veronica Rose *and* Meghan Reilly

Federal law strictly regulates machine guns (firearms that fire many rounds of ammunition, without manual reloading, with a single pull of the trigger).

Among other things, federal law:

1. requires all machine guns, except antique firearms, not in the U.S. government's possession to be registered with the Bureau of Alcohol, Tobacco, Firearms and Explosives (ATF);
2. bars private individuals from transferring or acquiring machine guns except those lawfully possessed and registered before May 19, 1986;
3. requires anyone transferring or manufacturing machine guns to get prior ATF approval and register the firearms;
4. with very limited exceptions, imposes a $200 excise tax whenever a machine gun is transferred;
5. bars interstate transport of machine guns without ATF approval; and
6. imposes harsh penalties for machine gun violations, including imprisonment of up to 10 years, a fine of up to $250,000, or both for possessing an unregistered machine gun.

The lawful transfer of a machine gun generally requires (1) filing a transfer application with ATF, (2) paying a transfer tax, (3) getting ATF approval, and (4) registering the firearm in the transferee's name. Transferees must pass an extensive criminal background investigation and meet the criteria for possessing firearms under state and federal law. Among those ineligible are felons and people (1) addicted to controlled substances, (2) discharged under dishonorable conditions from the U.S. Armed Forces, or (3) adjudicated mentally defective or committed to a mental institution.

Under Connecticut law, private citizens may own machine guns, provided the firearms are registered pursuant to federal law and with the Department of Public Safety (DPS). Failure to register a machine gun with DPS is presumed possession for an offensive or aggressive purpose. Possession of a machine gun for an offensive or aggressive purpose is punishable by a fine of up to $1,000, imprisonment for five to 10 years, or both.

There is no age requirement for "possessing" machine guns as a class of weapons

*Public document originally published as Veronica Rose and Meghan Reilly, "Summary of State and Federal Machine Gun Laws," https://www.cga.ct.gov/2009/rpt/2009-R-0020.htm (January 12, 2009).

under federal or state law. Age restrictions generally apply to handguns (pistols and revolvers) and long guns (shotguns and rifles) and transfer of these firearms. Federal law prohibits federal firearms licensees from transferring handguns to people under age 21. It generally prohibits nonlicensees from transferring them to people under age 18 and prohibits such minors from possessing them. Under state law, the effective age for possessing handguns appears to be 21. With regard to long guns, minors age 12 to 16 must obtain a Department of Environmental Protection (DEP) junior firearms hunting license, which allows them to hunt with firearms under supervision. People over age 16 can get a DEP license for unsupervised firearm hunting.

Federal Law and Machine Guns

Federal law defines a machine gun as "any weapon which shoots, is designed to shoot, or can be readily restored to shoot, automatically more than one shot, without manual reloading, by a single function of the trigger." This definition includes the frame or receiver, any part or combination of parts designed and intended, solely and exclusively, for use in converting a weapon into a machine gun, and any combination of parts from which a machine gun can be assembled (26 USC § 5845[b], 27 CFR §§ 478.11 & 479.11). It does not include "antique firearms" (26 USC § 5845[a] & [g]).

Since 1934, Congress has strictly regulated the manufacture, transfer, and possession of machine guns. The firearms are regulated by the 1934 National Firearms Act (NFA) (26 USC § 5801 *et seq.*) and the 1968 Gun Control Act as amended by the 1986 Firearms Owners' Protection Act (18 USC § 921 *et seq.*).

The agency responsible for administering and enforcing federal firearm laws, including machine gun laws, is the Bureau of Alcohol Tobacco, Firearms and Explosives. (Until January 24, 2003, Bureau of Alcohol, Tobacco and Firearms was within the Treasury Department. The 2002 Homeland Security Act transferred it to the Justice Department and changed its name to the Bureau of Alcohol, Tobacco, Firearms and Explosives.)

National Firearms Act

With limited exceptions, the NFA imposed (1) a $200 excise tax (making tax) on the manufacture of machine guns (other than by qualified manufacturers that pay a special occupational tax and on the manufacture of machine guns by or on behalf of a state or federal agency) and (2) a $200 excise tax on each transfer of a machine gun (transfer tax). It also imposed a special occupational tax on people and entities engaged in the business of importing, manufacturing, and dealing machine guns (26 USC §§ 5821, 5852[b], 5853[b], 5852[c], and 5811[a], and 5801).

The NFA also required all machine guns not in the possession, or under the control, of the U.S. government to be registered with the Treasury, including those possessed by states and political subdivisions (e.g., police departments) (28 USC § 5841).

For transfer tax purposes, a "transfer" involves "selling, assigning, pledging, leasing, loaning, giving away, or otherwise disposing of" the firearm (26 USC § 5845[j]). It does not apply to (1) transfers of registered firearms between licensees (importers, manufacturers, and dealers) who have paid the special occupational tax; (2) transfers to state or federal agencies; (3) exportation of firearms (provided appropriate proof of the export is provided to ATF and documentation completed); or (4) transfer of unserviceable firearms as defined in law (26 USC §§ 5851–5854 & 27 CFR §§ 479.88–91). ATF also does not consider any of the following activities as a transfer for tax purposes (1) possession of machine guns by employees who take custody of the firearms within the scope of their employment and for the licensee's business purposes, (2) distribution of registered firearms to lawful heirs, and (3) temporary transfers to federal firearm licensees for repair.

The registration requirement applies to manufacturers, importers, and anyone or entity transferring a machine gun. It applies when a firearm is made, transferred, or imported, and to functional and unserviceable firearms as well as curios and relics. The registration information required includes the (1) identification of the firearm, (2) registration date, and (3) identification and address of the person to whom the firearm is registered (26 USC § 5841). A registered owner who moves to a different in-state address must notify ATF of the new address.

The Firearm Owners' Protection Act

The Firearm Owners' Protection Act banned civilian transfer and possession of machine guns not in circulation before May 19, 1986. Specifically, it restricts the transfer and possession of machine guns except for:

> 1. "transfers to or by, or possession by or under the authority of, the United States or any department or agency thereof or a State, or a department, agency, or political subdivision thereof; or
> 2. any lawful transfer or lawful possession of a machinegun that was lawfully possessed before [May 19, 1986]" (18 USC § 922[o] & 27 CFR § 478.36).

Under ATF regulations, qualified manufacturers may make machine guns for sale to federal agencies or qualified licensees and special occupational taxpayers as "sales samples" for demonstration to prospective government customers (27 CFR § 479.105). They may also make them for export in compliance with the Arms Export Control Act and Department of State regulations (27 CFR § 479.105).

Procedure for Acquiring Machine Guns

An unlicensed individual may acquire machine guns, with ATF approval, from its lawful owner residing in the same state as the individual (27 CFR §§ 479.84 & 479.105). The transferor must file an ATF application, which must be completed by both parties to the transfer and executed under penalties of perjury, and pay a $200 transfer tax to ATF. The application must include detailed information on the firearm and the parties to the transfer (26 USC § 5812 & 27 CFR § 479.84).

The transferee must certify on the application that he or she is not disqualified from possessing firearms on grounds specified in law. He or she must submit with the application (1) two photographs taken within the past year; (2) fingerprints; and (3) a copy of any state or local permit or license required to buy, possess, or acquire machine guns (27 CFR § 479.85).

An appropriate law enforcement official must also certify whether he or she has any information indicating that the firearm will be used for other than lawful purposes or that possession would violate state or federal law (27 CFR § 479.85).

Approvals and Denials. Anyone acquiring a machine gun must, as part of the registration process, pass an extensive Federal Bureau of Investigation criminal background investigation. If ATF denies an application, it must refund the tax. Gun owners must keep approved applications as evidence of registration of the firearms and make them available for inspection by ATF officers.

Eligibility Criteria for Acquiring Machine Guns

ATF cannot approve an application if the transfer, receipt, or possession of the firearm would place the transferee in violation of law... (27 CFR § 479.65).

Federal Law. It is a violation of the NFA for any of the following to acquire or possess firearms, including machine guns:

1. anyone under indictment for or convicted of a felony,
2. fugitives from justice,
3. illegal aliens,
4. anyone unlawfully using or addicted to controlled substances,
5. anyone subject to a domestic violence restraining order (issued in accordance with specified terms),
6. veterans discharged under dishonorable conditions,
7. anyone who has been adjudicated mentally defective or committed to a mental institution,
8. people who have renounced their U.S. citizenship, or
9. anyone who has been convicted of misdemeanor crime of domestic violence (18 USC § 922g).

An applicant wanting to register a machine gun must certify, under penalty of perjury, on the required ATF form that he or she is not disqualified from acquiring or possessing firearms on any of these grounds.

The NFA also contains age requirements as they pertain to firearm transfers. These and state requirements are discussed at the end of the report.

State Law. It is a violation of state law for convicted felons and the following people to possess any firearms, including machine guns—anyone:

1. convicted of a serious juvenile offense;
2. who knows he or she is under a protective or restraining order in a case involving the use or threatened use of physical force;
3. subject to a firearm seizure order issued after notice and a hearing opportunity; or
4. prohibited under federal law from possessing or shipping firearms because he or she was adjudicated as a mental defective or committed to a mental institution, unless granted relief from this disability (CGS § 53a-217).

Machine Guns in Interstate Commerce

It is generally unlawful for anyone, other than a licensed importer, licensed manufacturer, licensed dealer, or licensed collector transporting relics or curios, to transport a machine gun in interstate or foreign commerce (18 USC § 922[a][4] and 27 CFR § 478.28[c]). But ATF may authorize a registered owner to transport a machine gun in interstate or foreign commerce where reasonably necessary and consistent with public safety and applicable state and local law (27 CFR § 478.28[a]).

Violations

Under federal law, it is illegal to do any of the following with regard to machine guns:

1. engage in business as a manufacturer, importer, or dealer without registering or paying a special occupational tax;
2. make, receive, possess, transport, deliver, or transfer the firearm in violation of the NFA;
3. receive a firearm not identified by a serial number as required;
4. obliterate, remove, change, or alter the firearm's serial number; or
5. make or cause to be made any false entry on any application, return, or required record (26 USC § 5861).

The criminal penalties in the Gun Control Act include both felonies and misdemeanors. Fines and penalties for felonies are at least $250,000 for individuals and $500,000 for organizations. For misdemeanors, the fines are up to $100,000 for individuals and $200,000 for organizations (18 USC § 924). The law also provides for forfeiture of firearms and ammunition involved in NFA violations (26 USC § 5872).

A willful attempt to evade or defeat the tax is a felony punishable by up to five years in prison and a $100,000 fine ($500,000 for corporations) under the general tax evasion statute (26 USC § 7201). For an individual, the $100,000 for tax evasion fine could be increased to $250,000 (18 USC 3571[b][3]).

State Law

State law defines a machine gun as any weapon, loaded or unloaded, that shoots, is designed to shoot or can be readily restored to shoot automatically more than one projectile by a single function of the trigger without manual reloading. This definition includes any part or combination of parts designed to assemble, or convert a weapon into, a machine gun (CGS § 53-202[a]).

With limited exceptions, the law requires anyone who owns a machine gun to register it with DPS within 24 hours of acquiring it and annually thereafter on July 1 (CGS § 53-202[g]). The registration requirement does not apply to machine guns (1) manufactured for sale or transfer to the U.S. government, states, territories, or political subdivisions or (2) rendered inoperable by welding.

Manufacturers must maintain a register of machine guns they manufacture or handle. For each firearm, the register must show the (1) model and serial number; (2) date of manufacture, sale, loan, gift, delivery, or receipt; (3) name, address, and occupation of the transferor and transferee; and (4) purpose for which it was acquired. Manufacturers must make their registers and gun stock available for inspection by law enforcement officials. Violations are punishable by a fine of up to $2,000 (CGS § 53-202[f]).

There is a presumption that a machine gun is possessed for an offensive purpose if it is:

1. located on premises not owned or rented as a business or residence by the person possessing it,
2. in the possession of an unnaturalized foreign born person,
3. possessed by anyone convicted of a violent crime,
4. not registered as required, or
5. when empty or loaded projectiles are found in the immediate vicinity of the firearm (CGS § 53-202[d]).

The presence of a machine gun in a room, boat, or vehicle is presumptive evidence of possession or use of the firearm by each occupant (CGS § 53-202[e]). Using or possessing a machine gun for an offensive or aggressive purpose is punishable by a maximum $1,000 fine, imprisonment for five and 10 years, or both (CGS § 53-202[c]).

The restrictions on machine guns do not apply to machine guns (1) manufactured for sale or transfer to the U.S. government, states, territories, or political subdivisions; (2) rendered inoperable by welding; or (3) acquired, transferred, possessed, and registered under the NFA (CGS § 53-202[h]).

Age Restrictions and Firearm Possession

There is no age requirement for "possessing" machine guns as a class of weapons under federal or state law. Age restrictions generally apply to handguns (pistols and revolvers) and long guns (shotguns and rifles) and transfer of these firearms, rather than possession.

Federal law prohibits dealers from transferring handguns to anyone under age 21. It generally prohibits nondealers from transferring them to anyone under age 18 and prohibits such minors from possessing them. Minors under age 18 may receive and possess handguns only with a parent or guardian's written permission for limited purposes (e.g., employment, ranching, farming, target practice, or hunting). Also, minors under age 18 who are members of the U.S. Armed Forces or National Guard can possess them on duty (18 USC 922x and 922b). Federal law prohibits FFLs from selling or transferring long guns to minors under age 18. But it does not address sales or transfers by nondealers or possession by minors (18 USC § 922[b] and 27 CFR § 178. 99[b][1]).

State law does not explicitly set a minimum age for possessing firearms. But the practical effect of three laws appears to make the minimum age 21. One law (with one minor exception) prohibits transferring a handgun to anyone under age 21 (CGS § 29-34). Another prohibits anyone from acquiring a handgun without an eligibility certificate or permit (CGS § 29-36f). A third prohibits carrying a handgun without a permit (CGS § 29-35). People under age 21 cannot get the permit or certificate.

The only age-related provision in state law pertaining to long guns (shotgun and rifles) allows minors age 12 to 16 to obtain a DEP junior firearms hunting license, which allows them to hunt with firearms under supervision. People over age 16 can get a DEP license for unsupervised firearm hunting (CGS § 26-27[a] and 26-38).

• C. Cities and Communities •

25. Gun Violence

It Can Happen Anywhere*

RON CARLEE

The above headline is from 2013. As people across the United States awoke on October 2, 2017, they learned it has happened again. This time in Clark County, Nevada, and the world-famous Las Vegas Strip. The number of dead and wounded is not yet confirmed. The latest reports as I write this on October 2 are over 58 dead and over 500 wounded.

In 2012, Norcross, Oakland, Seattle, Aurora, Oak Creek, Minneapolis, and Newtown—seven U.S. cities from coast to coast, all experienced mass shootings in 2012: 72 dead, 70 injured, and many others emotionally scarred for life. Since 2012, we have had five mass shootings in 2013, four in 2014, seven in 2015, six in 2016, and, thus far, seven in 2017. The count before the Vegas shooting were 187 dead and 173 injured. The deadliest events were at the Orlando nightclub in 2016 (49 dead and 53 injured) and at the Washington, D.C. Navy Yard in 2013 (12 dead, 8 injured), and at a public health department holiday party in San Bernardino in 2015 (14 dead, 12 injured).

What I wrote almost five years ago remains starkly true today: "The magnitude of gun violence in the United States is undeniable. As with all social phenomena, the extent of the problem and the dominant public attitudes vary dramatically from one community to another. The stark reality is that mass gun deaths can occur in any community on any day. The challenge for managers is to be prepared."

The following are key points from the 2013 article:

City managers who have experienced mass shootings in their communities have accumulated valuable experiences that can help other managers prepare for similar emergencies. Based on interviews and reports from these communities, here are 10 critical issues that have emerged.

1. **Stay involved**. Managers walk a line between disengagement and micromanagement, but at all stages—emergency preparedness, response, and recovery—the chief executive needs to be visible and engaged. Have you had a

---

*Originally published as Ron Carlee, "Gun Violence: It Can Happen Anywhere," https://icma.org/blog-posts/gun-violence-it-can-happen-anywhere (October 2, 2017). Reprinted with permission of the publisher.

conversation with your leadership team and elected officials on how your city would handle a mass-shooting event?

2. **Plan and train**. The Columbine High School murders in 1999 changed everything, showing how lessons can be learned and put into place. Active shooter plans are now commonplace and direct first responders to encounter and neutralize the shooter as the immediate priority. Most police departments now plan and train based on this model. Mass events, however, require responses across all of the assets of a local government. Planning, training, and testing cannot be limited to public safety. Does your city have mass shooter training for all employees? Do your schools and major employers have mass shooter training?

3. **Activate the plan**. The actual incident, however, will not match the plan and the scenario training. Having a strong foundation enables responders to improvise based on the uniqueness of the situation. Expect the unexpected; be prepared to be surprised. Dan Singer was city manager of Goleta, California, when seven people were killed at a mail processing plant. He noted that government is accustomed to "following the rules," which can help guide an organization in a time of crisis, but that not every scenario can be predetermined. Singer said that key participants must think creatively, intuitively, and non-bureaucratically. Has your city's team exercised sufficiently to act creatively?

4. **Take care of the victims and their loved ones**. This is one of the most critical and most challenging tasks. Once the scene is secured and people are out of danger, a new phase of difficult and emotional work begins. In everything that is done, it is critical to show the highest possible regard for the dignity of the people who may have died and the highest possible level of sensitivity to people who have lost loved ones. Family assistance is critical. Families need to have a number to call and someone with whom to talk. Many family members will gather at the scene. A safe, secure, and private location needs to be established for the families where they can get accurate information and support services and have their basic needs met. Delays in identifying victims and clearing the crime scene will seem endless and create considerable anxiety for family members. They need to know that people are aware of their needs and are doing everything possible to meet them. They need empathy with action. Skip Noe, city manager of Aurora, Colorado, where 12 people were killed and 58 injured in 2012 shooting, advised local government staff to take their time and follow the lead of victims. "Putting the victims first will always put responders and the local government in the best position." In addition to a response plan, does your city have a plan to cope with victims and their families in the aftermath? If so, has it been tested?

5. **Take care of your people, yourself, and the community**. It may seem strange that the community is listed last in this heading; however, if first responders and other officials, including the manager, are emotionally impaired, they cannot take care of others. A mass death event, however, presents images never imagined, images indelibly etched into everyone's memory. Early intervention can make a difference. Critical stress debriefing is an essential part of the preplanning and requires immediate deployment. It's a mistake to think that intervention is only needed for first responders. A mass death event takes an emotional toll and counseling needs to be rapidly available for everyone, including local government staff members. What is your city's plan for dealing with employees? Is there a trusted

entity prepared to provide the support services and will your employees use them?

6. **Manage the media and other outsiders**. The number of media outlets is overwhelming and their reach is global. Media transmit 24/7, with an insatiable appetite. Have a media management plan in place, including contingency resources from outside the organization. Be prepared to take these actions:

- Designate a media manager.
- Find a place to stage the media.
- Meet the media's basic safety and sustenance needs.
- Give the media visuals.
- Schedule regular briefings.
- Select a spokesperson; have a clear message and stick to it. What resources can your city devote to the media? Are they prepared for 24/7 international coverage? Do you have a communications consultant on retainer with experience in crisis communications? How will you deal with tweets from the President of the United States?

1. **Facilitate an ad hoc memorial and appropriate events**. People are compelled to demonstrate their sadness and hurt. Help make a memorial happen. Find a place for it and protect it. At an appropriate time, retire it and preserve the artifacts as appropriate. Who will have this responsibility in your city? How will site management decisions be made?

2. **Manage donations and volunteers**. Beyond the ad hoc memorial, a number of people will want to help, often with money, which needs a depository and a trustworthy administrator to oversee it. People will also want to make donations of goods and services, whether these are needed or not. Realize that these are good people with good intent who sincerely want to help. Give them a way to do so and have a strategy in place to accomplish it. Who will manage donations in your community? Is there a trusted third party? How will disbursement decisions be made?

3. **Plan a permanent memorial**. Involve the families of victims and others intimately connected to the event. Set realistic goals that are achievable within a reasonable period of time. How will your city honor those lost and those who responded?

4. **Learn and share**. The community will have to resolve a long list of tasks: clearing the crime scene; reopening or permanently closing the site of the incident; attending to such legal matters as lawsuits and trials; and handling the many requests from outside organizations for presentations about the event, with the heaviest demands likely to be on the police and fire chiefs. In the months after the incident, there will be official reviews—after-action reports, commission reports, legislative reports—any and all of which may second-guess what the manager and his/her team did and how they performed. Former Blacksburg City Manager Mark Verniel recommended embracing legitimate criticism and using it as a lesson for everyone. He noted that Columbine is a great example of how people learned to operate differently. What system and structure will your city establish to effectively manage post-shooting events while being able to return attention to other community needs?

Moving On

The ability to "move on" for the long-term may be the hardest task of all. Dealing with all of the above issues creates a new day-to-day reality that can become an obsession. All involved will be changed forever. "Surreal" is a word that has often been used to describe gun-violence tragedies. Managers must find the support to move on themselves, so that they can help the community move on, honoring those lost and building a community for the living, for their children, and for posterity.

Note: For downloadable database on mass shootings in the U.S., see motherjones.com.

26. Firearm Regulation and Cities*

League of Minnesota Cities

Understand how state laws affect a city's ability to prohibit guns on city property. Read options for regulation of city employees carrying firearms at work and restrictions on elected officials or volunteers carrying firearms when conducting city business. Get details about the permitting process and privacy status of permit data.

I. Regulation in General

A. Federal Law

The federal government's ability to regulate firearms comes from the commerce clause of the Constitution and the fact that all guns have likely traveled interstate. One significant limitation on federal gun control is the Second Amendment to the Constitution. The Second Amendment states "A well regulated Militia, being necessary to the security of a free State, the right of the people to keep and bear Arms, shall not be infringed." In a 2008 opinion, the United States Supreme Court held that the Second Amendment conferred a constitutional right to citizens to possess firearms in their home for traditionally lawful purposes such as self-defense. However, the court stated, and the Minnesota State Supreme Court recognized, that the right to possess a firearm does not extend to "any weapon whatsoever in any manner whatsoever and for whatever purpose."

While most of the gun laws affecting cities are state laws, federal firearm statutes cover many areas. Federal gun laws regulate individuals in the business of buying, selling, or manufacturing firearms, firearm taxation, and interstate transfer of firearms. They also provide for licensure of most firearm vendors. Federal law generally requires those in the business of selling firearms to perform background checks on purchasers, though there are exceptions.

Federal law also limits who may have a gun and what guns people may have. These laws ban certain individuals, such as convicted felons, from buying or possessing a firearm, and block sales of handguns to those under age 21. Federal law currently bans new sales of fully automatic firearms to citizens, as well as sales of firearms containing

*Originally published as League of Minnesota Cities, "Firearm Regulation and Cities," https://www.lmc.org/wp-content/uploads/documents/Firearm-Regulation-and-Cities.pdf (August 10, 2020). Reprinted with permission of the publisher.

minimal metal (including 3D-printer made guns). Federal registration is required of silencers (or suppressors), disguised or improvised firearms, and some more powerful firearms.

Firearms and other dangerous weapons are banned from federal facilities. "Dangerous weapon" is defined as a weapon, device, instrument, material, or substance, animate or inanimate, that is used for, or is readily capable of, causing death or serious bodily injury. It does not include a pocket knife with a blade of less than 2½ inches in length. There are exceptions for police and military officers, as well as any possession incidental to hunting or "other lawful purposes."

The major federal gun laws include the following:

- The National Firearms Act
- The Omnibus Crime Control and Safe Streets Act of 1968
- The Gun Control Act of 1968 (GCA)
- The Firearm Owners Protection Act
- The Undetectable Firearms Act
- The Gun-Free School Zones Act
- The Brady Handgun Violence Prevention Act
- The Protection of Lawful Commerce in Arms Act

B. State Regulation and Pre-emption of City Regulation

State authority to regulate firearms is broader than federal authority as a matter of states' rights, but it is also limited by the Second Amendment to the federal Constitution. In Minnesota, the state has significantly limited the authority of cities to regulate firearms.

Since 1985, the state legislature has explicitly preempted all cities, counties, towns and other governmental subdivision from regulating "firearms, ammunition or their respective components," with two exceptions. A governmental subdivision such as a city may regulate the discharge of firearms and it may adopt regulations identical to state law.

The term "firearm" is not defined for the purposes of the law. However, in the context of criminal law, Minnesota courts have relied on a statutory definition pertaining to fish and game. Under this definition, a firearm is "a gun that discharges shot or a projectile by means of an explosive, a gas, or compressed air."

Using this definition, case law has provided that neither BB guns nor paintball guns are considered firearms for purposes of criminal law.

Due to the state preemption, Minnesota cities have no authority to ban assault weapons, high-capacity magazines or any other firearm, ammunition or component thereof unless already banned by state law. Whether BB guns and paintball guns may be banned because they are not "firearms" within the context of criminal law is less clear.

C. Minnesota Citizens' Personal Protection Act of 2003

With limited exceptions, for many years, cities have been unable to regulate the carrying or possession of pistols. In 2003, the Minnesota Citizens' Personal Protection Act (MCPPA) imposed further limits on city regulation of pistols.

1. Firearms Regulated by the MCPPA

The MCPPA governs the carrying of "pistols." "Pistol" is defined as a weapon designed to be fired by the use of a single hand and with an overall length less than 26 inches, or having a barrel or barrels of a length less than 18 inches in the case of a shotgun or having a barrel of a length less than 16 inches in the case of a rifle (1) from which may be fired or ejected one or more solid projectiles by means of a cartridge or shell or by the action of an explosive or the igniting of flammable or explosive substances; or (2) for which the propelling force is a spring, elastic band, carbon dioxide, air or other gas, or vapor.

"Pistol" does not include a device firing or ejecting a shot measuring .18 of an inch, or less, in diameter and commonly known as a "BB gun," a scuba gun, a stud gun or nail gun used in the construction industry or children's pop guns or toys.

The MCPPA does not apply to antique firearms which are carried or possessed as curiosities or for their historical significance or value, or to ammunition or primers, projectiles, or propellant powder designed solely for use in an antique firearm.

2. Conduct Protected by the MCPPA

The MCPPA allows individuals to carry into a "public place" any number of pistols in their motor vehicle, snowmobile or boat; on or about their clothing or person; or otherwise in their possession or control so long as they have a valid permit to do so.

A "public place" is defined as property owned, leased, or controlled by a governmental unit and private property that is regularly and frequently open to or made available for use by the public in sufficient numbers to give clear notice of the property's current dedication to public use.

"Public place" does not include: a person's dwelling house or premises, the place of business owned or managed by the person, or land possessed by the person; a gun show, gun shop, or hunting or target shooting facility; or the woods, fields, or waters of this state where the person is present lawfully for the purpose of hunting or target shooting or other lawful activity involving firearms.

Further restrictions on public places where a permitted pistol may be carried are discussed later in this memo.

3. Authority with Respect to City Facilities

There is no general authority for a city to ban permitted pistols from being carried into city facilities. Under an exclusivity provision within the MCPPA, no city official or employee or other person or body acting under color of law or governmental authority may change, modify, or supplement the law, or otherwise limit the exercise of a permit to carry. Any city action to prohibit permitted pistols on public property would likely constitute an additional limit on the permit to carry.

When the MCPPA was reenacted in 2005, an amendment was proposed in the House to give cities authority to "restrict the possession or carry of a firearm, including prohibiting the possession of a firearm in local government property." The amendment did not pass; accordingly, this legislative history suggests there is an arguable presumption that cities lack authority to prohibit permitted pistols from being carried onto city property.

4. Counties as Sole Permit Issuing Authority

City police departments lost authority to issue permits to carry in 2003 though they still process permits to purchase or transfer firearms. Since then counties have been the sole authority to issue and process these permits to carry. The sheriff's office can contract with local police departments to process the permits on behalf of the county. In this case, "the sheriff remains the issuing authority and the police chief acts as the sheriff's agent."

The obligations associated with taking applications, conducting background checks and issuing the permits are significant. Accordingly, LMC recommends that cities carefully consider the risks and benefits before entering into such contracts. LMC also recommends that the contract makes it clear that the county would cover the liability for police chiefs' action.

There is potential liability if the chiefs do not follow procedures such as the mandatory background checks.

D. Peace Officer Firearms

Peace officers are authorized to carry firearms while on duty by inherent power of government entities. There are a number of state statutes which refer to this unwritten authority. For instance, firearm training is required by state law before the "agency head issues a firearm to the officer or otherwise authorizes the officer to carry a firearm in the course of employment." Additionally, departments must have a "use of force" policy that does not prohibit justified use of deadly force, including use of a firearm. Federal law allows concealed firearms to be carried if a person, among other things, "is authorized by the agency to carry a firearm." While cities have very little authority with regard to firearms, it's important to acknowledge this significant and fundamental power of cities and other government entities.

The city is not required to authorize police officers to carry, and there is a limit to who may be authorized to carry a firearm on behalf of the city.

When a city has authorized a licensed officer to carry a firearm while on duty, that officer may carry a firearm while on duty without any further authorization (e.g., permit). Whether the officer is on- or off-duty, that "authorized" officer may still carry a concealed weapon under federal law and regardless of state law unless they are intoxicated. However, despite considerable emergency powers in a crisis, cities cannot authorize an employee or agent to carry a firearm while on duty unless the person is a licensed peace officer.

II. Valid Firearm Regulation by Cities

Clearly, in most respects state law preempts city regulation of firearms. However, there are some valid regulatory options still available to cities.

A. Discharge

Cities may regulate the discharge of firearms within the city limits. Some cities prohibit discharge on public lands and roadways. In certain wildlife management areas, restrictions on discharge of shotguns may be invalid. Presumably, the Second Amendment would allow the discharge of firearms for self-defense purposes.

B. Provisions Identical to State Law

Cities may also adopt firearm regulations identical to state law. Cities cannot ban possession of permitted pistols in city facilities generally, but cities can adopt provisions already in law which prevent carrying firearms into some circumstances. Following are many of the state gun control laws that regulate locations, weapons or people, followed by some offenses specific to permitted pistols.

1. Regulation by Location

a. Private, nongovernmental establishments

Firearms, permitted or otherwise, cannot be carried into a private business if the business has posted placards banning them. Under state statute, a person who carries a pistol into a private, nongovernmental establishment that has a sign at the door banning firearms must follow an order to leave or face a petty misdemeanor.

b. Court facilities

Dangerous weapons are prohibited generally in "court complexes," though this statutory prohibition does not apply to permitted pistols. However, due to the constitutional separation of powers, the judiciary has its own authority, equal to that of the Legislature, to order by decree that all firearms, including permitted pistols, be prohibited from the court's facilities.

c. Jails, lockups, correctional facilities and "state hospitals"

Whoever introduces or in any manner causes the introduction of a dangerous weapon into any jail, lockup, or correctional facility without the consent of the person in charge, or is found in possession of a dangerous weapon while within the facility or upon the grounds thereof commits a felony. "Dangerous weapon" includes "any firearm, whether loaded or unloaded, or any device designed as a weapon and capable of producing death or great bodily harm."

It is also a felony to bring, send or in any manner cause to be introduced into a state correctional facility or hospital any firearms, weapons or explosives of any kind. For purposes of this law, "state hospital" or "hospital" means any state-operated facility or hospital under the authority of the commissioner of human services for (a) persons with mental illness, developmental disabilities, or chemical dependency, (b) sex offenders, (c) persons with a sexual psychopathic personality, or (d) sexually dangerous person.

d. Polling places (potentially)

There is no law explicitly banning firearms from polling places, and they are possibly considered "public places" under the MCPPA. However, it is likely many polling locations are also places where guns are not permitted under other law. Many polling places are held in schools and churches.

As discussed below, there is a statutory prohibition on carrying a firearm on school property. Churches are able to ban firearms from church property, but churches are not required to comply with the posting requirements other private establishments must follow in order to ban the carrying of firearms. Cities should confirm with polling place hosts whether firearms are permitted on the property.

e. Private use of city property

A private party that leases space in city buildings or facilities for a "private, nongovernmental establishment" may prohibit firearms in the leased spaced by following the posting and notice requirements described above. However, as a landlord, the city may not restrict the "lawful carry or possession of firearms by tenants or their guests."

f. Public places

With some exceptions, it is a crime to carry a BB gun, rifle, or shotgun (but not permitted pistols) to "public places" as defined by law. It is a very severe crime for a person under 21 to carry to a public place a "semiautomatic military-style assault weapon" as defined by the law. It's important to notice that through the broad exceptions, a lot of "carrying" is still allowed. This is presently a source of confusion in the law.

For example, one law states carrying "a BB gun, rifle, or shotgun" with a permit under the Personal Protection Act is not illegal "carrying" within the meaning of this law. One interpretation of this is that a permit authorizes carrying any BB gun, rifle, or shotgun into a public place. At the same time, the MCPPA permits the carrying of only "pistols," which includes a handgun less than 26 inches, a shotgun with a barrel or barrels less than 18 inches, or a rifle of less than 18 inches. Further, BB guns are explicitly excluded from the definition of "pistol" governed by the Act. As a result, there is ambiguity in the law.

It could be that a permit will authorize carrying of some smaller rifles or shotguns to a public place, but despite the statute, a permit cannot authorize carrying a BB gun to a public place. Given this legal ambiguity, cities are encouraged to consult their legal advisor if they encounter a situation involving carrying in a public place.

Again, the exceptions to the prohibition on carrying a BB gun, rifle or shotgun to a public place are broad. Other exceptions include carrying antique firearms, carrying firearms unloaded and in a gun case, and carrying firearms to a place where any lawful activity or ceremony involving firearms occurs.

g. Schools and child care property

It is a felony for an individual to carry any dangerous weapon, including a firearm, while knowingly on "school property." There are additional crimes for brandishing or possessing a BB gun or gun replica on "school property." "School property" is defined as including "a public or private elementary, middle, or secondary school building and its improved grounds, whether leased or owned by the school; a child care center licensed under chapter 245A during the period children are present and participating in child care programs; … and that portion of a building or facility under the temporary, exclusive control of a public or private school, a school district, or an association of such entities where conspicuous signs are prominently posted at each entrance that give actual notice to persons of the school related use." Accordingly, if city property is being used for any of these defined school related purposes, guns are prohibited.

h. Transportation by motor vehicle

It is generally forbidden to transport a firearm in a motor vehicle, though there are many exceptions. If the weapon is unloaded and kept in a case or the trunk, the transportation is allowed. The law also provides a "handgun" that is an antique or carried in compliance with the Personal Protection Act may be transported in a motor vehicle, though the term "handgun" is not defined. There is an exception under certain circumstances for persons with disabilities.

A person may transport an unloaded, uncased firearm (excluding pistols that are generally permitted) in a motor vehicle while at a shooting range where the person has received permission from the lawful owner or possessor to discharge firearms, while hunting on private or public land or travelling to or from a site the person intends to hunt lawfully or has hunted lawfully that day. However, this rule does not apply in Anoka, Hennepin or Ramsey Counties; within any city of population 2500 or more; on school grounds; or as otherwise restricted by law.

As noted in the context of employment later, a parked motor vehicle may be used to store an employee's permitted pistol during a work shift if the employer has banned employees from carrying pistols while working.

2. Regulation by Weapon

It is a crime under state law to have certain firearms, regardless of where. With some narrow exceptions, no one in Minnesota may own, possess or operate a machine gun, a trigger activator or machine gun conversion kit or a short-barreled shotgun as defined by the law.

Until 2015, silencers or "suppressors" were illegal in the state. A suppressor is defined as a device for "'silencing, muffling, or diminishing' the sound made by a firearm." They may now be possessed if a person fills out ATF paperwork, submits to a background check and pays a tax as required by the National Firearms Act.

3. Regulation by Individual

State law provides many categories of individuals who may not possess ammunition, a pistol, a semiautomatic military-style assault weapon or other firearms. These categories include persons convicted of violent or other crimes, those judicially determined to be mentally ill and generally persons under the age of 18. These categorical prohibitions of individuals do not generally apply to antique firearms which are carried or possessed as curiosities or for historical significance or value, or to ammunition or primers, projectiles, or propellant powder designed solely for use in an antique firearm.

Under state law, employers, including cities, may establish policies that restrict the carry or possession of firearms by its employees while acting in the course and scope of employment. This exception does not apply to parking areas. This exception is further discussed below.

4. Crimes Under the Personal Protection Act

The following are some of the crimes specific to permitted pistols.

- It is a gross misdemeanor for a person to carry a pistol in a public place without a permit.
- It is a petty misdemeanor for a person authorized to carry a gun to not have the "permit card" in immediate possession. The charge must be dismissed if the person later demonstrates in court or in the office of the arresting officer that the person was authorized to carry the pistol at the time of the alleged violation. A violation of this provision does not result in a forfeiture of the person's gun.
- It is a petty misdemeanor for a permit holder to fail to notify the issuing sheriff of a change of address or a lost or destroyed card. A violation of this provision does not result in a forfeiture of the person's gun.
- It is illegal to carry even a permitted pistol while under the influence of alcohol or a controlled substance. The processes and procedures are very similar to those for driving while under the influence of alcohol or a controlled substance. Any individual with an alcohol concentration of .04 or more can face criminal charges. An individual's permit to carry may also be revoked. If the individual

has an alcohol concentration of .10 or more, the gun may also be subject to forfeiture.
- As noted before, it is a petty misdemeanor for a person carrying a permitted pistol to refuse to follow a private establishment's request to leave if the establishment has posted placards banning guns.

III. *The Personal Protection Act and City Personnel*

A. Restricting Possession

1. EMPLOYEES

The Personal Protection Act specifically allows an employer, public or private, to "establish policies that restrict the carry or possession of firearms by its employees while acting in the course and scope of employment." The law also allows the city to discipline employees for violations of the policy.

This means that cities can establish a policy that prohibits employees from carrying or possessing firearms while:

- Working on city property.
- Working in any location on behalf of the city.
- Driving on city business.
- Riding as a passenger on city business.
- Performing emergency or on-call work after hours on behalf of the city.
- Attending training or conferences on behalf of the city.

The law also states that an employer cannot prohibit the lawful carry or possession of firearms in a parking facility or parking area. For many employees, this means that they will leave any firearms in their cars during the workday if the city has a policy prohibiting possession while at work. This could raise issues of security for city parking facilities.

2. CITY OFFICIALS

The MCPPA does not specifically address whether the city can restrict elected officials from carrying firearms while conducting city business.

Therefore, it depends on whether elected officials would be considered "employees" of the city under this particular law. This determination could be different from city to city, depending on a number of factors. For example, some cities have specifically taken actions to designate their elected officials as "employees" in order to offer them certain types of benefits such as workers' compensation coverage, group health and life insurance and coverage in pension and retirement plans. These cities are more likely to be able to make an argument that the elected officials should be treated as employees under this law.

On the other hand, many state and federal employment laws tend to exempt elected officials from coverage. For example, elected officials are not considered employees for purposes of the Fair Labor Standards Act, which governs minimum wage and overtime. They are also specifically exempt from the state law that defines public employees for purposes of collective bargaining rights.

The best practice is for the city to examine how it has treated elected officials in the past on various types of issues and remain consistent with those practices. For example, if the city has designated elected officials as employees for purposes of workers' compensation coverage and other benefits, it should probably designate them as employees for purposes of this law as well.

3. City Volunteers

The city probably cannot restrict volunteers from carrying firearms when performing duties on behalf of the city based on the MCPPA, but a city is not required to use volunteers who carry handguns.

A true "volunteer" probably cannot be restricted from carrying firearms on the basis of being an employee of the city. However, the city may be able to adopt a policy stating that it will not use volunteers unless they sign an agreement that they will not carry a firearm while acting on behalf of the city.

In defining city volunteers, the city should take a particularly careful look at its volunteer firefighters. Many fire departments in the state compensate their volunteer firefighters in a manner that would probably be seen by the Department of Labor as making them ineligible for volunteer status under wage and hour laws. The city should attempt to be consistent in its definition of volunteer firefighters either as true volunteers or as "paid on call" city employees.

If the city determines that its volunteer firefighters are actually employees, they can be included in the city's general policy prohibiting employees from carrying firearms while on duty. A similar argument could possibly be made with respect to positions such as ambulance attendants, first responders, police reserves, and emergency response volunteers, all of whom are categorized as employees under Minnesota's workers' compensation laws. If they are true volunteers, the city may be able to require them to sign an agreement that they will not carry a firearm while acting on behalf of the city.

B. Role of City Officials

1. Peace Officers

The MCPPA removed permit issuance responsibility from local police chiefs and placed it with the county sheriffs. However, when an application for a permit is filed with the county sheriff, the sheriff is required to notify the chief of police of the municipality where the applicant resides. The chief of police is then authorized, but not required, to provide "any information relevant to the issuance of the permit." While the law does not impose an obligation to provide information, local law enforcement officials may want to adopt policies that articulate what sources of information they will review in responding to notification of a permit application from a county sheriff.

Upon request by an officer, permit holders are required to display their permit card with identification, provide a sample signature in the officer's presence as well as disclose whether they are currently carrying a firearm.

2. Prosecutors

When a person is charged with an offense that would, upon conviction, prohibit the person from possessing a firearm, the prosecuting attorney is required to ascertain whether the person is a permit holder. If the person is a permit holder, the prosecutor is required to notify the issuing sheriff that the person has been charged with a prohibiting offense. The prosecutor must also notify the sheriff of the final disposition of the case. In addition to the felony charges that would trigger this reporting obligation for county attorneys, local prosecutors will also have this obligation for certain offenses such as violations of orders for protection; domestic assault; and harassment and stalking. There could be potential liability to the city and its prosecutor if these responsibilities are not carried out.

3. Responsible Authority

All permit-application data collected by state agencies, political subdivisions, or statewide systems are classified as private under the Minnesota Government Data Practices Act. As a result, only the applicant and individuals within the state or local governmental entity whose work assignments reasonably require access will be able to access this data.

However, law enforcement agencies will be able to verify whether permits are valid. The commissioner of public safety is required to maintain an automated database of persons authorized to carry pistols under this new law that is available 24 hours a day, seven days a week. This database will only be available to law enforcement agencies, including prosecutors verifying the validity of permits.

Limited permit data will also be available to the public. On an annual basis, the commissioner of public safety must report to the legislature specific data regarding permits issued under the new law. Sheriffs and police chiefs are specifically permitted to release private data to the department of public safety for this purpose. The report will be available to the public at its actual cost of duplication. The report will not contain any personally identifiable data. For example, although the report will contain the number of permits applied for, issued, suspended, revoked, and denied, it will only be categorized by the age, sex, and zip code of the applicant or permit holder.

IV. Municipal Liability Exposure

There are a number of ways in which municipal liability exposure may arise due to the MCPPA.

A. Immunity

The law includes an "immunity" section, but it likely does not protect the city from all possible claims or lawsuits that may be brought as a result of the law. The immunity states that "… a police chief, any employee … of a police chief involved in the permit issuing process, is not liable for damages resulting or arising from acts with a firearm committed by a permit holder unless the person had actual knowledge at the time the permit was issued or the instruction was given that the applicant was prohibited by law from possessing a firearm." So there is protection from claims or lawsuits where the permit holder shoots someone and the injured party tries to sue the city for the information that it gave to the county to issue the permit.

This immunity does not apply if it can be shown that the city employee had actual knowledge that the applicant was prohibited by law from possessing a firearm.

Therefore, if the police knew that the applicant was dangerous or mentally ill and did not say anything to the sheriff after being notified, there may be potential liability.

The immunity also does not specifically apply to cities. Cities would have to argue that they are immune through vicarious immunity because of the actions of their employees.

Finally, the immunity does not apply to lawsuits not involving acts with a firearm such as a defamation lawsuit as discussed below.

B. Defamation

Under the law, after notification by the sheriff of a person's application for a permit, the local police chief may provide relevant information on the issuance of the permit.

There is a potential for defamation claims by the applicant. Defamation is where you tell someone something in writing (libel) or orally (slander) that is proved to be false and resulted in damages to the person's reputation or in obtaining some benefit (such as a gun permit). In this situation, damages could also be argued to include physical injury if the person can show that if they had had a gun, they would not have been injured.

C. Injuries to Third Parties

If a person or a city employee carrying a gun with a permit uses the gun to hurt someone on city premises, the city could be liable for those injuries. Under common law, the city could be liable if the city knew that the person or the employee was dangerous for other reasons. Carrying a gun legally with a permit would not give the city sufficient reason to act on the person's ability to be on the city premises. There must have been some other action indicating danger, such as a threat or a fight.

If the city had such knowledge, it had a duty to protect other users by kicking the dangerous person out of the building or premises at that time or for a period of time. If the city didn't do this, there could be potential liability for negligent supervision of the premises. There also is the argument that the dangerous action was foreseeable because of the past acts of the person. LMC recommends that you have a procedure in place for expelling people or employees who may be a danger to other users of the city premises. The procedure should afford some level of due process.

D. Training

If the city provides training through a certified instructor to people who apply for permits and later use the firearm, is there liability for the city? The certified instructor individually would be immune from these types of claims and the city could argue vicarious immunity if the instructor was working in the course of his or her city employment. As stated before, the immunity doesn't apply if the instructor had actual knowledge that the person was not eligible for a permit at time of application.

E. Chemical Testing

Under state law there is a specific procedure established for chemical testing to determine if a person is carrying a firearm while under the influence of alcohol or drugs.

Is there liability if city police do not follow this procedure? Potentially, if it resulted in wrongful revocation of a permit or wrongful conviction.

V. Further Information

For more information, see the following resources.

- Federal Bureau of Alcohol, Tobacco, Firearms and Explosives
- Minnesota Bureau of Criminal Apprehension
- Resources on Minnesota Issues: Firearm Carry Laws from the Minnesota Legislative Reference Library.
- Sample employment policies from Minneapolis and MNSCU

27. Forget Lanes

*We All Need to Head Together Toward
Preventing Firearm Injury**

Michael Hirsh

Many of us working in the "Gun Sense" field—that is, finding a middle ground position to advance firearm safety and reduce preventable injury in our patients—had an "a-ha" moment that led us to toil in these fields.

Mine was on November 2, 1981, when my friend and co-resident Dr. John C. Wood II was shot right in front of our hospital emergency room at Columbia Presbyterian Hospital in Washington Heights, New York City.

I have taken care of many gunshot wound victims since then, but none so difficult emotionally as this one. I participated in cracking my friend's chest to start open cardiac massage and saw his heart devoid of blood from a through-and-through gunshot wound into his heart with a Saturday night special.

The survivability of a cardiac gunshot wound like this is close to zero, even though he was minutes away from the ER. He was in the OR and placed on cardiac bypass within 10 minutes of arrival. But his pupils were fixed and dilated and he had exsanguinated, or bled out, into his chest cavity. He did not survive despite our best efforts. It was an event that rocked Columbia and all who knew John, a fully boarded pediatrics-turned-surgical resident, a world-class Juilliard-trained French horn player and former Columbia rugby team captain.

The urgency of the firearm violence issue facing our country was heightened this past week when nine people were killed in three separate mass shootings over an 18-hour period in the U.S. In the past month, there have been attacks at places of worship, yoga studios and hospitals. Add these to the shootings in schools and in movie theaters and the tremendous sense of unease our citizenry is experiencing is completely understandable.

As physicians and surgeons on the front lines, many of my colleagues and I feel that it is no longer acceptable to treat this problem like our trauma team is a MASH unit. We have an obligation and an opportunity to reach out and speak out, and my hope is the country is listening. Because this is indeed our lane.

---

*Originally published as Michael Hirsh, "Forget Lanes—We All Need to Head Together Toward Preventing Firearm Injury," *The Conversation*, https://theconversation.com/forget-lanes-we-all-need-to-head-together-toward-preventing-firearm-injury-107399 (November 28, 2018). Reprinted with permission of the publisher.

Watching the Violence Grow

My training took me to other cities, and everywhere the tragedy of firearm injury seemed to follow. I knew after that night in November '81 I could no longer practice in New York City, but I could not escape the parade of firearm tragedies. Children shot accidentally. Teens shot in gang wars. Teens and elders shooting themselves in impulsive moments of despair, yielding nearly 100 percent completion of their suicide task.

Gun violence increasingly became my focus when I heard Sarah Brady explain the concept of limiting access to lethal means. Sarah is the wife of Jim Brady, Ronald Reagan's press secretary shot in the 1981 presidential assassination attempt. Brady spent the rest of his life partially paralyzed. He died in 2014, and the medical examiner ruled his death a homicide.

The Brady approach to gun control is limiting access. It is based on the premise that we might not be able to deal with the root causes of the violence—racism, poverty, mental illness—but that we could perhaps deal with the vector of violence that elevates all these factors into lethality—access to firearms. This is the philosophy behind the Brady Campaign, which aims to limit gun violence in the U.S. I began to wonder what I as an individual trauma surgeon could do to make a difference.

Looking for Answers

In the 1990s, I was working in Pittsburgh as a pediatric trauma surgeon. A gang turf war over control of the crack cocaine trade broke out between the Bloods and the Crips. Both sides were heavily armed. As the body count rose on the north side of Pittsburgh where I was working, legislators tried to help by establishing a mandatory sentence for anyone in possession of a firearm when arrested for drug trafficking.

This caused the dealers to push the age of the drug runners to preteens and young teens, and they were equally armed. Our pediatric gunshot-wound patient victim numbers soared. When an 11-year-old was shot with an AK-47 in front of the mayor's house, suddenly the city responded. Pittsburgh held community meetings. As director of a Robert Wood Johnson Injury Prevention Program, I was selected to represent the Allegheny General Hospital. The community disparaged our hospital as being insensitive and uncaring. Many believed we were "profiting" from the carnage and just sending the patients back out into the street to face more mayhem even if they had survived.

Our hospital encouraged my practice partner, Dr. Matt Masiello, and me to do something. We were both transplanted New Yorkers in the 'Burgh, and we had heard about a new kind of gun buyback program in Washington Heights where a carpet store owner, Fernando Mateo, had emptied his inventory in exchange for locals bringing in their firearms. Previously, gun buybacks had only offered cash for the weapons. We decided to build a version of the program exchanging the guns for gift certificates to local merchants rather than actual merchandise. We collected 1,400 weapons that first year in 1994 and about 10,000 since then.

The buyback program has become much more than just a way to give the patrons the ability to rid their homes of unwanted or unsecured weapons. We built a public information blitz about the responsibility that goes along with the right to own a firearm, and we built awareness of the increased risk of suicide, homicide, femicide, accidental shooting, or breaking and entering for the purpose of stealing a firearm.

We have now reproduced the program in a number of cities across the U.S. In my hometown of Worcester, Massachusetts, working out of the UMass Memorial Medical Center, our multi-pronged approach to gun safety education coupled with the gun buyback has given us the distinction of having the lowest-penetrating trauma rate in New England.

In calendar year 2017, we had zero firearm fatalities, down from five the year before.

This was an astounding number, in view of national stats showing a rise from 33,000 deaths in 2010 to 38,000 in 2018. We faculty at the University of Massachusetts have built a curriculum for students at our medical school to empower doctors to ask the right questions in the proper way.

I am truly excited about the response my fellow physicians have demonstrated in their reaction to the National Rifle Association's "stay in your lane" comments.

The NRA has already tried and failed to gag doctors in Florida from talking with their patients about gun safety.

In 2011, it backed a bill ultimately passed by the Florida legislature that would have forbidden doctors from asking patients about gun ownership or gun storage unless the doctor had a specific reason to do so. Doctors in violation could have been punished by loss of license and up to a US$10,000 fine.

"Physicians interrogating and lecturing parents and children about guns is not about gun safety," read a letter from the NRA in support of the bill. "It is a political agenda to ban guns. Parents do not take their children to physicians for a political lecture against the ownership of firearms, they go there for medical care."

Though it took six years to do so, the parts of the law that gagged doctors were overturned by the 11th Circuit Court of Appeals in February 2017.

And now, even more than in previous years, doctors are saying they have seen enough—actually, way too much.

Now the awakening of the M.D.s gives me a sense of encouragement and hope that we as a profession can lead our country away from the intransigent position in which nothing gets done. Gun buyback is a middle-ground Gun Sense position that can rally a community around the cause that I have been fighting for since that dark day in November 1981. I hope other municipalities will join us, as these programs do work.

28. Battling the Bullets from the Operating Room to the Community*

Laura Ungar

ST. LOUIS—Dr. Laurie Punch plunged her gloved hands into Sidney Taylor's open chest in a hospital's operating room here, pushing on his heart to make it pump again after a bullet had torn through his flesh, collarbone and lung. His pulse had faded to nothing. She needed to get his heart beating.

She couldn't let the bullet win.

Bullets are Punch's enemy. They threaten everything the 44-year-old trauma surgeon cherishes: her patients' lives, her community, even her family. So, just as she recalled doing two years ago with Taylor, Punch has made it her life's mission to stem the bleeding and the damage bullets cause—and excise them if she can.

In the operating rooms at Barnes-Jewish Hospital, Punch treats gunshot victims, removing bullets that studies show can poison bodies with lead and fuel depression. And in her violence-racked community, she teaches people how to use tourniquets to stop bleeding, creating a legion of helpers while building trust between doctors and community members.

Punch feels a calling to St. Louis, a place with the nation's highest murder rate among big cities, where at least a dozen children were shot to death this summer alone, including a 7-year-old boy playing in his backyard. Punch believes all she's learned has prepared her for now, when gun violence kills an average of 100 Americans a day and mass shootings are so common that two this summer struck less than 24 hours apart.

To her, the battle is personal, in more ways than one.

Besides being a surgeon, she's a multiracial single mom living in Ferguson, Missouri, just over a mile from where Michael Brown, a black teenager, was shot and killed by a white police officer five years ago.

She has a son the same age as the little boy killed in the backyard in August. And she said, "I hear the gunshots echoing through my 2-acre backyard all the time."

*Originally published as Laura Ungar, "Battling the Bullets from the Operating Room to the Community," *Kaiser Health News*, December 12, 2019. Reprinted with permission of the publisher. *Kaiser Health News* is a nonprofit news service covering health issues. It is an editorially independent program of the Kaiser Family Foundation that is not affiliated with Kaiser Permanente.

Stopping a Deadly Disease

In September, Punch brought her message to Washington, D.C., testifying before the House Ways and Means Oversight subcommittee on gun violence. Wearing a jacket and tie, she faced lawmakers to share the story of Shannon Hibler.

The 23-year-old was brought to Punch's hospital last summer, shot seven times. While the nurses gave him blood, Punch said, she cut open his chest, trying to force life back into his body—to no avail.

"I watched his wife sink, as the floodwaters of vulnerability and risk came into her eyes, thinking about the life of her and her child and how they would live without him," Punch told the assembled lawmakers. "I watched his father rage. And I heard his mother wail."

Punch placed the black-and-yellow, blood-splattered Adidas sneakers she'd worn the day of the shooting on the table before her in the hearing room.

"I can't wash these stains out," she told lawmakers.

The trauma surgeon was adamant: Violence is a true medical problem doctors must treat in both the operating room and the community. Until they do that, she said, violence victims will continue to be vectors who spread violence.

"The disease that bullets bring does not yet have a name," she told Congress that day. "It's like an infection, because it affects more than just the flesh it pierces. It infects the entire family, the entire community. Even our country."

But healing also can be contagious—spreading among victims, families and the physicians themselves.

Punch, who regularly visits the neighborhoods where her patients live, attended an event last year for Saint Louis Story Stitchers, an artist and youth collective working to prevent gun violence. She remembers spotting a volunteer she knew—Antwan Pope, who'd been shot some years earlier but had found renewed purpose helping young people.

Punch told Pope about Hibler's case, and learned Hibler was Pope's cousin. Hibler's dad was at the community event, too, and he handed Punch a lapel pin with his son's picture.

She wore it on her white coat for months.

Two Worlds

Punch was born in Washington, D.C., the only child of a Trinidadian father and white Midwestern mother. They separated six months after her birth.

Until she was 7, Punch moved every year with her mom. They eventually settled with Punch's grandmother in the tiny town of Wellsville, Ohio, a close-knit but segregated community.

Classmates bullied her for being different, Punch recalls.

"I was different in every way because I wasn't black; I wasn't white," said Punch, who later came out as gay.

From the time Punch was 9, she took $2 piano lessons from Elizabeth Carter. The local music teacher had transformed former drug dens into places with music lessons, free clothes and meals, and put all the kids who sought her help to work. Punch's assignment was serving food.

"You show someone that they can help," Punch said, "it's revolutionary."

That lesson guided her life as a child and when Punch moved on to Yale University, the University of Connecticut's medical school and then the University of Maryland Medical Center in Baltimore, where poverty and trauma scarred many of her patients' lives.

Punch spent her early career in the shock trauma center in Baltimore, throwing everything she had into saving others.

After marrying a woman she met as a medical intern, Punch became pregnant with twins at 35.

The next few years were marked by highs and lows in her personal life and the unrelenting stress of dealing with the aftermath of violence at work.

She miscarried at five months. No one could tell her why.

Five months later, she became pregnant again, this time giving birth to a healthy boy, Sollal Braxton Punch. But not long later, she and her wife separated. Now she found herself as a single parent as the pressures of her job mounted.

One morning, three shooting victims arrived at the trauma center, quickly followed by a car crash victim who was pregnant. Punch's nanny texted her, saying Sollal had a fever of 102.3.

"I realized I can't do this anymore," Punch said. "I just can't."

The Call of Community

So, she took a break from trauma for more than two years, focusing on general surgery at Houston Methodist Hospital in Texas.

But in 2015, a former colleague contacted her about a job as a trauma surgeon and educator at Washington University in St. Louis.

She feared going back to another troubled city. Michael Brown had been killed in Ferguson, Missouri, a little more than a year earlier, triggering unrest and riots in that city just outside St. Louis.

Despite the area's well-known history of violence, she flew to St. Louis for interviews, then rode around Ferguson with Dr. Isaiah Turnbull, an assistant professor. He pointed out the spot on Canfield Drive where Brown's body had lain in the road for more than four hours.

"It was almost like seeing Ground Zero," Punch said. "This is where it all went down. And it went down because of deep structural realities that caused the experience of black and brown people in north St. Louis to be fundamentally different. I went from not wanting to go to wanting to be right in the middle of it."

And now she is.

On a recent hot summer evening, 20 people—some black, some white—gathered around Punch. A few feet away, a doctor, a trauma nurse and a medical student stood near tables stacked with "pool noodles," the long foam cylinders kids play with in swimming pools—these happened to be about the width of a human arm.

Punch told the class that a person can bleed to death in a minute, but an ambulance can take 15 minutes to arrive.

"If you can stop the bleed, you can save a life," she said. "Time is life and minutes matter."

Participants practiced packing wounds by pressing gauze into holes in the pool noodles. They tightened tourniquets—first on the foam cylinders, then on each other.

Punch knows one of the doctors who created the "Stop the Bleed" training sessions after the mass shooting at Sandy Hook Elementary School in Connecticut. She realized the same training could save lives after street shootings, too.

Since March 2018, she and her team have trained more than 7,000 community members in the St. Louis metropolitan area. Many come to a rented space she dubbed "The T," for trauma, tourniquet and time. But Punch's team has also held classes in schools, a juvenile detention center and a firing range.

"It's far more than teaching people what to do," Punch said. "They learn: 'I am not simply a victim or a perpetrator or an observer; I'm a helper. I have the capacity to help.'"

Contagious Healing

Two years ago, Sidney Taylor was shot outside his brother's comedy club in north St. Louis County while trying to help a friend who was drunk. When Taylor arrived at Punch's hospital, profuse bleeding had left his blood pressure dangerously low.

At one point, the father of four technically died on the operating table, but Punch and her team pulled him back.

After 10 days in intensive care, the longtime wrestling coach was still in physical and mental agony.

That's the point when many patients slip back to their communities unhealed. But Taylor, now 47, showed up in Punch's clinic a month after he had been shot, and they bonded during a 25-minute visit. Punch described to him how her team had removed part of his lung and inserted a breathing tube.

"Wow," he told her. "I have another chance at life."

Punch mulled a thought, then asked. "Would you ever want to share your story?"

Taylor agreed.

Punch recruited his hospital caregivers to create a video of their memories of saving him. When the taping finished, Taylor hugged each one.

Punch uses the video during talks, sometimes inviting Taylor to join her. Giving back to the community in that way has saved him a second time, he said.

After getting shot, "I could've basically turned to the dark side and done straight revenge," Taylor said. "But I didn't because of her."

29. DC's Harllee Harper Is Using Public Health Tools to Prevent Gun Violence

*Will It Work?**

Amanda Michelle Gomez

After four people were murdered in one week in early September—all in the same Washington, D.C., neighborhood—residents made a plea for help.

"We've been at funerals all week," said Janeese Lewis George, a City Council member who represents the neighborhood. "What can we do as a community?"

She was speaking to dozens of people at a vigil site, a tree adorned with teddy bears and candles along a street lined with rowhouses. According to police, the area, known as Brightwood Park, has been plagued by several dozen violent, gun-related crimes over the past year. When Lewis George asked whether the crowd had known anyone who'd been shot, most people raised their hands.

Earlier that day, five council members joined Lewis George in asking Mayor Muriel Bowser for assistance—not in the form of more police, but from the city's first-ever gun violence prevention director, Linda Harllee Harper.

Harllee Harper knows Brightwood Park, having grown up near the heavily Black and Latino neighborhood, which has recently begun to attract white residents, too. She knows the local stories, both good and bad. Some families have lived there for decades, witnessing generational poverty and government neglect. During the 1990s, parts of it were considered a "war zone" because of rampant drug- and gang-related activity. She still lives in the same ward with her husband and son, who plays basketball at the local recreation center with the children of a recent murder victim.

Her investment in finding a solution is clear. "It's not a new development," Harllee Harper told KHN. "My view of gun violence is shaped by how much loss I've experienced. I've had friends who have been killed and I also have had young people that I have worked with be killed."

D.C. began 2021 with two crises: the coronavirus pandemic and a gun violence epidemic. To respond to the latter, Bowser advanced plans to draw on lessons learned from

*Originally published as Amanda Michelle Gomez, "DC's Harllee Harper Is Using Public Health Tools to Prevent Gun Violence. Will It Work?," *Kaiser Health News*, October 21, 2021. Reprinted with permission of the publisher. *Kaiser Health News* is a nonprofit news service covering health issues. It is an editorially independent program of the Kaiser Family Foundation that is not affiliated with Kaiser Permanente.

the former. She started by creating a position, one that anti-gun violence groups had long requested and became too urgent to ignore: gun violence prevention director. Enter Harllee Harper, who was appointed January 28.

About three weeks later, the mayor declared a public health emergency over gun violence and created an "emergency operations center" that mirrored the city's Covid-19 response. No part of the U.S. has been spared from an increase in murders during the pandemic. And in the nation's capital the murder toll is outpacing last year's, which reached 198, a 16-year high. Per capita, that's about 29 murders per 100,000 residents.

The City Council has directed unprecedented funding to support the efforts.

Harllee Harper, 56, started her 20-plus-year career at D.C. Public Schools as a substance abuse prevention and intervention coordinator. Most recently, she was senior deputy director for the D.C. Department of Youth Rehabilitation Services, where she helped overhaul the agency.

"I've run programs before, but this was a different level of limelight" than something she would have signed up for on her own, she said.

Nine months into this new role, Harllee Harper's most powerful tool is the mayor's initiative, Building Blocks. Drawing on public health strategies to contain the spread of gun violence, it's designed to treat the immediate symptoms and root causes of community violence.

Its workers operate almost as contact tracers, whose methods have become familiar during the pandemic. They enter targeted communities to form relationships and connect high-risk residents to violence interrupters, who are trained to de-escalate conflict. They also arrange for resources, like drug addiction treatment and housing assistance. The idea is to reach the small number of people who engage in dangerous behavior and invest in them and their neighborhood.

"Hopelessness combined with a gun, combined with substance abuse, is a really bad combination. And I think that's what we are seeing right now," said Harllee Harper.

Building Blocks is up and running in about a third of its targeted 151 blocks—2 percent of the city—that were connected to 41 percent of last year's gunshot-related crimes last year. (Brightwood Park is not on this list but is included in the city's fall crime prevention initiative run by the police department.)

These diverse neighborhoods are home to people who tend to be poorer and lack access to resources and opportunities. Statistics among Covid and murder victims look similar: The same neighborhoods were hit hardest and the vast majority of deaths have befallen Black people.

D.C. stemmed the spread of Covid far more efficiently than the nation as a whole, in part through government action. The city's crash course on public health during the pandemic could mean it's better situated to address gun violence. "We can explain certain things through this public health lens and people can understand it a bit better," said David Muhammad, executive director of the National Institute for Criminal Justice Reform.

He said D.C.'s approach is unique and Harllee Harper's position is rare. "If you claim to want to reduce gun violence in your city, prove it. Whose full-time job is it in your city to do that? In most cities, it is zero," he said. "Don't tell me the police chief. That's a small portion of their job."

For the few dozen cities that have some sort of anti-violence czar, the position is relatively new. Richmond, California, is an exception, with an agency dedicated to reducing gun violence since 2008. Richmond's Office of Neighborhood Safety has been heralded as a model. By 2013, Richmond went from more than 40 homicides a year to 16, according to Giffords Law Center to Prevent Gun Violence—its lowest number in three decades.

Harllee Harper's position is housed not within the public safety agency but the city administrator's office, presumably affording her more authority and oversight of government programs.

And Building Blocks created a mobile app with which its employees can flag requests during walk-throughs of select neighborhoods. An employee could make a request using the city's "311" service line to repair a streetlight that is out, for example, and the agency responsible would prioritize it because it came from Building Blocks.

There's no guarantee these interventions will work, though multiple studies have shown positive outcomes of violence interrupters or infrastructure improvements, such as cleaning and transforming vacant lots and abandoned buildings.

But Daniel Webster, director of the Johns Hopkins Center for Gun Violence Prevention and Policy in Baltimore, said it's important to track successes and failures because efforts like the one Harllee Harper is spearheading don't "always work in all places" and there are lessons to learn when they don't.

"We can't expect the workers to just perform miracles," said Webster.

While expectations are high, Harllee Harper's success depends on whether government and business leaders will respond with the same urgency as they did when the health director requested action.

"The biggest hurdle really is getting all of government to buy into a new day and a new way to get things done," said council member Charles Allen, who chairs a committee that created Harllee Harper's position. "Bureaucracy is not nimble."

"My colleagues in the sister agencies across the city, when Building Blocks calls, they are very, very responsive," said Harllee Harper. "We're working together to create performance metrics for agencies related to gun violence prevention."

Some residents remain skeptical. Residents of the first Building Blocks neighborhood said the follow-up continues to lag. Jamila White, an elected member of the Advisory Neighborhood Commission, said she had several conversations with Harllee Harper and gave her a tour to point out the needs, including quick fixes like adding or fixing streetlights and regular street-sweeping. White has yet to see expedited results, she said, but respects Harllee Harper and admits that no one could address all the issues, many rooted in poverty, alone.

"There's a lot of shared agreement. But you know, having a shared agreement and having political will and power to do something is a different thing," said White.

30. Civic Engagement, Guns, Constitutional Rights and ASPA*

Don Klingner

The recent shootings of black men by police officers and of Dallas police officers at a "Black Lives Matter" rally present profound threats to U.S. civil society.

Professional public administration and public service require informed and engaged citizens, and cooperation between public administrators and elected officials. Democracy requires citizens to articulate their policy preferences (backed by facts or personal experience), genuinely consider others' preferences, work together to develop public policies and make sure these are implemented correctly and fairly. At present, American society does not meet these standards. Media sound bites, political attack ads and web-based misinformation—all funded by dark money and shadow organizations—fuel an increasingly shallow, self-congratulatory and ideologically driven shouting match. Growing income disparities, continued racial and ethnic discrimination and unfocused anger at social change and economic uncertainty all stir the pot.

The U.S. Constitution is short and riddled with dilemmas that the judicial branch must resolve. The Dallas shootings highlight the conflict between the First Amendment right to peacefully assemble and to petition the government for a redress of grievances, and the Second Amendment right to keep and bear arms. Supporters of "Black Lives Matter" had assembled to protest earlier police shootings. Dallas police were providing crowd control and ensuring public safety. Then a disturbed and disgruntled black Army Reservist, targeting white police officers, killed five and wounded others before being killed. Under Texas law, open carry of long guns is legal and many people at this event carried assault rifles. But once the shooting started and given the initial assumption that several coordinated shooters were in place, how were officers who had been trained to react to the presence of a weapon expected to distinguish shooters from gun-carrying bystanders?

Open carry laws also present a broader threat to U.S. society. Their underlying assumption is that public-spirited and trained civilians who carry can help maintain public safety. Those who carry assume they meet these qualifications. Those who don't carry may disagree, and feel less (rather than more) safe when others around them have guns.

We must respond to these events by continuing to teach and model civic engagement, social justice and inclusion. However, these are not a sufficient response to the

*Originally published as Don Klingner, "Civic Engagement, Guns, Constitutional Rights and ASPA," *PA Times*, https://patimes.org/civic-engagement-guns-constitutional-rights-aspa/ (September 30, 2016). Reprinted with permission of the publisher.

danger of living in a country where shooting others is becoming an acceptable alternative to public dialog. Why not just fund shooting ranges instead of public universities?

We can stop this devolution to an armed society by adopting laws and policies that limit the corrosive effect of openly carried weapons on citizens' First Amendment rights without unconstitutionally abridging their Second Amendment rights:

- Prohibit the sale of military-grade assault weapons and high-capacity magazines. These are intended to kill the maximum number of people possible, not self-defense, target shooting or hunting.
- Require gun owners to carry liability insurance policies for their guns. This would encourage them to store guns safely and to report gun thefts quickly, as with cars.
- Require fingerprint identification so that guns intended and sold for civilian use can only be fired by their registered owners. This would reduce accidental deaths, gun thefts and illicit arms trafficking. Many cell phones have this feature; why not guns?

However, the killing of young black men by law enforcement officers requires different responses. We should accept the validity of objective data and public perceptions that blacks are more likely than whites to be the subjects of police interest as citizens or as drivers and more likely to be subjected to force during these encounters. We should also accept that the expectations placed on law enforcement have toughened considerably due to a social safety net weakened by years of budget cuts, and may not be realistic. Of course "all lives matter," but those who say this should acknowledge that this may deflect legitimate demands to address institutional racism.

ASPA is a "big tent." Our professional staff, volunteer leaders and members "walk the talk" of civic engagement by working together with mutual trust and shared values. But supporting and modeling civic engagement as part of our wider mission to support professional public administration and public service is not enough. We as ASPA must also support open discussion of these policy issues, and add our policy recommendations to the national dialog:

President Gooden can select speakers and direct the program committee to use the 2017 annual conference in Atlanta to highlight these issues. How about U.S. Rep. John Lewis or Dallas Police Chief David Brown as speakers? How about Founders' Forums or other panels focused on the social justice, civil engagement and guns?

The National Council and president can create an advisory group to consider whether ASPA is really walking the talk on social equity, social justice and accountability issues, and make policy recommendations for consideration by the National Council.

Past presidents can lend their individual support to these efforts. We may choose to make recommendations as a body to the president and National Council, particularly if asked.

Public Administration Review could commission a symposium on these issues, encouraging research articles (co)written by leaders of community-based organizations and law enforcement; and academic experts in criminal justice, program evaluation, leadership and ethics. Other ASPA journals can do likewise.

With the approval of the president and the National Council, ASPA could advocate policies and programs, and aggregate and articulate shared interests with counterpart associations like NAPA, NASPAA and ICMA.

31. How the Gun Control Debate Ignores Black Lives*

Lois Beckett

On a drizzly afternoon in January 2013, almost a month after the school shooting in Newtown, Connecticut, that left 20 first-graders dead, more than a dozen religious leaders assembled in Washington, D.C.

They had been invited by the Obama administration to talk about what the country should do to address gun violence. Vice President Joe Biden had been meeting with victims and advocates all day, and he arrived so late that some in the room wondered whether he would come at all. When he finally walked in, the clergy started sharing their advice, full of pain, some of it personal. "The incidents of Newtown are very tragic," Michael McBride, a 37-year-old pastor from Berkeley, California, recalled telling Biden. "But any meaningful conversation about addressing gun violence has to include urban gun violence."

McBride supported universal background checks. He supported an assault weapons ban. But he also wanted something else: a national push to save the lives of black men. In 2012, 90 people were killed in shootings like the ones in Newtown and Aurora, Colorado. That same year, nearly 6,000 black men were murdered with guns.

Many people viewed inner-city shootings as an intractable problem. But for two years, McBride had been spreading awareness about Ceasefire, a nearly two-decades-old strategy that had upended how police departments dealt with gang violence. Under Ceasefire, police teamed up with community leaders to identify the young men most at risk of shooting someone or being shot, talked to them directly about the risks they faced, offered them support, and promised a tough crackdown on the groups that continued shooting. In Boston, the city that developed Ceasefire, the average monthly number of youth homicides dropped by 63 percent in the two years after it was launched. The U.S. Department of Justice's "what works" website for crime policy had a green check mark next to Ceasefire, labeling it "effective"—the highest rating and one few programs received.

McBride wanted President Obama to make Ceasefire and similar programs part of his post–Newtown push to reduce gun violence. He had brought a short memo to give to White House staffers, outlining a plan to devote $500 million over five years to scaling

*This story was originally published by ProPublica as Lois Beckett, "How the Gun Control Debate Ignores Black Lives," https://www.propublica.org/article/how-the-gun-control-debate-ignores-black-lives (November 24, 2015). Reprinted with permission of the publisher.

such programs nationwide. His pitch to Biden that day was even simpler: Don't ignore that black children are dying too.

In response, the vice president agreed urban violence was very important, McBride said. But it was clear that "there was not a lot of appetite for that conversation by folks in the meeting," McBride recalled.

Michael McBride, a pastor who has been pushing the president and other politicians to increase support for programs like Ceasefire. (Deanne Fitzmaurice for ProPublica)

Later, other ministers who worked with McBride would get an even blunter assessment from a White House staffer: There was no political will in the country to address inner-city violence.

When McBride spoke to administration staffers again about dramatically increasing money for programs like Ceasefire, he said, "People were kind of looking at me like, 'Are you crazy?' No, I'm not crazy. This is your own recommendation. You should do it!"

Mass shootings, unsurprisingly, drive the national debate on gun violence. But as horrific as these massacres are, by most counts they represent less than 1 percent of all gun homicides. America's high rate of gun murders isn't caused by events like Sandy Hook or the shootings this fall at a community college in Oregon. It's fueled by a relentless drumbeat of deaths of black men.

Gun control advocates and politicians frequently cite the statistic that more than 30 Americans are murdered with guns every day. What's rarely mentioned is that roughly 15 of the 30 are black men.

Avoiding that fact has consequences. Twenty years of government-funded research has shown there are several promising strategies to prevent murders of black men, including Ceasefire. They don't require passing new gun laws, or an epic fight with the National Rifle Association. What they need—and often struggle to get—is political support and a bit of money.

A week after McBride and the other faith leaders met with Biden, Obama announced his national gun violence agenda. He called for universal background checks, which experts say could prevent some shootings. Other key elements of his plan—a ban on assault weapons and funding to put police officers in schools—were unlikely to save a significant number of lives.

At the press conference where Obama announced the plan, a diverse group of four children sat on the podium with him: two girls and two boys who had written letters begging the president to do something about gun violence. "Hinna, a third-grader—you can go ahead and wave, Hinna—that's you—Hinna wrote, I feel terrible for the parents who lost their children. I love my country, and I want everybody to be happy and safe," the president said.

Obama went over the litany of school shootings—Columbine, Virginia Tech, Newtown—and made a brief nod to the deaths of "kids on street corners in Chicago." But his plan included no money for the urban violence strategies his Justice Department described as effective. His platform didn't refer to them at all.

McBride, who was in the audience, said he was not surprised. He supported the president's other proposals, and, when it came to urban violence, he had "realistic expectations." In his fight to save the lives of black men, McBride has kept running up against the same assumption: that "urban violence is a problem with black folk. It's not a problem for this country to solve."

Gun violence in America is largely a story of race and geography. Almost two-thirds of America's more than 30,000 annual gun deaths are suicides, most of them committed by white men. In 2009, the gun homicide rate for white Americans was 2 per 100,000—about seven times as high as the rate for residents of Denmark, but a fraction of the rate for black Americans. In 2009, black Americans faced a gun homicide rate of nearly 15 per 100,000. That's higher than the gun homicide rate in Mexico.

To liberals, gun violence among African Americans is rooted in economic disadvantage and inequality, as well as America's gun culture and lax gun laws. Conservatives, meanwhile, often focus on black "culture." "The problem is not our gun laws," a member of the Wall Street Journal editorial board wrote last year about Chicago's murder rate. "Nor is it our drug laws, or racist cops, prosecutors and judges. The problem is black criminality, which is a function of black pathology, which ultimately stems from the breakdown of the black family."

Lost in the debate is that even in high-crime cities, the risk of gun violence is mostly concentrated among a small number of men. In Oakland, for instance, crime experts working with the police department a few years ago found that about 1,000 active members of a few dozen street groups drove most homicides. That's .3 percent of Oakland's population. And even within this subgroup, risk fluctuated according to feuds and other beefs. In practical terms, the experts found that over a given stretch of several months only about 50 to 100 men are at the highest risk of shooting someone or getting shot.

Most of these men have criminal records. But it's not drug deals or turf wars that drives most of the shootings.

Instead, the violence often starts with what seems to outsiders like trivial stuff—"a fight over a girlfriend, a couple of words, a dispute over a dice game," said Vaughn Crandall, a senior strategist at the California Partnership for Safe Communities, which did the homicide analysis for Oakland.

Somebody gets shot. These are men who do not trust the police to keep them safe, so "they take matters into their own hands," he said. It's long-running feuds, Crandall said, that drive most murders in Oakland.

Men involved in these conflicts may want a safer life, but it's hard for them to put their guns down. "The challenge is that there is no graceful way to bow out of the game," said Reygan Harmon, the director of Oakland Police Department's violence reduction program.

These insights led a group of Boston police, black ministers and academics to try a new approach in 1996. Since group dynamics were driving the violence, they decided to hold the groups accountable. The plan was simple: Identify the small groups of young men most likely to shoot or be shot. Call them in to meet face-to-face with police brass, former gang members, clergy and social workers. Explain to the invitees that they were at high risk of dying. Promise an immediate crackdown on every member of the next group that put a body on the ground—and immediate assistance for everyone who wanted help turning their lives around. Then follow up on those promises.

The results of Operation Ceasefire were dramatic. Soon after Boston held its first meeting—known as a call-in—on May 15, 1996, homicides of young men plummeted along with reports of shots fired.

The Rev. Jeff Brown, one of the ministers who worked on the project, remembers people were outside more, barbecuing in the park. At Halloween, kids were able to trick-or-treat on the streets again.

The team behind the effort quickly started getting calls from other cities—even other countries—about how to replicate what became known as the Boston Miracle. With the support of the Justice Department under Presidents Bill Clinton and George W. Bush, many cities tried the strategy and some got dramatic results. Stockton saw a 42 percent reduction in monthly gun homicides over several years. Indianapolis experienced a 34 percent drop in monthly homicides. Lowell, Massachusetts, saw gun assaults fall by 44 percent.

A 2012 review of the existing research evidence found that seven of eight cities that had rigorously implemented Ceasefire and similar strategies had seen reductions in violence.

Other cities have tried Ceasefire, or half-tried it, and then abandoned it. The strategy requires resources, political buy-in, and ongoing trust between unlikely partners. The effort in Boston had "black and Latin and Cape Verdean clergy working with white Irish Catholic cops in a city that had a history of race relations leading up to that point that was abysmal," Brown said. "It was really a shift in behavior, in the way we did business."

These partnerships can be fragile. Boston's own Ceasefire effort fell apart in 2000, researchers said. There was infighting and the police official who led it got another assignment. In subsequent years, homicides of young men crept up again.

An endless number of variables can affect crime, making it hard to know how much a particular effort works. Daniel Webster, director of the Johns Hopkins Center for Gun Policy and Research, noted that the current research only evaluates the short-term effects of the program, so it's still unclear how well it works over the long term.

Still, Webster said, if you're interested in reducing shootings among young black men, the Boston Ceasefire model is one of the strategies that has shown "the most consistent positive response."

Jim Bueerman—head of the Police Foundation, which focuses on crime research—said that while the evidence is only "highly suggestive," Ceasefire is still worth doing.

"It's going to be a long time before you get the perfect evidence," said Bueerman, a former police chief of Redlands, California. "When you come across a strategy like Ceasefire that appears to be working, you owe it to people to try it in your local community."

Part of what seems to make Ceasefire effective is that it treats the men it targets as both dangerous and also in need of help. Such initiatives, however, fit into no political camp and thus have few powerful champions.

"It has no natural constituency," said Thomas Abt, a Harvard Kennedy School researcher who has worked on crime policy at the Justice Department. "To vastly oversimplify, progressives want more prevention and conservatives want more enforcement. Focused deterrence"—what academics call Ceasefire and similar approaches—"challenges the orthodoxy on both sides. It makes everybody uncomfortable."

Ceasefire has often been greeted with skepticism in the neighborhoods it's supposed to help, where residents have reason to distrust the police. To buy into Ceasefire, McBride had to weigh the data against his own experience. In 1999, as a college student studying theology, McBride was stopped as he drove home by two white San Jose police officers. He said they forced him to get out of his car, groped him, and made him lie on the ground while threatening him.

It didn't matter that he was a youth pastor, that he was involved in local politics, that he had just helped to get San Jose's new mayor elected. That night, he was just another black man lying on the ground. (The police chief at the time told ProPublica that while the officers and McBride gave conflicting accounts, he decided to launch a study of racial profiling during traffic stops, one of the nation's first.)

When McBride moved to Berkeley in 2005, fresh out of divinity school at Duke University, he thought he would focus his social justice work on education—mentoring young people struggling to graduate from high school.

Then a few of the young people he was mentoring were murdered. One was Larry Spencer, a charismatic 19-year-old—funny, popular, "someone that everyone just really loved," McBride said. Spencer was shot to death outside a liquor store in nearby Oakland. It was the city's 39th gun homicide in a year that left 110 dead.

Hundreds of mourners attended Spencer's funeral, McBride said. McBride asked the congregation how many had attended a funeral before. Everyone raised their hands. How many had been to two funerals? Three? Four? He continued to count upward. "I got as high as 10," he recalled. "Half of the young people started to cry and still had their hands in the air."

Oakland had tried Ceasefire on and off for years but struggled to make it work. "There wasn't a true commitment to the strategy," said Lt. LeRonne Armstrong, who managed the city's program in the mid–2000s while working in the criminal investigations unit. "We did not have the political support."

McBride and others pushed city leaders and pastors to embrace the strategy.

Many of them were skeptical, but McBride thought working with the police was crucial. "We realized that in order for us to do any of this work, we were going to have to be in some relation with the police department. We pay taxes. We're paying for the police department, whether we like it or not," he said.

In 2012, Oakland recommitted itself to Ceasefire. It hired a full-time manager for the program, using both city dollars and part of a 2013 Justice Department grant. The city also dedicated funds to work with a team of experts who had helped other cities implement Ceasefire. The experts helped Oakland do a detailed data analysis homing in on the men who needed to be called in. There were only 20 guys at the first relaunched call-in—"but they were 20 of the right guys," said Armstrong.

Murders dropped from 126 in 2012 to 90 in 2013, according to police department data. Last year, Oakland had 80 murders.

McBride traveled across the country as part of a national campaign to reduce urban violence using Ceasefire. Every city had its own challenges. Money was one of them. Ceasefire was not particularly expensive, but hiring outreach workers and providing social services to the men involved required a little support, as did hiring outside consultants. Outside funding also made it easier for city leaders to move ahead with a different approach to gun violence.

The Obama administration has several grant programs aimed at helping urban neighborhoods reduce violence, but the demand for grants far outstrips funding. For one 2012 grant, the Justice Department received over 140 applications and had money for just 15.

"It is a brutal process to apply for these grants. Most of them don't get funded, and I think that's a bit of a tragedy," said Bueerman, the head of the Police Foundation. "You have agencies that are highly willing to do the work. You don't have to sell them on the efficacy of the strategy. You just have to empower it through a relatively small amount of money to help them get the program started."

The Obama administration has consistently asked for more money than Congress has authorized. In 2012, the White House requested $74 million for five grants for Ceasefire and similar programs. It got $30 million.

Advocates of Ceasefire have tried to press Congress for more money. Some legislators "really like these programs," one former Hill staffer said, but not enough to take on an uphill battle for additional funding. "I think the one sort of antidote to that was if you had massive political pressure from some organization or group that felt really strongly about something and could get people riled up about it," the staffer said. "Honestly speaking, if we are talking about urban violence, there is less of that."

The national groups that spend the most money and do the most advocacy related to gun violence have concentrated almost exclusively on passing stricter gun control laws. Dan Gross, the president of the Brady Campaign to Prevent Gun Violence, said he's "very supportive," of strategies like Ceasefire, but "it's not our lane."

A spokeswoman for Michael Bloomberg's Everytown for Gun Safety said much the same. "We're focused on what we know, which is how to improve the laws," said Erika Soto Lamb.

Declines in violent crime over the last two decades have made it harder to galvanize support for gun violence prevention. The number of Americans murdered by guns peaked in 1993, then dropped sharply until 2000 for reasons that are still not fully understood. Since then, the number of Americans killed in gun homicides has remained remarkably consistent, about 11,000 to 12,000 a year.

Another constant: About half of those killed this way are black men, though they make up just 6 percent of the U.S. population. In 2001, when George W. Bush took office, 5,279 black men were murdered with firearms, according to estimates from the Centers for Disease Control and Prevention. In 2012, it was 5,947.

These deaths are concentrated in poor, segregated neighborhoods that have little political clout.

"I think that people in those communities are perceived as not sufficiently important because they don't vote, they don't have economic power," said Timothy Heaphy, a former U.S. attorney who has spent much of his career focused on urban violence. "I think there's some racism involved. I don't think we care about African-American lives as much as we care about white lives."

The few congressional efforts to advance gun legislation in recent years have been prompted by mass shootings, violence that is seemingly random and thus where everyone can feel at risk.

"Congress has only moved in response to galvanizing tragedy, and galvanizing tragedy tends to not involve urban, run-of-the-mill murder," said Matt Bennett, a gun policy expert at Third Way, a centrist think-tank. "The narrative about the need for gun violence prevention generally is driven by these black swan events, and those often involve white people," he added. "It is horrific and tragic, but that's the fact."

When Adam Lanza shot his way into the Sandy Hook Elementary School with a military-style rifle and handguns in December 2012, it wasn't clear if any laws would have stopped him. Lanza had taken the guns from his mother, who had purchased them legally.

The package of proposed legislation and policy initiatives recommended by the Obama administration in the aftermath of Sandy Hook centered on closing loopholes in background checks and renewing the federal ban on assault weapons that expired in

2004. The president also called for increased spending on mental health, crackdowns on the trafficking networks that sell illegal guns, and more than $150 million for a new program to put more cops and psychologists in schools.

Obama and gun control advocates made universal background checks the focus of their push. It wasn't a policy that was relevant to Newtown, but they saw it as the most likely way to reduce everyday gun violence and save lives. Most researchers agree that a better background check system could help curtail both urban gun violence and mass shootings, though there's no hard data to indicate how much.

There was less evidence proving that the other elements of the president's plan would reduce gun violence. Though the public quickly focused on one weapon Lanza used, a Bushmaster XM15-E2S, experts knew the assault weapons ban hadn't saved many lives. The effects of a renewed ban "are likely be small at best, and perhaps too small for reliable measurement," a report funded by the Justice Department concluded.

A former senior White House official agreed. While a ban on high-capacity magazines could help some, the official told ProPublica, the assault weapons ban "does nothing." Though Obama endorsed it as part of the post–Newtown package, "we did the bare minimum," the official said. "We would have pushed a lot harder if we had believed in it."

Some gun control advocates who worked with the administration on gun legislation said they saw the endorsement of the assault weapons ban as a bargaining chip. "It's all a dance, it's a kabuki thing, and right from the beginning the White House understood that they weren't going to get a ban done," said Bennett, the gun policy expert. "They had to talk about it. It would have been insane not to. Every news report after Sandy Hook had this horrible looking AR-15, and noted that it had been a banned weapon that now wasn't."

Adding police at schools has popular appeal, but classroom homicides are exceedingly rare.

"Any given school can expect to experience a student homicide about once every 6,000 years," said Dewey Cornell, a University of Virginia professor who studies school safety.

"Children are in far more danger outside of schools than in schools. If we had to take officers out of the community to put them in schools, then actually children will be less safe rather than more safe."

Two former administration staffers who worked on the gun violence platform said the $150 million proposal for cops and counselors in schools—which "may have been a bit outsized," one said—was driven by Vice President Biden's history of championing federal grants for hiring cops.

It also seemed like "something that people might be willing to, you know, give us money for," a former senior White House official said.

The staffers said they could not remember why funding to support strategies like Ceasefire was not included in the plan. "Look, if it was some deliberate conversation not to do it, I would remember," the former senior official said.

Though Justice Department grants for community violence prevention weren't part of the post–Sandy Hook platform, a staffer said, "we were watching the fiscal year 2014 budget process and making sure we were continuing to push for those resources at DOJ." Bruce Reed, Biden's chief of staff at the time, said budget concerns likely kept funding for innovative local efforts out of the package.

"We didn't want to turn this into an appropriations bill, because that would be ..." he said, shrugging. "That would cost us whatever Republicans we had hoped for."

"The appropriations climate was, if possible, more divisive than the gun debate," Reed added later. "We were always between shutdowns."

Webster, the Johns Hopkins gun violence researcher, said that it would have been "more justifiable" to devote federal dollars to supporting Ceasefire and similar programs than it was to put the money toward school security. "I don't know of any evidence that putting police in schools makes them safe, and I do know of evidence that having police in schools leads to more kids being arrested," he said.

Two weeks after Obama unveiled his plan, McBride and dozens of other clergy members, many of them from cities struggling with high rates of gun violence, met again with staffers from Vice President Biden's task force.

The mood at the January 29 meeting was tense. Many of the attendees, including McBride, felt the president's agenda had left out black Americans.

"The policy people working for Biden worked with the reality of Congress," said Teny Gross, one of the original Boston Miracle outreach workers who now leads the Institute for Nonviolence Chicago. "What they were proposing to us was very limited and was not going to help the inner city."

Gross said he "blew a gasket." The clergy members in the room were pleading for help. "We bury hundreds of kids every year in the inner city," Gross recalled them telling the administration representative. "Some of the solutions need to apply to us."

A staffer said that the political will of the country was not focused on urban violence, several ministers who attended the meeting recalled.

"What was said to us by the White House was, there's really no support nationally to address the issue of urban violence," said the Rev. Charles Harrison, a pastor from Indianapolis. "The support was to address the issue of gun violence that affected suburban areas—schools where white kids were killed."

The Rev. Jeff Brown, from Boston, was angered by the administration's calculated approach. "When you say something like that and you represent the President of the United States, and the first African-American President of the United States, you know, that's hugely disappointing," he said.

Former administration officials said they thought it was tragic that the everyday killings of black children did not get more political attention. "I totally agree with their frustrations," a former official said. "At the same time, when the nation listens, you've got to speak, and you don't get to pick when the nation listens."

It would turn out there was little political will to realize the administration's gun-violence proposals either. Measures to expand background checks and ban assault weapons died on April 17, 2013, when they couldn't muster the votes necessary to advance in the Senate.

In his 2014 budget recommendations around the same time, Obama again asked for more money for local grant programs to combat urban gun violence. He recommended tripling the funding for a Justice Department grant that helped cities adopt Ceasefire from $8 million to $25 million. Overall, he requested $79 million for grants to support similar initiatives. Obama had asked for almost twice that much to put more cops and psychologists in schools.

Congress slashed Obama's requests across the board. Instead of approving $150 million to help schools hire cops and psychologists, it created a $75 million school safety research program.

It also rejected his proposed increases for Ceasefire and similar programs. Instead,

Congress took many of the small grants and made them even smaller. One program was cut from $8 million to $5.5 million. Another shrank from $2 million to $1 million.

In all, Congress spent $31 million on five urban violence-related grants—less than half of what it approved for research on how to make schools safer.

There have been increasing concerns about rising murder rates over the past year in cities across the country. Some have blamed the increases on the "Ferguson Effect,"—the theory that increased scrutiny of cops has made them reluctant to do their jobs—although there is "no data" to support this claim, as Attorney General Loretta Lynch said recently. It's not clear how much murders have increased nationwide. Each city has its own trend. Some have seen an uptick only in comparison to the historic lows they had last year. In other cities, violence is truly spiking. Baltimore recently recorded its 300th homicide this year, the most since 1999.

In Indianapolis, where homicides are set to increase for the third straight year, more federal funding might have made a difference. In early 2012, Indianapolis applied for a Justice Department grant to help implement Ceasefire, requesting $1.5 million over three years. But just four of more than roughly 60 cities that applied received funding. Indianapolis was not among them.

"Absolutely, there's no doubt in my mind, if we had been awarded the grant we would have had the financial carryover to move the program forward," said Shoshanna Spector, the executive director of IndyCAN, a local faith-based advocacy group that pushed for Ceasefire.

Douglas Hairston, who works on private-public partnerships at the Indianapolis mayor's office, said the city is currently doing "60 to 70 percent" of the Ceasefire strategy.

"Federal funds would have helped," he said. "We know that we could do more, and we're striving to find ways to do it."

Earlier this year, Indianapolis Police Chief Rick Hite said the city was doing the strategy "with modifications" and that the city is always using the "tenets of Ceasefire."

There have been 133 murders so far this year in Indianapolis, according to police department data, up from 96 in 2012.

In Baltimore, Ceasefire appears to have struggled. The program's manager resigned in March, the Baltimore Sun reported. Webster, the researcher evaluating the effort, told the paper he questioned whether the rollout of Ceasefire in the Western District was "being done on the cheap and being done in a way that is not even resembling the program model."

Other cities have seen more success. New Orleans and Kansas City both saw drops in violence that researchers have credited to their new Ceasefire programs. Chicago has been rolling out call-ins to an increasing number of police districts. Gary, Indiana, and Birmingham, Alabama, both launched new Ceasefire programs this year. Cities have often paid for the programs using money from a variety of sources: federal dollars, local governments, and, increasingly local foundations.

Obama has launched an initiative to support young men and boys of color. One of the stated goals of My Brother's Keeper, which was launched last year, is reducing violence. The initiative is backed by more than $500 million in corporate and philanthropic commitments. But most of that money has been devoted to mentoring and education programs.

Organizers said they would reduce violence, too, albeit indirectly. "I would challenge this notion that violence reduction resources or targeting is only to be looked at through the lens of reducing violence per se," Broderick Johnson, the chair of the My Brother's Keeper Task Force, told ProPublica. "It is just as important to look at it in terms of opportunities for young people to stay in school or get jobs or to get second chances."

Last year, the Justice Department also launched a modest effort called the Violence Reduction Network, which provides cities with training and advice from former police chiefs and other crime-fighting experts. Many of the needs the network meets are basic: It helped Wilmington, Delaware, police create a homicide unit. Wilmington, with 70,000 mostly black residents, has a higher murder rate than Chicago.

Running the network is inexpensive. It costs about $250,000 per city annually. But once again, it's not meeting the greater need. The program is targeted at the roughly four-dozen cities with the nation's highest violent crime rate. The government is only working with 10 of them.

The White House did not comment on questions about the administration's overall response to urban violence. The Justice Department offered the following statement: "In addition to focusing on violent crime reduction in cities, the department also responded to one of the worst mass shootings in our nation's history in Newtown by identifying funding for school resource officers to help keep kids safe in schools and to assist the many victims of this heinous crime."

Biden's office also offered a statement: "Whether it's by banning assault weapons, incentivizing local police to create better relationships with residents of America's cities, or finding alternatives to jail, including diversionary programs like drug courts, the Vice President has worked to support any viable solutions to reduce gun violence in our cities."

When Jeff Brown was at the White House recently for an initiative on extremism, he ran into Biden.

"The vice president walked up to me and said, 'Reverend Brown, good to see you,'" Brown said. Biden said he remembered meeting Brown back in the '90s, when he visited Boston to hear more about Operation Ceasefire and the Boston Miracle.

"I hope we can bring back some of what we did in Boston," Brown said he told the vice president.

"I hope so, too," Biden replied.

Brown laughed at the memory. "You're the vice president—can't you do something about it?"

This story was co-published with The New Republic. *Produced by Emily Martinez and Hannah Birch.*

32. The Final Cut*

Chaseedaw Giles

BALTIMORE—The barber had with him his tools of trade: a black leather smock, a razor, clippers, scissors and tufts of black locks he had collected from the floor of his shop.

He would use them to try to cover the bullet hole that tore through his client's head.

Antoine Dow owns a barbershop in the Druid Heights neighborhood of West Baltimore and has often been called upon to provide clients who have been gunned down with their final haircut. It's a ritual that he says helps bring some dignity to the young black men whose lives are disproportionately affected by gun violence, many of whom Dow knew and serviced while they were still alive.

"When I walked into the room and saw his body, I didn't recognize him because the trauma to the skull was so bad," Dow said of Deontae Taylor, 20, a young man who was killed last fall. "The entry wound was a hole and the exit wound was sewed up in the back like a football," he said.

After he finished, he called Taylor's mother. "I did the best I could do."

The decline in gun deaths in some major cities across the country has made headlines, but in places like Baltimore, the numbers remain high. There were 348 homicides in Baltimore last year, up more than 12 percent from the year before, and only five fewer than the record set in 1993. Firearms were involved in 312 of the 348 killings, according to an analysis of the latest numbers in the Baltimore Police Department Crime Stats Open Data database by Kaiser Health News.

Dow has been cutting hair for 24 years. He started when he was 19, giving haircuts to friends in his father's basement. In 2001, at age 27, he found a small shop with a reasonable rent that had only enough room for one barber. He had the shop remodeled and has been open ever since. On Saturdays, he can be found cutting hair for as many as 70-odd clients, his barber chair positioned at the shop entrance, where he can greet each person as they enter.

"I always wanted my own barbershop. I pretty much knew what I wanted to do, because I enjoyed it, and people would pay me for it," he said.

The issue of gun violence has followed Dow for years. In 2000, at a barbershop on the corner of Lafayette and Division streets in West Baltimore where he worked, Dow was shot in the leg after he tried to intervene in an argument between a client and another man. His client, Howard Robinson, 35, was shot in the back and died later that day.

*Originally published as Chaseedaw Giles, "The Final Cut," *Kaiser Health News*, March 20, 2020. Reprinted with permission of the publisher. *Kaiser Health News* is a nonprofit news service covering health issues. It is an editorially independent program of the Kaiser Family Foundation that is not affiliated with Kaiser Permanente.

Typically, funeral homes dress the bodies of the deceased and cut their hair, if necessary. But sometimes a favored barber is brought in.

Dow was 26 when he performed his first haircut for a deceased client. In that case, it was an older man who had died of natural causes, circumstances that Dow said are much easier to manage than a shooting victim. He has continued to take on the difficult task of providing haircuts for clients who have been killed, for a straightforward reason, as he sees it—"because I cut their hair while they were alive."

And as his business has expanded, Dow has hired other barbers who have also learned the trade of post-mortem hair cutting.

Quant'e Boulware, 24, has worked for Dow the past four years and has cut the hair of two customers no longer alive. One was a 2-year-old child who died in a car crash—his godson. "I rather me cut his hair than somebody else," he said softly.

When clients leave Dow's shop, he said he tells them to "please be safe," but he knows that can be hard in a city like Baltimore. He estimates that as many as eight of his clients were murdered in the last year alone.

Dontae Breeden, one of Dow's younger clients, said that he and his peers often feel invisible in a city where violence is so common and that some young men turn to gun violence out of desperation. "People just want to be known for something," said Breeden, 22. "They just want recognition."

Rashad Jones has been a client of Dow's for three years. In March 2019, he was shot at a bus stop on East Northern Parkway after work. Not only has Jones lost two of his best friends to gun violence this year, but in 2013 his brother was shot and paralyzed from the waist down at age 25.

The barbershop is one of the few places in West Baltimore where Jones, 29, said he feels safe and Dow has tried to provide that comfort to his clients, both in life and in death.

He talks to his clients while cutting their hair, even those who have passed away, like the young man who had been shot in the head.

"I was talking to him while I was cutting his hair, like I do a lot of my deceased clients," said Dow. "I just said, you know, 'I hope you rest well.'"

KHN reporter Victoria Knight contributed to this article.

• *D. Firearms Industry and Associations* •

33. The Road to Responsible Gun Ownership**

National Shooting Sports Foundation

Owning a Firearm, Whether for Target Shooting, Hunting or Personal Protection, Is a Right Every Law-Abiding American Enjoys

It comes with an ongoing commitment to safety and responsibility—something that should be fully understood before buying your first firearm. This is at the heart of our message: "Own it? Respect it. Secure it."

To help, we've provided a "road map" of the milestones toward responsible gun ownership that should be considered. Following these guidelines can help you be a responsible firearms owner, including following the many laws regarding purchasing, ownership, storage and use. By doing so, you will be contributing to a culture of firearms safety that has produced a dramatic decline in firearms accidents.

Make an Informed Purchasing Decision

Buying a firearm involves understanding what type, model, caliber and more are suitable and the best fit for your intended use. You have many ways to conduct research, including reading reviews and handling and testing products yourself. Many organizations that support Project ChildSafe can offer advice and guidance, and you can speak with experts at a local firearms retailer or shooting facility near you. If possible, try various models at a local range. Click here to see a list of ranges by state, and learn more about safety with this Range Safety and Etiquette video (https://vimeo.com/220814809).

---

*Originally published as National Shooting Sports Foundation, "The Road to Responsible Gun Ownership," https://projectchildsafe.org/join-us-on-the-road-to-responsible-gun-ownership/ (2020). Reprinted with permission of the publisher.

You've Decided Which Firearm Is Right for You, But Do You Know How You're Going to Store It Safely?

Securely storing firearms when not in use is a key element of responsible gun ownership and the #1 way to help prevent firearm accidents, thefts and misuse.

As a firearms owner, you have lots of options for storage devices to fit your lifestyle and home circumstances. The Safe Storage Options infographic (https://33safe.org/wp-content/uploads/2020/07/PCS_SafeStorage_19.pdf), Gun Lock Safety brochure (https://projectchildsafe.org/wp-content/uploads/2020/05/PCSBrochure_Adstar.pdf), and 10 Tips for Firearm Safety in Your Home fact sheet (*https://projectchildsafe.org/wp-content/uploads/2020/05/PCS_FirearmsSafety_2020_web.pdf*) are packed with helpful resources to help you explore storage options and determine what will work best for you. Experts at your local range or firearms retailer can also help answer questions.

Taking a Firearms Safety Training Class at Your Local Range or Firearms Retailer Is a Great Idea for New Gun Owners and a Good Refresher Even If You've Been a Gun Owner for Years

Classes usually cover safe handling and use, proper maintenance, storage and other helpful information for getting the most out of your firearm and being a safe and responsible firearm owner.

Find a safety training course close to home with this list of ranges by state. Additionally, the firearms dealer from whom you purchased your gun can point you in the right direction for a class or possibly provide one on-site. Think you already know all the gun safety rules? Double-check with this list of tips for safe gun handling (https://projectchildsafe.org/safety/safe-handling/).

Strike Up a Conversation with Your Family About Safe Firearms Handling, Your Household Rules for Firearms and Your Firearm Storage Plan

To help you get started, shooting champion Julie Golob and Project ChildSafe teamed up to make the video "How to Talk to Kids About Firearm Safety" (*https://projectchildsafe.org/talking-to-kids/*). Our Firearms Responsibility in the Home brochure also provides tips for discussing firearm safety with kids. You can encourage them to sign the Child's Pledge to make safety a mutual responsibility.

Part of Being a Responsible Firearm Owner Includes Keeping Your Skills Sharp

It's important to be sure you understand the mechanical characteristics and safe operation of the firearm you've chosen. Be sure to read and understand the instructions, warnings and safety devices the manufacturer includes with your firearms. If you have any questions, contact them or seek the advice of a firearms safety instructor or licensed retailer in your area. Also, practice and periodically reassess your training and skills.

Find safety classes and other training opportunities through the NRA's list of safety courses, a Project ChildSafe supporter organization in your area or the firearms dealer from whom you purchased your gun.

Treat your storage plan as evolving and ongoing to stay on top of your safety needs and those of your family. There are numerous storage options out there. A good place to start researching is the Safe Storage Options infographic which outlines a range of storage options for many lifestyles and budgets, ranging from gun locks to gun cases, lock boxes and gun safes. You can also refer to these safe storage tips (*https://childsafe-wp.devbox24.com/parents-and-gun-owners/*) and download the brochure from the Project ChildSafe storage kit for more information.

Families Change and Evolve, and So Does Your Conversation with Your Family About Firearms Safety

New family dynamics—like new family members, teenagers exploring their boundaries or loved ones experiencing a difficult time—can pose questions about firearms storage and uncover new or additional needs. Revisit the conversation of firearm safety with "How to Talk to Kids About Firearm Safety," a video with shooting champion Julie Golob. It is a helpful resource to break the ice or get tips for having a conversation with kids. Our Firearms Responsibility in the Home brochure also discusses how you can deter access available to children and at-risk persons. Sign the Child's Pledge (*https://projectchildsafe.org/wp-content/uploads/2020/05/PCS_Pledge_July2020.pdf*) with your child to make safety a mutual responsibility.

As You Know, Responsible Firearms Ownership Is a Lifelong Journey

An important part of that journey is sharing what you know with others. As a responsible gun owner, you can be a powerful voice in building a culture of firearms safety within your house, your neighborhood and your community. We urge you to share the firearm safety message with our easy-to-use web and social media badges, by taking the Project ChildSafe pledge and by sharing this information with friends and family.

Thank you for making the commitment to be a responsible gun owner. We hope you and your family will safely enjoy the shooting sports for many years. Along the way, you can always find all of our Project ChildSafe tools and resources here: *https://childsafe-wp.devbox24.com/resource-library/*.

34. The American Public Has Power Over the Gun Business

Why Doesn't It Use It?*

BRIAN DELAY

As teenagers in Parkland, Florida, dressed for the funerals of their friends—the latest victims of a mass shooting in the U.S.—weary outrage poured forth on social media and in op-eds across the country. Once again, survivors, victims' families and critics of U.S. gun laws demanded action to address the never-ending cycle of mass shootings and routine violence ravaging American neighborhoods.

The 14 children and three adults shot dead on February 14 at Marjory Stoneman Douglas High School were casualties of the nation's 30th mass shooting this year—defined by the Gun Violence Archive as involving at least four victims including the injured—and one of the deadliest in U.S. history. A question on many minds is whether this massacre will finally compel Washington to act. Few commentators seem to believe so.

If advocates for reform despair, I can understand. The politics seem intractable. It's easy to feel powerless.

But what I've learned from a decade of studying the history of the arms trade has convinced me that the American public has more power over the gun business than most people realize. Taxpayers have always been the arms industry's indispensable patrons.

The U.S. arms industry's close alliance with the government is as old as the country itself, beginning with the American Revolution.

Forced to rely on foreign weapons during the war, President George Washington wanted to ensure that the new republic had its own arms industry. Inspired by European practice, he and his successors built public arsenals for the production of firearms in Springfield and Harper's Ferry. They also began doling out lucrative arms contracts to private manufacturers such as Simeon North, the first official U.S. pistol maker, and Eli Whitney, inventor of the cotton gin.

The government provided crucial startup funds, steady contracts, tariffs against foreign manufactures, robust patent laws, and patterns, tools and know-how from federal arsenals.

*Originally published as Brian DeLay, "The American Public Has Power Over the Gun Business—Why Doesn't It Use It?," *The Conversation*, https://33434.com/the-american-public-has-power-over-the-gun-business-why-doesnt-it-use-it-92005 (February 16, 2018). Reprinted with permission of the publisher.

The War of 1812, perpetual conflicts with Native Americans and the U.S.-Mexican War all fed the industry's growth. By the early 1850s, the United States was emerging as a world-class arms producer. Now-iconic American companies like those started by Eliphalet Remington and Samuel Colt began to acquire international reputations. Even the mighty gun-making center of Great Britain started emulating the American system of interchangeable parts and mechanized production.

Profit in War and Peace

The Civil War supercharged America's burgeoning gun industry.

The Union poured huge sums of money into arms procurement, which manufacturers then invested in new capacity and infrastructure. By 1865, for example, Remington had made nearly US$3 million producing firearms for the Union. The Confederacy, with its weak industrial base, had to import the vast majority of its weapons.

The war's end meant a collapse in demand and bankruptcy for several gun makers. Those that prospered afterward, such as Colt, Remington and Winchester, did so by securing contracts from foreign governments and hitching their domestic marketing to the brutal romance of the American West.

While peace deprived gun makers of government money for a time, it delivered a windfall to well-capitalized dealers. That's because within five years of Robert E. Lee's surrender at Appomattox, the War Department had decommissioned most of its guns and auctioned off some 1,340,000 to private arms dealers, such as Schuyler, Hartley and Graham. The Western Hemisphere's largest private arms dealer at the time, the company scooped up warehouses full of cut-rate army muskets and rifles and made fortunes reselling them at home and abroad.

More Wars, More Guns

By the late 19th century, America's increasingly aggressive role in the world insured steady business for the country's gun makers.

The Spanish American War brought a new wave of contracts, as did both World Wars, Korea, Vietnam, Afghanistan, Iraq and the dozens of smaller conflicts that the U.S. waged around the globe in the 20th and early 21st century. As the U.S. built up the world's most powerful military and established bases across the globe, the size of the contracts soared.

Consider Sig Sauer, the New Hampshire arms producer that made the MCX rifle used in the Orlando Pulse nightclub massacre. In addition to arming nearly a third of the country's law enforcement, it recently won the coveted contract for the Army's new standard pistol, ultimately worth $350 million to $580 million.

Colt might best illustrate the importance of public money for prominent civilian arms manufacturers. Maker of scores of iconic guns for the civilian market, including the AR-15 carbine used in the 1996 massacre that prompted Australia to enact its famously sweeping gun restrictions, Colt has also relied heavily on government contracts since the 19th century. The Vietnam War initiated a long era of making M16s for the military, and the company continued to land contracts as American war-making shifted from Southeast Asia to the Middle East. But Colt's reliance on government was so great that it filed for bankruptcy in 2015, in part because it had lost the military contract for the M4 rifle two years earlier.

Overall, gun makers relied on government contracts for about 40 percent of their revenues in 2012.

Competition for contracts spurred manufacturers to make lethal innovations, such as handguns with magazines that hold 12 or 15 rounds rather than seven. Absent regulation, these innovations show up in gun enthusiast periodicals, sporting goods stores and emergency rooms.

NRA Helped Industry Avoid Regulation

So how has the industry managed to avoid more significant regulation, especially given the public anger and calls for legislation that follow horrific massacres like the one in Las Vegas?

Given their historic dependence on U.S. taxpayers, one might think that small arms makers would have been compelled to make meaningful concessions in such moments. But that seldom happens, thanks in large part to the National Rifle Association, a complicated yet invaluable industry partner.

Prior to the 1930s, meaningful firearms regulations came from state and local governments. There was little significant federal regulation until 1934, when Congress—spurred by the bloody "Tommy gun era"—debated the National Firearms Act.

The NRA, founded in 1871 as an organization focused on hunting and marksmanship, rallied its members to defeat the most important component of that bill: a tax meant to make it far more difficult to purchase handguns. Again in 1968, the NRA ensured Lyndon Johnson's Gun Control Act wouldn't include licensing and registration requirements.

In 1989, it helped delay and water down the Brady Act, which mandated background checks for arms purchased from federally licensed dealers. In 1996 the NRA engineered a virtual ban on federal funding for research into gun violence. In 2000, the group led a successful boycott of a gun maker that cooperated with the Clinton administration on gun safety measures. And it scored another big victory in 2005, by limiting the industry's liability to gun-related lawsuits.

Most recently, the gun lobby has succeeded by promoting an ingenious illusion. It has framed government as the enemy of the gun business rather than its indispensable historic patron, convincing millions of American consumers that the state may at any moment stop them from buying guns or even try to confiscate them.

This helps explain why the share price of gun makers so often jumps after mass shootings. Investors know they have little to fear from new regulation and expect sales to rise anyway.

A Question Worth Asking

So with the help of the NRA's magic, major arms manufacturers have for decades thwarted regulations that majorities of Americans support.

Yet almost never does this political activity seem to jeopardize access to lucrative government contracts.

Americans interested in reform might reflect on that fact. They might start asking their representatives where they get their guns. It isn't just the military and scores of federal agencies. States, counties and local governments buy plenty of guns, too.

Take Smith & Wesson, maker of the AR-15 Nikolas Cruz just used to kill his teachers and classmates at the Marjory Stoneman Douglas High School. Smith & Wesson is well into a five-year contract to supply handguns to the Los Angeles Police Department, the second-largest in the country. In 2016 the company contributed $500,000 (more than any other firm) to a get-out-the-vote operation designed to defeat candidates who favor tougher gun laws.

Do voters in LA—or in the rest of the country—know that they are indirectly subsidizing the gun lobby's campaign against regulation? Concerned citizens should begin acting like the consumers they are and holding gun makers to account for political activities that imperil public safety.

35. How the U.S. Government Created and Coddled the Gun Industry*

Brian DeLay

After Stephen Paddock opened fire on Las Vegas concertgoers on October 1, many people responded with calls for more gun control to help prevent mass shootings and the routine violence ravaging U.S. neighborhoods.

But besides a rare consensus on restricting the availability of so-called bump stocks, which Paddock used to enable his dozen semi-automatic rifles to fire like machine guns, it's unclear if anything meaningful will come of it.

If advocates for reform despair after such a tragedy, I can understand. The politics seem intractable right now. It's easy to feel powerless.

But what I've learned from a decade of studying the history of the arms trade has convinced me that the American public has more power over the gun business than most people realize.

The U.S. arms industry's close alliance with the government is as old as the country itself, beginning with the American Revolution.

Forced to rely on foreign weapons during the war, President George Washington wanted to ensure that the new republic had its own arms industry. Inspired by European practice, he and his successors built public arsenals for the production of firearms in Springfield and Harper's Ferry. They also began doling out lucrative arms contracts to private manufacturers such as Simeon North, the first official U.S. pistol maker, and Eli Whitney, inventor of the cotton gin.

The government provided crucial startup funds, steady contracts, tariffs against foreign manufactures, robust patent laws, and patterns, tools and know-how from federal arsenals.

The War of 1812, perpetual conflicts with Native Americans and the U.S.-Mexican War all fed the industry's growth. By the early 1850s, the United States was emerging as a world-class arms producer. Now-iconic American companies like those started by Eliphalet Remington and Samuel Colt began to acquire international reputations. Even the mighty gun-making center of Great Britain started emulating the American system of interchangeable parts and mechanized production.

---

*Originally published as Brian DeLay, "How the U.S. Government Created and Coddled the Gun Industry," *The Conversation*, https://theconversation.com/how-the-us-government-created-and-coddled-the-gun-industry-85167 (October 9, 2017). Parts of this contribution repeat sections of DeLay's contribution preceding this one. Reprinted with permission of the publisher.

Profit in War and Peace

The Civil War supercharged America's burgeoning gun industry.

The Union poured huge sums of money into arms procurement, which manufacturers then invested in new capacity and infrastructure. By 1865, for example, Remington had made nearly US$3 million producing firearms for the Union. The Confederacy, with its weak industrial base, had to import the vast majority of its weapons.

The war's end meant a collapse in demand and bankruptcy for several gun makers. Those that prospered afterward, such as Colt, Remington and Winchester, did so by securing contracts from foreign governments and hitching their domestic marketing to the brutal romance of the American West.

While peace deprived gun makers of government money for a time, it delivered a windfall to well capitalized dealers. That's because within five years of Robert E. Lee's surrender at Appomattox, the War Department had decommissioned most of its guns and auctioned off some 1,340,000 to private arms dealers, such as Schuyler, Hartley and Graham. The Western Hemisphere's largest private arms dealer at the time, the company scooped up warehouses full of cut-rate army muskets and rifles and made fortunes reselling them at home and abroad.

More Wars, More Guns

By the late 19th century, America's increasingly aggressive role in the world insured steady business for the country's gun makers.

The Spanish American War brought a new wave of contracts, as did both World Wars, Korea, Vietnam, Afghanistan, Iraq and the dozens of smaller conflicts that the U.S. waged around the globe in the 20th and early 21st century. As the U.S. built up the world's most powerful military and established bases across the globe, the size of the contracts soared.

Consider Sig Sauer, the New Hampshire arms producer that made the MCX rifle used in the Orlando Pulse nightclub massacre. In addition to arming nearly a third of the country's law enforcement, it recently won the coveted contract for the Army's new standard pistol, ultimately worth $350 million to $580 million.

Colt might best illustrate the importance of public money for prominent civilian arms manufacturers. Maker of scores of iconic guns for the civilian market, including the AR-15 carbine used in the 1996 massacre that prompted Australia to enact its famously sweeping gun restrictions, Colt has also relied heavily on government contracts since the 19th century. The Vietnam War initiated a long era of making M16s for the military, and the company continued to land contracts as American war-making shifted from southeast Asia to the Middle East. But Colt's reliance on government was so great that it filed for bankruptcy in 2015, in part because it had lost the military contract for the M4 rifle two years earlier.

Overall, gun makers relied on government contracts for about 40 percent of their revenues in 2012.

Competition for contracts spurred manufacturers to make lethal innovations, such as handguns with magazines that hold 12 or 15 rounds rather than seven. Absent regulation, these innovations show up in gun enthusiast periodicals, sporting goods stores and emergency rooms.

NRA Helped Industry Avoid Regulation

So how has the industry managed to avoid more significant regulation, especially given the public anger and calls for legislation that follow horrific massacres like the one in Las Vegas?

Given their historic dependence on U.S. taxpayers, one might think that small arms makers would have been compelled to make meaningful concessions in such moments. But that seldom happens, thanks in large part to the National Rifle Association, a complicated yet invaluable industry partner.

Prior to the 1930s, meaningful firearms regulations came from state and local governments. There was little significant federal regulation until 1934, when Congress—spurred by the bloody "Tommy gun era"—debated the National Firearms Act.

The NRA, founded in 1871 as an organization focused on hunting and marksmanship, rallied its members to defeat the most important component of that bill: a tax meant to make it far more difficult to purchase handguns. Again in 1968, the NRA ensured Lyndon Johnson's Gun Control Act wouldn't include licensing and registration requirements.

In 1989, it helped delay and water down the Brady Act, which mandated background checks for arms purchased from federally licensed dealers. In 1996 the NRA engineered a virtual ban on federal funding for research into gun violence. In 2000, the group led a successful boycott of a gun maker that cooperated with the Clinton administration on gun safety measures. And it scored another big victory in 2005, by limiting the industry's liability to gun-related lawsuits.

Most recently, the gun lobby has succeeded by promoting an ingenious illusion. It has framed government as the enemy of the gun business rather than its indispensable historic patron, convincing millions of American consumers that the state may at any moment stop them from buying guns or even try to confiscate them.

Hence the jump in the shares of gun makers following last week's slaughter in Las Vegas. Investors know they have little to fear from new regulation and expect sales to rise anyway.

A Question Worth Asking

So with the help of the NRA's magic, major arms manufacturers have for decades thwarted regulations that majorities of Americans support.

Yet almost never does this political activity seem to jeopardize access to lucrative government contracts.

Americans interested in reform might reflect on that fact. They might start asking their representatives where they get their guns. It isn't just the military and scores of federal agencies. States, counties and local governments buy plenty of guns, too.

For example, Smith & Wesson is well into a five-year contract to supply handguns to the Los Angeles Police Department, the second-largest in the country. In 2016 the company contributed $500,000 (more than any other company) to a get-out-the-vote operation designed to defeat candidates who favor tougher gun laws.

Do taxpayers in L.A.—or the rest of the country—realize they are indirectly subsidizing the gun lobby's campaign against regulation?

36. Is the NRA an Educational Organization? A Lobby Group? A Nonprofit? A Media Outlet? Yes*

SAMUEL BRUNSON

The National Rifle Association has hit more turbulence since 17 people died in the shooting at Marjory Stoneman Douglas High School in Parkland, Florida, than the nation's biggest gun advocacy group is accustomed to after such tragedies.

Anti-NRA memes implying that the nonprofit abuses its tax-exempt status went viral. A petition calling on the authorities to audit the group and consider revoking its exemption circulated. At least 10 companies dropped the special deals they used to offer its millions of members amid widespread concern about the NRA's role in squelching gun control and a growing interest in how the group operates.

As a law professor who teaches and writes about tax-exempt organizations, I would like to explain how the NRA retains its nonprofit status despite the vast amount of influence it exerts over politicians.

Social Welfare

The NRA is actually a bundle of organizations. The largest one, in terms of how much it spends, is the National Rifle Association of America. Originally formed in 1871, this NRA branch claims to have about 5 million members, although some investigative reporters question that assertion.

It has operated as a social welfare organization since 1944.

Like public charities, these groups, are exempt from taxation on the money they take in. Also known as 501(c)(4), based on language in the tax code, they differ from public charities in a few ways.

First, donors to social welfare organizations can't deduct their gifts from their taxable income. Second, these organizations may support and oppose political candidates. Third, social welfare organizations can engage in unlimited lobbying, as long as that effort to sway lawmakers and policymakers is related to their core mission.

*Originally published as Samuel Brunson, "Is the NRA an Educational Organization? A Lobby Group? A Nonprofit? A Media Outlet? Yes," *The Conversation*, https://theconversation.com/is-the-nra-an-educational-organization-a-lobby-group-a-nonprofit-a-media-outlet-yes-92806 (March 12, 2018). Reprinted with permission of the publisher.

Like charities, social welfare groups must spend all their revenue on work tied to their mission or shoring up their endowments. They can't, in other words, distribute any profits left over after paying their bills to their leaders, their funders or anyone else.

The NRA has five main missions: protecting the Second Amendment, promoting public safety, training for marksmanship and gun safety, promoting competitive shooting and improving hunter safety. Among other things, it publishes the American Rifleman, American Hunter, America's 1st Freedom and Shooting Illustrated magazines and produces NRATV programs. It also has a lobbying arm, created in 1975, called the Institute for Legislative Action.

In 2016 this social welfare group raised almost US$337 million in revenue, with about half coming from membership dues. The rest largely came from its media operations, donations and grants. It draws a growing share of its income, reportedly, from gunmakers rather than gunowners.

Politicking and Lobbying

The NRA also runs a political action committee, the NRA Political Victory Fund, through which it backs electoral candidates.

The NRA's political spending more than doubled between the 2012 and 2016 electoral cycles, rising to $54.4 million, according to the Center for Responsive Politics, a nonpartisan group that tracks the money reported to the government in federal elections. About $31 million of that sum supported Trump's candidacy.

The gun group's lobbying arm, which is technically a division of its social welfare group, spent more than $5 million in 2017, actively seeking to influence politicians or public officials regarding specific policies or pieces of legislation. It roughly tripled those expenditures in the last decade.

Charities

The NRA also runs four affiliated charities: the NRA Foundation, Inc., the NRA Civil Rights Defense Fund, the NRA Freedom Action Foundation and the NRA Special Contribution Fund.

Like thousands of churches, universities, museums and advocacy groups of other stripes, these are 501(c)(3) groups. That means they are excused from paying taxes on most of their income. In addition, their donors may get tax breaks when they deduct the value of their gifts to charities from their taxable income. To maintain that coveted incentive, these nonprofits can't endorse or oppose political candidates. They also can't do more than minimal amounts of lobbying.

What Do the NRA's Charities Do?

The NRA Foundation does public outreach to promote marksmanship and gun safety through grants to shooting programs run by everyone from the Boy Scouts to local police departments. It also advocates for protecting the constitutional right to bear arms, as does the NRA Freedom Action Foundation.

The NRA Civil Rights Defense Fund provides legal and financial aid to people and groups dealing with lawsuits related to the NRA's goals, and backs legal research on federal and state constitutional provisions that have to with guns.

The NRA Special Contribution Fund focuses on marksmanship and firearm safety, and operates the Whittington Center in New Mexico, a vast shooting range.

Common but with a Caveat

This multilayered structure isn't unique. For instance, the Sierra Club, a social welfare organization that advocates for environmental protection, is affiliated with the Sierra Club Foundation, a charity. The American Civil Liberties Union, a civil rights group partners with the ACLU Foundation and Planned Parenthood Federation of America, a charity that runs reproductive health care clinics, is affiliated with the Planned Parenthood Action Fund, a social welfare group that lobbies.

This arrangement helps charities preserve donors' tax breaks without sacrificing the ability of their affiliated membership groups to engage on the day's issues. Taken to its logical extreme, however, this dynamic can flout restrictions on what the government defines as legitimate charitable gifts.

Without such limits, what's to stop me or anyone else from getting tax breaks for donations that will pay for lobbying? I could give it to the charity of my choice, which in turn could hand my dollars to its related social welfare organization. I'd get my tax deduction, and the group that supports my policy preferences could use the money I donated for lobbying.

The IRS prohibits these financial switcheroos. While charities may contribute to their affiliated social welfare organization, both parties must keep records that prove the charitable gifts don't fund lobbying or political candidacies.

The NRA Foundation made a nearly $20 million grant to the National Rifle Association of America, in 2016. But that did not necessarily flout any tax laws.

Still, the NRA may sometimes let donations flow too freely between its affiliates, as Yahoo News has reported, in ways that violate federal electoral laws.

Running so many different kinds of organizations, each subject to different rules, is an immense and difficult undertaking. It's worth keeping an eye on the NRA to ensure that it manages to stay within the lines the law has painted.

37. The NRA's Video Channel Is a Hotbed of Online Hostility*

Adam G. Klein

As the National Rifle Association, the most influential gun rights advocacy group in the U.S., comes under pressure from victims' groups and gun control advocates, internet companies like Amazon, Apple and YouTube are finding themselves uncomfortably close to the center of the controversy. These are among the companies that currently stream the NRA's official video channel, NRA TV.

NRA TV has become a central focus in what could be a threshold moment in the national gun debate. In the wake of the school shooting in Parkland, Florida, that claimed 17 lives, a consumer activist movement has worked to peel back the tight grip the NRA holds over the country's gun policy. The effort has driven some airlines, insurance companies, car rental companies and banks to sever their commercial and professional ties with the NRA. Now gun control activists are turning their full attention to the internet.

In the world of online politics, it's not unusual to find videos inciting hostility. On February 12, just days before the Parkland shooting, one such YouTube video featured a pundit smashing a sledgehammer through a TV set that featured liberal commentators, later declaring, "If we want to take back this nation from socialists who are out to destroy it ... you better believe we'll be pushing the truth on them." But that video was not the seething production of an obscure far-right blogger. It was the latest episode of the official video channel of the NRA.

NRA TV is not merely a platform for promoting Second Amendment rights or engaging gun enthusiasts. As a researcher of online extremism, I'd contend it has become one of the web's most incendiary hotspots for stoking outrage at liberal America, attacking perceived enemies like Black Lives Matter and the Women's March, and promoting the message that America is under threat from the so-called "violent left"— an especially alarming term, coming from a gun lobby.

What Is NRA TV?

Given the channel's association with the NRA, a newcomer to NRA TV might reasonably expect information on gun safety, Second Amendment rights and a community

---

*Originally published as Adam G. Klein, "The NRA's Video Channel Is a Hotbed of Online Hostility," *The Conversation*, https://theconversation.com/the-nras-video-channel-is-a-hotbed-of-online-hostility-92477 (March 1, 2018). Reprinted with permission of the publisher.

for firearms enthusiasts and collectors. Its focus is none of those things. Instead, visitors find a virtual hornet's nest of hard-right politics.

In my work, I came across NRA TV while tracking far-right and far-left groups' activities on Twitter. One such group had retweeted a video from NRA TV featuring host Dana Loesch calling the mainstream media "the rat bastards of the earth" whom she was happy to see "curb stomped."

The acidic tone of NRA TV represents an astonishing evolution of an organization that began as a rifle club to promote marksmanship. Even the NRA of the 1980s, which ran TV ads on the right to bear arms, would be hard to recognize as a forebear to today's version. My study of 224 NRA TV videos and tweets over two months in 2017 found that only 34 dealt with topics related to direct gun advocacy or gun ownership. The remaining 190, or about five out of every six posts, were trained on perceived political enemies, trading the core mission of gun rights for incessant attacks on "crazed liberals" and "hateful leftists."

A TV Ad from the NRA from the 1980s

It is hard to recall an NRA that once viewed itself as a bipartisan body. Its current online hosts warn that opponents of President Donald Trump will "perish in the political flames of their own fires." Even more provocative is the portrayal of the NRA's declared adversaries, framed not as political foes, but as ideological and even existential threats. The Women's March is labeled "a bigoted, fake feminist, jihad-supporting" movement, while Black Lives Matter is described as "a dangerous, hateful, destructive ideology."

The dystopian picture that NRA TV portrays includes government officials encouraging violent protests against conservative groups, and a media-sponsored "war on cops." The NRA believes it must be ready to defend itself and the country against these and other forces.

In addition to publishing its own material, NRA TV also retweets others' hostile messages.

In a video that streamed to NRA TV's 260,000 Twitter followers in August 2017, host Grant Stinchfield asked his audience,

"What scares me more than the North Korean crazed tyrant? The violent left and the crazed liberals who lead them. They like North Korea also pose a clear and present danger to America…. Make no mistake, the lying leftist media, the elitist cringe-worthy celebrities, and the anti–American politicians—who make up the violent left—don't just hate President Trump, they hate you."

The insinuation that left-wing forces are out to destroy the country by sabotaging its institutions is a demagogic refrain with echoes of the anti-communist McCarthy era. But it is particularly unsettling when it emanates from a lobby that simultaneously promotes the necessity of gun ownership. Which brings us back to Amazon.

Pulling the Plug

After another shooting at an American high school at the hands of a 19-year-old with an AR-15, the gun-control advocacy movement has turned its attention to its chief opponent, the NRA. The strategy is to dislodge the influence of the NRA by going after its support system. That has led activists to Amazon, Apple, Roku and other services that stream NRA TV content. While other companies support the NRA financially, these internet giants provide perhaps a more valuable currency in their prominent platforms that allow the NRA to distribute its message.

Moms Demand Action for Gun Sense in America is one organization leading the charge for internet companies to drop NRA TV, citing its "violence-inciting programming." The group is joined by some of the survivors of the Parkland shooting, such as David Hogg, who is encouraging people to boycott tech companies that carry NRA TV. A petition on Change.org, with 240,000 signatures as of March 1, is simultaneously calling on Amazon CEO Jeff Bezos to purge NRA content from his site's offerings. And on Twitter, #dropNRATV is gaining steam, even as the channel continues to host controversial content.

The growing wave of consumer activists has effectively placed the internet's biggest gatekeepers in the middle of America's hyperpolarized gun debate. As web hosts, their power to amplify or quiet controversial messages is unmatched in the modern media landscape. But in many ways, this is not strictly a gun issue. Rather, a closer look at NRA TV suggests that this is also an issue of community standards, which are well within a web host's domain.

And in recent months, YouTube and Twitter have each demonstrated a willingness to enforce stricter terms of service prohibiting hateful, dangerous or abusive material from their networks. So the real question that these internet companies now face is whether an NRA tirade about American liberals posing a "clear and present danger" is legitimate gun advocacy, or barefaced incitement.

• E. Schools and Children •

38. Arming Non-Teaching Staff*

Ian Smith

Historical Perspective

According to Cornell, Matthew (2010), although the weapons have changed student violence can be traced back to 2000 BCE. They cited numerous accounts of assaults, riots, and shooting in European schools from the Middle Ages into the 19th Century. The 1927 School Dynamiter, in Bath, Michigan, killed 44 including 38 students (Boissoneault, 2017). During 1966 a University of Texas engineering student went on a shooting rampage killing 16 people and wounded 31 (Lavergne, 1997). This historical trend has been replicated at an alarming rate inside Americas classrooms and school yard resulting in 37 active shooter incidents at elementary/secondary schools and 15 active shooter incidents at postsecondary institutions from 2000 to 2017 (Musu, Zhang, Wang, Zhang, Oudekerk, Barbara 2019, p. 22).

According to the Centers for Disease Control and Prevention (CDC), 7.4% of high school students in 2011 reported being threatened or harmed with a weapon on school grounds. The National Center for Education Statistics notes that between 1992 and 2009, there were between 14 and 34 homicides among children ages 5 to 18 at school each year. According to Janet Reno, former Attorney General of The Unites States "Youth violence has been one of the greatest single crime problems we face in this country" and in the same publication, Louis Freeh, former Director of The Federal Bureau of Investigation (FBI) stated "It is imperative that, community by community, we find the ways to protect our children and secure for them the safe places they need to learn the hard business of growing up, to learn right from wrong, to learn to be good citizens" (O'Toole 1999).

Good citizens do not murder children therefore many attributions include mental health. However, school shootings cannot be resolved with a single public policy. The issue of school safety and security involves a variety of problems and challenges that range on a continuum that is influenced by school culture, teacher attrition, classroom engagement, community poverty, sociocultural disenfranchisement (Cornell and Mayer 2010). Therefore, these varied stakeholders continuously exert considerable pressure to

---

*Published with permission of the author.

influence public policy decision makers because they want a solution to this shooting pandemic that is destabilizing their communities.

Politics, Parkland, and Marjory Stoneman Douglas High School

The community of Parkland, Florida, and its students at Marjory Stoneman Douglas High School mourned the execution of 14 students and three adults on February 14, 2018, when a 19-year-old former student attacked students, during school with an AR-15 style weapon. The public outcry and political pressure culminated with the subsequent passage of the Florida School Safety Act of 2018. The act authorizes non-teaching staff to carry guns during school operation. The right to bear arms and gun violence are volatile public health issues in many communities around The United States. Therefore, this synergy of public outcry, pressure group preferences, and personal political ambitions ensured the hasty enactment of Marjory Stoneman Douglas High School Public Safety Act within 23 days following the shooting.

According to Plakon, (2020), responding to widespread movements and a personal desire to hold a United States Senate seat in a few short months, Governor Rick Scott, very quickly signed The Marjory Stoneman Douglas Public Safety Act into law on March 9, 2018. On February 21, 2018—one week after the shooting, Governor Rick Scott announced his major action plan to combat school violence. The Act included many provisions to enhance school safety, implemented new policies, procedures, and added safety personnel at the state and local levels. The Act also revised and created new capital funding policies and allocated four hundred million dollars to implement those provisions (p. 681).

Marjory Stoneman Douglas Public Safety Act-2018

- Prevented gun ownership by individuals who have been adjudicated mentally defective or who have been committed to a mental institution.
- Bans anyone under twenty-one years old from purchasing a firearm and prohibits bump-fire stock possession.
- Established prevention, intervention, and emergency preparedness planning administered by the Office of Safe Schools.
- Created the Florida Safe Schools Assessment Tool, requiring the Department of Education to contract with a security consulting firm that specializes in developing risk assessment software solutions and has experience conducting security assessments of public facilities to develop, update, and implement a risk assessment tool.
- Allocated $400 million to implement the Act.
- Developed several new agencies, programs, and networks. These agencies include: a Commission on School Safety and Security within the Florida Department of Law Enforcement, an Office of Safe Schools within the Department of Education, a Multiagency Service Network for Students with Severe Emotional Disturbance (SEDNET).
- Created the Guardian Program, named after Coach Aaron Feis, who selflessly

sacrificed his life to save students at Marjory Stoneman Douglas during the massacre.

The Guardian Program funds the training and arming of non-teaching school staff. However, this controversial provision has the potential to create significant, negative, unintended consequences because the Guardianship Program has a primary focused on weapons and police training tactics. The perceived militarization of non-teaching school staff has the potential to exacerbate school safety concerns among many stakeholders around Florida.

Currently, it is not yet known how teachers, students, and community stakeholders perceive current levels of security preparedness for acts of violence within their schools. Although feeling safe while in school is a concern for every stakeholder, more guns represent more conflict. Therefore, those on the frontlines may display reduce commitment to the institution, student welfare, and their educational responsibilities. Additionally, students may disengage, misbehave or stay away from school. Communities will be paralyzed with fear, unease, and become burdened with a yearning for solutions to the trauma associated with having its members murdered in the secure space of their children's classrooms.

The Marjory Stoneman Douglas School Safety Act, especially the Guardian Program has been described as reactionary, emotionally driven, and a shooting cycle phenomenon (Plakon 2020, p. 681). The author claims that the act has become one of many other reactionary rapid, response, sociopolitical legislation that targets a tragic event with rare occurrence. As media hype and focus fades and switch to the next news headline, communities are abandoned to heal only to be jolted with the recurring nightmare from the next American school shooting and more emotional policy decision.

Purpose of the Study

The goal of this research was to examine, analyze and evaluate whether the decision by the State of Florida to allow armed non-teaching staff on school property, during school operation would increase school safety and security. Specifically, this study sought to determine whether the arming of non-teaching staff members would protect the schools from armed intruders. This report targeted the local South Florida, agricultural community of Clewiston, known as *"America's sweetest town"* because it is home to the corporate headquarters of U.S. Sugar Corporation.

The corporation has a private-public partnership with Hendry County School District. "*Take Stock in Children* is so proud to have U.S. Sugar as a partner in our work to provide students in Hendry County and across the state with the support to pursue their dreams through college and career success," said Veronica Roquette, Take Stock in Children Student Services Coordinator at Clewiston High School. "Take Stock really does change the lives of our students, families and the entire community" (https://www.ussugar.com/news/u-s-sugar-proud-support-academic-success-partnership-take-stock-children/).

About Hendry County School District

The district's student population of 7, 266 has benefited greatly from its public-private partnership with U.S. Sugar Corporation and *Take Stock in Children program.* The partnership has enhanced the district's ability to achieve its mission to *provide students the opportunity to achieve at high academic levels, equipping them to successfully pursue college or career goals.* Compared to other communities in Florida, Hendry County has the largest percentage of people without any formal schooling and the rural farming community is characterized by the following demographic statistics:

- Ranks 1st with residents younger than 18 years of age
- Ranks 2nd with Latin/American Indian residents
- Ranks 3rd with foreign born residents
- Student teacher ratio 18:1
- Smallest proportion (%) of people with undergraduate degrees.

Research Methodology and Findings

Research data was collected via structured interviews with key informant, subject matter experts and community convenience surveys from members of the Hendry County School District. Below is a summary of the research findings:

1. Arming of non-teaching staff is not the preferred method for protecting students in the Hendry County school system.
2. School security is the single most important defense for preventing a mass school shooting like the attack at Marjorie Stoneman Douglas High School.
3. Most teachers are uncomfortable with the arming of school staff.
4. Several community leaders expressed preference for trained police officers.
5. Other stakeholders prefer a focus on student behavior and student access to guns in the community

Analysis

The arming of school staff is not a new phenomenon since several states have legalized this procedure. However, the presence of guns in classrooms to protect students is refuted by Brandt (2016) in a study which showed no reduction in crimes on campus, even with increased armed security. According to the author, guns on campus introduce the unfavorable impact of suicide by gun and accidental shooting occurrences, at the expense of the increased communal feelings of safety (p. 64).

Additionally, on campus security is ineffective if a shooter with a high-powered weapon attacks a school by shooting from off-campus. Regardless of the source, students and teachers are prime targets and one teacher vehemently stated that *since teachers are on the frontline of any attack, they should be armed.* Others were more concerned that essential instructional funds will be diverted to pay for school security. However, any consideration and empathy for a shooters' mental health were vehemently rejected based on the shooters premeditated activities. There was also a consensus among community stakeholders that school shootings are the product of America's culture of glorifying violence in music, movies and entertainment.

Finding a solution for the complex issue of guns and mass shootings in America has generated attention and response across multiple sectors and disciplines. Many scholars and professionals are advocating for an interdisciplinary approach that involves mental health and allied systems of professionals (Cornell and Mayer 2010). The authors state that a Public Health Approach may play a more permanent and important role in averting school shootings. "We need a comprehensive public health approach to gun violence that is informed by scientific evidence and free from partisan politics" (Interdisciplinary Group on Preventing School and Community Violence 2018). A scientific approach to solving school shooting requires rigor, time, and rational reaction.

Recommendations

Although physical school security measures are important for students and staff feeling safe during school, preparing and guarding the school against an active shooter should not be the sole area of focus. There needs to be a change in school culture and a changed mindset from reaction to prevention and eventually early intervention. Early intervention entails more than simple security measures. It requires school campuses evolving into community centers for learning and innovation where confidentiality with honest communication are encouraged and respected. Preemptive measures include:

1. Adopting a school culture with professional student support services and teamwork
2. Implement a personal safety and security curriculum
3. Reintroduction of the vocational skills education for technically gifted students
4. Develop an active-progressive parent-led, parent teacher organization
5. Institute a mandatory monthly parent-school communication
6. Coordinate an annual physical security inspection by local law enforcement

References

Boissoneault, Lorraine (2017). *The 1927 Bombing That Remains America's Deadliest School Massacre.* Retrieved Nov. 28, 2020, from https://www.smithsonianmag.com/history/1927-bombing-remains-americas-deadliest-school-massacre-180963355.
Brandt, Jonathan R (2016). *Does Concealed Handgun Carry Make Campus Safer? A Panel Data Analysis of Crime on College and University Campuses.* The University of Texas at Austin.
Call for Action to Prevent Gun Violence in the United States of America Interdisciplinary Group on Preventing School and Community Violence (2018). Retrieved November 30, 2020, from https://curry.virginia.edu/prevent-gun-violence.
Cornell, Dewey, and Mayer, Matthew (2010). *Why Do School Order and Safety Matter?* Educational Researcher. Vol. 39. No. 1. p. 7–15.
Marguez, Yvonne (2020). *Florida Gov. Cuts Millions from Guardian Training Program. Campus Security and Life Safety.* Retrieved November 29, 2020, from https://campuslifesecurity.com/articles/2020/07/02/-florida-gov-cuts-millions-from-guardian-training-program.aspx.
Musu, L., Zhang, A., Wang, K., Zhang, J., and Oudekerk, B.A. (2018). *Indicators of School Crime and Safety.* (NCES 2019-047/NCJ 252571). *National Center for Education Statistics,* U.S. Department of Education, and Bureau of Justice Statistics, Office of Justice Programs, U.S. Department of Justice. Washington, D.C. http://nces.ed.gov/pubsearch/pubsinfo.asp?pubid=2019047.
Niche, Henry County Schools Rankings. https://www.niche.com/k12/d/hendry-county-schools-fl/.
O'Toole, Mary Ellen (1999). *School Shooter. A Threat Assessment Perspective.* Critical Incident Response Group (CIRG) National Center for the Analysis of Violent Crime (NCAVC) FBI Academy https://www.fbi.gov/file-repository/stats-services-publications-school-shooter-school-shooter.
Plakon, Emily (2020). *Reactionary Legislation: The Marjory Stoneman Douglas High School Public Safety*

Act. Stetson Law Review, Vol. 49. Is. 4. Articles and Symposia Editor. Candidate for Juris Doctor, Stetson University College of Law, 2020.

Texas State Historical Association. *The Southwestern Historical Quarterly*, Volume 101, July 1997–April 1998, periodical, 1998; Austin, Texas. (https://texashistory.unt.edu/ark:/67531/metapth117155/: accessed December 1, 2020), University of North Texas Libraries, The Portal to Texas History, https://texashistory.unt.edu; crediting Texas State Historical Association.

Town Charts, Hendry County, Florida Education Data. https://www.towncharts.com/Florida/Education/-Hendry-County-FL-Education-data.html.

"U.S. Sugar Proud to Support Academic Success through Partnership with Take Stock in Children," *U.S. Sugar*. https://www.ussugar.com/u-s-sugar-proud-support-academic-success-partnership-take-stock-children/.

Weigel, Margaret (2014). *Violence in Schools: Research findings on underlying dynamics, response and prevention. Journalist's Resource* https://journalistsresource.org/studies/society/education/mass-killings-schools-research-roundup/.

39. Searching for Safety

*Where Children Hide When Gunfire Is All Too Common**

CARA ANTHONY

ST. LOUIS—Champale Greene-Anderson keeps the volume up on her television when she watches 5-year-old granddaughter Amor Robinson while the girl's mom is at work.

"So we won't hear the gunshots," Greene-Anderson said. "I have little bitty grand-babies, and I don't want them to be afraid to be here."

As a preschooler, Amor already knows and fears the sounds that occurred with regularity in their neighborhood before the pandemic—and continue even now as the rest of the world has slowed down.

"I don't like the pop, pop noises," Amor explained, swinging the beads in her hair. "I can't hear my tablet when I watch something."

And when the television or her hot-pink headphones and matching tablet can't mask the noise of a shooting? "She usually stops everything," said her mother, Satin White. "Sometimes she cries, sometimes she covers her ears."

Her grandmother has even watched Amor hide inside a narrow gap between the couch and recliner.

In communities across the United States this spring, families are dealing with more than just the threat of the coronavirus outside their homes. In the midst of violence that does not stop even during a pandemic, children like Amor continually search for safety, peace and a quiet place. "Safer at Home" slogans don't guarantee safety for them.

More than two dozen parents and caregivers who spoke with *Kaiser Health News* attested that the kids hide underneath beds, in basements and dry bathtubs, waiting for gunfire to stop while their parents pray that a bullet never finds them.

In St. Louis, which has the nation's highest murder rate among cities with at least 100,000 people, the reasons are especially stark. More than 20 children in the St. Louis area were killed by gunfire last year, and this year at least 11 children have died already.

While some of the children's deaths were caused by accidental shootings inside a home, regular gunfire outside is a hurtful reminder that adults have to find ways to keep children safe. And while parents hope their kids grow into healthy adults, evidence

---

*Originally published as Cara Anthony, "Searching for Safety: Where Children Hide When Gunfire Is All Too Common," *Kaiser Health News*, May 28, 2020. Reprinted with permission of the publisher. *Kaiser Health News* is a nonprofit news service covering health issues. It is an editorially independent program of the Kaiser Family Foundation that is not affiliated with Kaiser Permanente.

shows that children who grow up around violence or witness it frequently are more likely to have health problems later in life.

Although the mental health of children around the world has been taxed these past few months, for some children the stress has been going on far longer. Regularly hearing shootings is one example of what's called an "adverse childhood experience." Americans who have adverse childhood experiences that remain unaddressed are more likely to suffer heart disease, cancer, chronic respiratory diseases and stroke, according to a 2019 Centers for Disease Control and Prevention report.

St. Louis mental health counselor Lekesha Davis said children and their parents can become desensitized to the violence around them—where even one's home doesn't feel safe. And, research shows, black parents and children in the U.S., especially, often cannot get the mental health treatment they may need because of bias or lack of cultural understanding from providers.

"Can you imagine as a child, you are sleeping, you know, no care in the world as you sleep and being jarred out of your sleep to get under the bed and hide?" Davis asked.

"We have to look at this, not just, you know, emotionally, but what does that do to our body?" she added. "Our brain is impacted by this fight-or-flight response. That's supposed to happen in rare instances, but when you're having them happen every single day, you're having these chemicals released in the brain on a daily basis. How does that affect you as you get older?"

But future health problems are hard to think about when you're trying to survive.

At This Day Care, "Dora" Means Drop

The children at Little Explorers Learning Center are getting reacquainted with their daily routine now that the day care facility has reopened for families of essential workers as the Covid pandemic stay-at-home orders loosen. And there's a lot to remember.

Teachers at the center remind the children of their hand-washing, mealtime and academic routines. They also make sure the kids remember what to do when gunfire erupts nearby. Assistant director Tawanda Brand runs a gunfire safety drill once a month. First, she tells the children to get ready. Then, she shouts: "Dora the Explorer!"

"Dora" is a code word, Brand explained, signaling the kids to drop to the floor—the safest place—in case gunfire erupts nearby.

During a drill one morning before the pandemic, most of the children got down. Others walked around, sending Brand on a chase as she tried to corral the group of 3- to 5-year-olds.

The drill may sound playful, but sometimes the danger is real.

The Little Explorers protocol isn't like the "active shooter" drills that took place in schools around the country on the rare chance someone would come inside to shoot—as at Columbine, Parkland or Sandy Hook. The day care program performs these drills because nearby shootings are an ongoing threat.

Day care director Tess Trice said a bullet pierced the window in November while the children were inside. Then, the very next day, bullets flew again.

"We heard gunshots, we got on the floor," Trice said. "Eventually, when we got up and looked out the window, we saw a body out there."

Trice called parents that day to see if they wanted to pick up their children early. Nicollette Mayo was one of the parents who received a call from the teachers. She knows the neighborhood faces challenges, but can't see her 4-year-old daughter, Justice, and infant son, Marquis, going anywhere else.

"I trust them," Mayo said. "And I know that, God forbid, if there is an incident that I'm going to be contacted immediately. They're gonna do what they need to do to keep my children safe."

Trice considered bulletproof glass for the day care center but could not afford it. A local company estimated it would cost $8,000 to $10,000 per window. So she relies on the "Dora" drills and newly installed cameras.

Still, in a city with such an alarming homicide rate, such drills aren't happening only at the few day care facilities that have reopened. They also happen at home.

"You Live Better If You Sit on the Floor"

Long before the coronavirus pandemic pushed the world to isolate at home, the Hicks family had their own version of sheltering in place. But it was from gun violence. When they hear gunshots outside their home in East St. Louis, Illinois, everyone hides in the dark.

The goal is to keep the family out of sight, because bearing witness to a shooting could put them at a different kind of risk, mom Kianna Hicks said.

So when trouble erupts, they do their best to remain unseen and unheard.

"We turn the TV down," said 13-year-old Anajah Hicks, the oldest of four. "We turn the lights off, and we hurry up and get down on the ground."

A few times each month, the family practices what to do when they hear gunshots. Hicks tells the kids to get ready. Then, their grandmother Gloria Hicks claps her hands to simulate the sound of gunfire.

"I need them to know exactly what to do, because in too many instances, where we've been sitting around, and gunshots, you know, people start shooting, and they'll just be up walking around or trying to run," Kianna Hicks said. "I'll tell 'em, 'Naw, that's not what you do. You hear gunshots, you hear gunshots. No matter where you at, you stop—you get on the ground and you wait until it's over with and then you move around.'"

And this summer, Hicks wants to make sure the kids are ready. At least twice a week in past years when the weather warmed up, the family got on the floor in response to real gunfire. Violence spikes in summer months, according to the Giffords Law Center to Prevent Gun Violence. And she knows they could be spending more time in the house if football camp for her boys is canceled because of coronavirus fears.

Other families in tough neighborhoods sit on the floor more often, even amid moments of relative quiet. The first time Gloria Hicks saw a family sitting on the floor, she was visiting her godson in Chicago decades ago. It was hot that summer, Hicks recalled, so families kept their apartment doors open to stay cool.

"They were sitting on the floor watching TV and I wondered, Why is it like that?" Hicks recalled. "Then I learned that you live better if you sit on the floor than on the couch, because you don't know when the bullets gon' fly."

"I Immediately Dropped to the Floor"

Although 16-year-old Mariah knows what to do when bullets fly, she said, she still has a difficult time processing the sound of violence. The honor student was babysitting her little cousins at her St. Louis home last winter when she heard gunshots.

"It couldn't have been no further than, like, my doorstep," recalled Mariah, whose mother asked that the teen's last name not be printed so the discussion of the trauma doesn't follow her into adulthood. "I immediately dropped to the floor, and then in a split second the second thing that ran through my head is like, 'Oh, my God, the kids.'"

When Mariah walked into the next room, she saw her two younger cousins on the floor doing exactly what their mother had taught them to do when gunfire erupts.

Get down and don't move.

"I was so worried," Mariah recalled. "They're 6 and 3. Imagine that."

The three kids walked away physically OK that day. But later that night, Mariah said, she pulled out strands of her hair, a behavior associated with stress.

"Pulling my hair got really bad," she said. "I had to oil my hair again because when I oil it, it makes it hard to pull out."

Davis, the mental health counselor who has worked for 20 years with children experiencing trauma, encourages parents to comfort their kids after a traumatic event and for the kids to fully explore and discuss their emotions, even months after the fact.

She said getting on the floor explains only how families are maintaining their physical safety.

"But no one's addressing the emotional and the mental toll that this takes on individuals," said Davis, vice president of the Hopewell Center, one of the few mental health agencies for kids in the city of St. Louis.

"We get children that were playing in their backyard and they witnessed someone being shot right in front of them," Davis said. "These are the daily experiences of our children. And that's not normal."

Carolina Hidalgo contributed to this report as a journalist at St. Louis Public Radio.

40. Why Trump's Idea to Arm Teachers May Miss the Mark*

AIMEE HUFF *and* MICHELLE BARNHART

President Donald Trump's proposal to arm teachers has sparked substantial public debate.

As researchers of consumer culture and lead authors of a recent study of how Americans use and view firearms for self-defense, we argue that while carrying a gun may reduce the risk of being powerless during an attack, it also introduces substantial and overlooked risks to the carrier and others.

Where Bullets Land

One of the biggest risks involved with arming teachers would be missing the target—literally. Despite the fact that police must undergo extensive professional training, particularly for high-pressure situations, one study notes that police involved in gunfights shoot with an accuracy rate of just 18 percent.

Assuming teachers can achieve the same level of accuracy as police, and that an armed teacher were able to get into position to fire, just one in five or six bullets would hit the shooter. The other four or five bullets would hit something or someone else. While an armed and trained teacher may be able to stop a shooter, the teacher may also shoot an innocent person.

Why Might They Miss the Target?

Our recent study about people who keep and use handguns for self-defense can help to explain why someone using a gun against an attacker has difficulty hitting their target.

Over 24 months, the research team monitored 6,879 threads in four online discussion forums focused on armed self-defense. One author completed concealed handgun license training. Two contributing authors attended the annual NRA convention. The lead authors attended two gun shows, and interviewed two police officers and nine civilians who keep and/or carry handguns for self-defense.

*Originally published as Aimee Huff and Michelle Barnhart, "Why Trump's Idea to Arm Teachers May Miss the Mark," *The Conversation*, https://theconversation.com/why-trumps-idea-to-arm-teachers-may-miss-the-mark-92335 (February 26, 2018). Reprinted with permission of the publisher.

Individuals in our study expressed concern about effectively using their training during an actual event. They spoke of the possibility of "freezing up" or clumsily drawing their weapons. Many, including police and military personnel, acknowledge that the fear and chaos caused by a threatening situation produce involuntary physical responses, such as a racing heart and loss of fine motor skills. They believe these responses could impede their ability to accurately fire and could expose themselves and bystanders to the risk of being shot. They engaged in regular rehearsals in an attempt to address these concerns.

Individuals in our study note other risks of using a gun for self-defense, such as mistaking an innocent person for an assailant or being targeted by an assailant who sees that you are armed. Indeed, if arming teachers becomes commonplace, shooters may target teachers first, further decreasing teachers' firing ability and accuracy.

We contend that other factors could inhibit teachers from effectively using their firearms training. The majority of shooters at high school and middle school incidents are current students. Recognizing the shooter as a student could emotionally inhibit a well-intentioned teacher from rapidly and accurately firing at him. Individuals in our study describe their reluctance to respond with firepower because they worry about being mistaken for assailants by law enforcement who respond to the scene. In the case of teachers, this fear could further inhibit them from engaging in a firefight.

The Day-to-Day Risks of Arming Teachers

Our findings show that handgun owners perceive a host of other physical, legal, psychological and moral risks associated with day-to-day preparedness for armed self-defense. These risks include unnecessarily drawing or firing in a moment of fear or someone taking their gun to injure others. However, handgun owners express a willingness to accept these risks as a trade-off for decreasing their risk of being victimized.

Teachers who carry firearms would assume a variety of similar day-to-day risks. For instance, armed teachers could unintentionally discharge their firearm or have their guns taken by an angry student while trying to break-up a fight. The potential for having their gun taken is very real. Research on shootings that took place in hospital emergency departments shows that 23 percent involve a gun that is taken from an armed security guard.

Reducing these day-to-day risks is taxing on individuals. Our data show that carrying a firearm responsibly involves continuous awareness of the weapon and the situation, understanding complex laws around self-defense, and mental preparedness to end a human life if necessary. More than half of the concealed carry license holders we interviewed and dozens of online discussants stated that they sometimes leave their firearms at home to avoid the burden of having to maintain this mindset.

Based on this finding, we assert that carrying a firearm would be equally taxing on teachers, if not more since they also must engage in the duties of their profession.

Do the Benefits Outweigh the Risks?

Despite the widespread news coverage of mass shootings at schools, the reality is that school shootings are still a rare occurrence. In an FBI study of 160 active shooter incidents that FBI identified between 2000 and 2013, 27—or about 17 percent—occurred at elementary, middle and high schools. Given that rarity, the challenges of effectively using a gun to neutralize a shooter without taking additional lives and added day-to-day risks, we argue that Trump's proposal would not be effective in making schools safer overall for teachers or students.

It is difficult to address the question of whether, in the moment of a school shooting, the presence of an armed teacher is preferable to an unarmed one.

At least eight states currently permit teachers and school staff to carry firearms. However, the small percentage of schools with armed personnel combined with the small percentage of schools experiencing mass shootings limits the opportunity for a quantitative study of the risks and benefits of arming teachers. A recent review of the available data on the effectiveness of armed security and school resource officers in deterring or responding to a school shooting was inconclusive.

One of the most compelling findings comes from the same FBI report that found between 2000 and 2013, it was unarmed civilians that stopped more active shooter events than armed civilians—13.1 percent versus 3.1 percent, respectively. "Of note, 11 of the incidents involved unarmed principals, teachers, other school staff and students who confronted shooters to end the threat (9 of those shooters were students)," the report states.

This shows arming teachers isn't the only way to stop active shooters at schools. Often active school shooters are stopped by unarmed educators with the will to act.

41. Books, Binders, Bleed-Control Kits

How School Shootings Are Changing Classroom Basics*

SANDY WEST

When a student recently opened fire at a California high school, staff members did what they were trained to do. They shepherded students to safe spaces, barricaded doors, pulled shades—and, when gunfire struck, used techniques adapted from the battlefield to save lives.

The staffers used two bleeding-control kits in the November 14 shooting in Santa Clarita, in which two students were killed and three injured before the gunman fatally shot himself, said Dave Caldwell, spokesman for the William S. Hart Union High School District. The kits, a recent addition to the district northwest of Los Angeles, are equipped with tourniquets, compression bandages and blood-clotting hemostatic gauze to prevent excessive blood loss.

Such kits have been pushed in school districts across the country. Georgia pioneered a statewide initiative to equip schools with Stop the Bleed Kits, for the 2017–18 academic year. This year, Texas, Arkansas, and Indiana passed legislation to put them into schools. The Arkansas law requires public school students to be trained on the kits as part of the health curriculum to graduate.

Some gun control advocates say the efforts sap the political energy needed to reduce the actual violence. Most of the policies on bleeding-control kits have occurred in Republican-led states, where gun control may be especially unlikely to pass. Still, Democrat-controlled Illinois is among those to have picked up the campaign, with the Illinois Terrorism Task Force announcing in September plans to distribute 7,000 of the kits to the state's public schools.

There is no statewide mandate for the kits in California. Rather, two students in the William S. Hart Union High School District took the initiative there.

Sisters Cambria, 15, and Maci Lawrence, 13, were worried about school shootings and natural disasters. They said they wanted to help keep students safe. After sharing their worries with their father, Dr. Tracy "Bud" Lawrence, who directs the emergency department of the Henry Mayo Newhall Hospital in Santa Clarita, the sisters raised $100,000 through the "Keep the Pressure" nonprofit they established to get bleeding-control kits into every classroom in the district.

"We just wanted to get them into as many hands as possible," Bud Lawrence said.

*Originally published as Sandy West, "Books, Binders, Bleed-Control Kits How School Shootings Are Changing Classroom Basics," *Kaiser Health News*, December 11, 2019. Reprinted with permission of the publisher. *Kaiser Health News* is a nonprofit news service covering health issues. It is an editorially independent program of the Kaiser Family Foundation that is not affiliated with Kaiser Permanente.

1.5 Million Trained

Stop the Bleed kits were developed following the 2012 mass shooting at Sandy Hook Elementary School in Newtown, Connecticut, in which 20 children and six adults were killed. Dr. Lenworth Jacobs, who was a surgeon at the trauma center closest to Sandy Hook, said he and his staff prepared for an influx of patients from the attack, but none came to the hospital. They had not survived.

Jacobs, through a coalition known as the Hartford Consensus, led military leaders, law enforcement, trauma surgeons and emergency responders to develop recommendations on how to improve the survival rate in mass casualty events. Among the recommendations was the development of a Stop the Bleed campaign.

The American College of Surgeons, a member of the Hartford Consensus, launched the Stop the Bleed campaign to distribute the kits and to promote training so that more people understand how to stop bleeding if responding to an emergency. Jacobs said the effort has reached 100 countries and trained 1.5 million people.

Advocates for the campaign stress that the kits can help any type of significant traumatic injury.

Most fatal injuries, in fact, aren't caused by gunfire, said Billy Kunkle, deputy director for the Georgia Trauma Commission. Kunkle said the No. 1 cause of such deaths is falls, followed by car crashes.

In 2018, for example, a fourth-grade student in Georgia was playing with friends on the playground when she fell and a friend fell on top of her. According to news reports, the girl broke her arm and severed her artery. The school's nurse, using the Stop the Bleed kit her school had received less than 24-hours earlier, applied a tourniquet that the surgeons who treated Lopez credited with saving her life.

Kunkle said the kits should be viewed as an extension of a first aid kit. He likened them to other lifesaving tools, such as defibrillators, that have been installed throughout public spaces.

"We know it works. We know it saves lives," said Republican Indiana state Rep. Randy Frye, a retired firefighter who authored legislation to put the kits in the state's public schools. "You can't wait for 911, even in the best system."

Limited Reach of Gun Control

Still, gun control advocates say bleeding-control kit efforts allow lawmakers to avoid dealing with the cause of school shootings.

"On the one hand, anything we do to save lives is good. But, on the other hand, fundamentally, it is allowing lawmakers and officials to ignore the root cause of gun violence," said Kyleanne Hunter, vice president of programs for Brady, formerly known as the Brady Campaign to Prevent Gun Violence.

"Yes, we need to deal with mental health. Yes, we need to deal with first aid and medical care. And we need to address how easy it is to get guns," Hunter said. "We don't believe it should be an either-or."

Legislators have ignored numerous proposals aimed at reducing gun violence, including Brady's "End Family Fire," she said. According to a Wall Street Journal analysis, 75 percent of school shootings involved guns that shooters found unsecured in their homes. End Family Fire encourages the safe storage of weapons to make it more difficult for children to access unsecured guns.

"I am sure that a lot of school safety legislation allows some legislators to say, 'We are doing something,' and that allows a release valve for them to not focus on gun control," said Democratic Texas state Rep. Diego Bernal, who was a co-sponsor on the Stop the Bleed legislation in his state.

Still, he added, "I suspect, even if there was gun control legislation, we would pursue this bill. I don't think this is an either-or proposition."

Among the advantages of having the kits in schools and more people trained on methods to stop bleeding, Jacobs said, is that a lockdown often follows a shooting. That prevents emergency responders from getting in or the injured from getting out. In every kind of trauma, he said, minutes count.

"If, God forbid, something happens, you really want to know there is someone right there beside you who can do something," said Jacobs. "If you can keep the blood inside the body until you reach the hospital, you have a phenomenal chance for survival."

In Georgia, the governor allocated $1 million from fees generated by the state's Super Speeder traffic safety law to pay for the kits. To date, Kunkle said, the kits are in about 2,100 of the state's 2,300 schools, and have been used seven times.

In Arkansas and Indiana, the cost of supplying kits to schools was covered largely by private donations.

Dr. Marlon Doucet, a Little Rock, Arkansas, trauma surgeon, is leading efforts to expand access and training on Stop the Bleed kits in schools and elsewhere in his state. He believes strongly that training more people—including cops, teachers and students—will save lives.

Twenty-five people were shot in the July 2017 Little Rock Power Ultra Lounge shooting, and all survived, Doucet said.

"No one died because law enforcement officers were using tourniquets and packing wounds," he said. "This just makes sense."

42. Fired!

Is Your Community Ready
for an Active Shooter?*

Rod Gould *and* Jack Brown

Active shooter incidents are increasing in America and around the globe. Local government managers and assistants have an affirmative duty to guide preparation, prevention, and response actions to limit the loss of life in the face of this alarming trend.

Not only must these efforts knit together first responders, including police, fire, and EMS personnel, into an integrated response, but research and experience indicates that local governments must increasingly involve and educate residents and business people in what to do when confronted with such a threat or an actual shooting itself.

Big or small, no community is immune from this deadly behavior. According to the Gun Violence Archive, there were 277 mass shootings in 2014, 332 in 2015, and 191 mass shootings in 2016 up through July 16, 2016.[1]

Time and learning from experience teaches that there are a number of actions a local government can take to preempt a lethal shooting or effectively cope when one occurs.

Emergency Preparedness

Make sure your organization's general emergency preparedness plan, including equipment, is up-to-date. Get elected and management support to make it happen.

Equip and practice setting up an emergency operations center (EOC), which will be the nerve center that manages the local response to the active shooter and mass casualty incident. An EOC does not need to be a stand-alone building. It requires a large enough space that can be set-up with the necessary furniture and equipment in a reasonable period of time.

*Originally published as Rod Gould and Jack Brown, "Fired! Is Community Ready for an Active Shooter?," *PM Magazine*, November 2016. Reprinted with permission of the publisher.

Invest in emergency training. Understand the National Incident Management System (NIMS).[2] All too often, city officials give lip service to this system and its proven techniques. This system really works. Train on it so it becomes second nature.

Orient your disaster service workers and plan to meet their needs during an emergency. Most importantly, exercise your plans and check your equipment quarterly, if possible, using different scenarios, including an active shooter. This way your staff will be able to move into emergency response mode with confidence and speed.

For too long, law enforcement, fire, and EMS have perceived their first-responder roles as independent of one another. This is a major mistake. All three need to train together to provide an integrated response and must be comfortable with an integrated Incident Command Structure.

The manager must get the buy-in of the chiefs to overcome institutional bias in emergency planning and response. This is critical. Use the Rescue Task Force (RTF) concept.[3] The RTF is essentially a simple response model made up of multiple four-person teams that move forward into the unsecured scene along secured corridors to provide stabilizing care and evacuation of the injured.

There is also a need for common operations language using simple terms to avoid confusion during the pressure of an active shooter incident. Consider cross training law enforcement, fire, and EMS dispatchers.

Provide the necessary equipment for your first responders, including ballistic vests, helmets and eye wear, and assault rifles for your law enforcement officers. Get your first responders into major public and private facilities so that they are familiar with their layouts and train in them when possible.[4]

Similarly, make sure your radio and communications systems are up to snuff. This means that they are interoperable so that police, fire, public works, the schools, local cities, and the county can all talk with one another seamlessly. Create redundant systems.

It is a best practice to provide direct and simple training for residents and business people about what to do in the event of an active shooter. Many jurisdictions are using instructional videos on local cable television and at community events, service clubs, and other gatherings and are encouraging employers to show them to their employees.

The common advice is to run, hide, or fight when the shooter is active. Good examples include a video provided by Houston, Texas: "RUN. HIDE. FIGHT.® Surviving an Active Shooter Event" (https://www.youtube. com/watch?v=5VcSwejU2D0). Or one titled "Surviving an Active Shooter" by the Los Angeles, California, Sheriff's Department: https://www.youtube.com/ watch?v=DFQ-oxhdFjE.

These videos can be disturbing, but the information they contain can help prevent folks from freezing up and becoming easy targets.

Advanced active shooter prevention requires regular and structured communication between law enforcement, mental health and social workers, schools, and community nonprofits dealing with at-risk populations. Too often, there are danger signs that are not shared that could have been acted upon.

Unless these agencies and their staffs actively collaborate, there is a chance that a potentially dangerous person can fall between institutional cracks and become an active shooter. Sharing concerns and warning signals can lead to interventions that end up saving lives. This takes a shared commitment on the part of organizations that don't always work well together.

Saving Lives, Coping Strategies

Empirical evidence indicates that the speed of the emergency medical response is key to saving lives. That means moving properly trained, armored (not armed) medical personnel, who are accompanied by law enforcement officers, into areas of mitigated risks—sometime referred to as "warm zones"—as quickly as possible.

Early aggressive hemorrhage control is essential for better outcomes. All first responders need to know how to use tourniquets and hemostatic agents like gauze for severe bleeding. Rendering life-saving care in warm zones by EMS, fire, and law enforcement is a relatively new paradigm supported by data.[5]

The American College of Surgeons studied lessons learned from the battlefield and the responses to active shooter events in the U.S. and has made recommendations known as the Hartford Consensus about how emergency workers should respond in these situations. The white paper (http://bulletin.facs. org/2015/07/the-hartford-consensus-iii-implementation-of-bleeding-control) is well worth reading and boils down to the acronym THREAT:

T—Threat Suppression
H—Hemorrhage Control
RE—Rapid Evacuation
A—Assessment by medical personnel
T—Transport to definitive care.

This involves tactical emergency casualty care (TECC) and the need for integrated planning, preparation, response, treatment, and care.[6] The analysis deserves careful consideration. Public managers should work with their chiefs and labor groups to institutionalize these practices and procedures.

After the tragic event, the community will need time and space to grieve and heal. Social workers, therapists, and faith community members must be involved to assist individuals and groups to process their losses.

Community gatherings to remember and unite must be organized. First responders will also need help in dealing with the trauma of the shooting. Having good relationships with these support groups in place prior to an active shooter event will be beneficial when the time comes. Expect media saturation for at least a week after the shooting incident. The public information officer will be stretched to his or her limits, so be sure the individual gets the requisite training in advance.

Be Prepared

Sadly, active shooters are increasingly common in civil society. Local governments must prepare for, prevent where possible, and respond to mass shootings as an important subset of public safety and emergency service.

ICMA has put together a useful compendium of articles and papers on this topic, which can be found at ICMA. org/Active_Shooter. Local government managers and assistants must educate themselves and staff members to protect their communities from the scourge of active shooters.

This involves tactical emergency casualty care (TECC) and the need for integrated planning, preparation, response, treatment, and care.[7] The analysis deserves careful consideration. Public managers should work with their chiefs and labor groups to institutionalize these practices and procedures.

NOTES

1. www.gunviolencearchive.org: Definition of mass shooting: four or more shot and/or killed in a single incident at the same general time and location, not including the shooter.

2. www.fema.gov/national-incident-management-system.

3. "Improved Active Shooter/ Hostile Event Response," A Report by the Interagency Board, September 2015, p.16, and "Arlington County, Virginia, Task Force Rethinks Active Shooter Incident Response," *Journal of Emergency Medical Services*, Blake Iselin, November 30, 2009.

4. "Improved Active Shooter/ Hostile Event Response," a report by the Interagency Board, September 2015, pp 8–12.

5. "First Responder Guide for Improving Survivability in Improvised Explosive Devises and/or Active Shooter Incidents," Homeland Security Office of Health Affairs, June 2015.

6. Fire/Emergency Medical Services Department, *Operational Considerations and Guide for Active Shooter and Mass Casualty Incidents*, FEMA, U.S. Fire Administration, September 2013.

7. "See Something, Do Something: Improving Survival," American College of Surgeons, September 2015 *Bulletin*, Volume 100, Number 15.

43. Most Mass Killers Are Men Who Have Also Attacked Family*

LISA ARONSON FONTES

What do most mass killers have in common?

As a researcher who studies coercive control in intimate relationships, I can point out a few key characteristics. First, they are men. Additionally, they have a history of controlling and abusing their wives and girlfriends—and sometimes other family members—before "graduating" to mass killings.

Considering a few recent examples makes the pattern clearer.

Mass Shooters Practice at Home

Devin P. Kelley, 26, who shot to death 26 people and injured 20 more at a Texas church on November 5, had kicked, beaten and choked his first wife and infant stepson, fracturing the baby's skull. In the following years, he was investigated for other charges of violence against women including sexual assault and rape.

Since 1996, those convicted of domestic violence—even misdemeanor offenses—are supposed to be entered into the National Criminal Information Database and permanently barred from legally purchasing guns. However, Air Force officials neglected to register Kelley's conviction, leaving him free to walk into a sporting goods store and purchase the rifle used to murder Texas churchgoers. A congressional report determined such registration failures happen at least 30 percent of the time.

Esteban Santiago, charged with killing five travelers in a mass shooting at the Fort Lauderdale airport in January 2017, was previously accused of assaulting and strangling his girlfriend.

Spencer Hight shot and killed his estranged wife and seven of her friends who had gathered to watch football on TV in Plano, Texas. These family-based mass shootings rarely gain the same kind of publicity as those conducted in public, perhaps because the average person mistakenly thinks they can avoid being victimized if the shooting occurs "in the family."

From January 1 to November 5, 2017, the U.S. experienced 307 mass shootings, which the government defines as a shooting that kills or injures four or more people.

*Originally published as Lisa Aronson Fontes, "Most Mass Killers Are Men Who Have Also Attacked Family," *The Conversation*, https://theconversation.com/most-mass-killers-are-men-who-have-also-attacked-family-87230 (November 14, 2017). Reprinted with permission of the publisher.

However, not all domestic violence perpetrators who become mass killers use guns.

Tamerlan Tsarnaev, who planned and executed the Boston Marathon bombing along with his younger brother, had been arrested for assaulting his girlfriend.

Mohamed Lahouaiej-Bouhlel, who plowed a truck through a crowd in Nice, France in 2016, killing 82, and Khalid Masood, who killed five and injured 50 driving through a crowd in Westminster, London, both controlled and abused the women in their lives.

An obvious question arises. If domestic violence laws were more effective, could perpetrators be caught earlier? Could they be deprived of their access to weapons, jailed when necessary and given the kinds of intensive intervention and supervision that would curb their behavior? In other words, could stronger domestic violence laws prevent some mass shootings?

Less Family Violence, Fewer Mass Shootings

The laws in the U.S. that are currently used to address domestic violence were developed for attacks by unrelated people. They don't work so well for what happens in families.

A bar fight is over when the violence ends, but abusive violence in couples does not end. In as many as 40 percent of cases, the abuser assaults his partner several times a week and sometimes daily, often over many years. Most domestic violence incidents involve pushes, slaps, kicks, pulling hair and the like. If police wait for broken bones, they miss more than 95 percent of domestic violence incidents. As Evan Stark of Rutgers University points out, the seriousness of partner violence derives from the cumulative weight of all previous abuse, rather than the severity of a particular assault. U.S. law does not adequately address these "minor" violent incidents, nor the constant intimidation, harassment, monitoring and the limiting of a partner's freedom that is so typical of violent control in couples.

In 2015, England and Wales made controlling a current or former partner a serious crime. This new offense recognizes the harm that can result from an ongoing pattern of controlling behavior. A relative of Westminster car attacker Masood's ex-wife is quoted in The Guardian describing their relationship: "He was very violent towards her, controlling in every aspect of her life—what she wore, where she went, everything."

Masood's behavior is an example of coercive control. Coercive control combines tactics designed to instill fear, like violence and threats, with tactics that isolate a partner, degrade her and deprive her of basic rights. Eighty percent of abused women are being coercively controlled and not simply hit. In the U.K., police and prosecutors have undergone intensive training related to the criminalization of coercive control. Police have learned to use an incident of reported domestic violence as a window through which to examine the entire relationship.

One of the earliest convictions for coercive control concerns a 30-year-old named Nigel Wolitter, who was arrested for vandalizing machinery belonging to his partner's family to punish her for refusing to give him money for marijuana. As a result of their new training, police traced Wolitter's vandalism to a 13-year pattern of dominating his girlfriend. The prosecution linked photos of injuries from his partner's cellphone with her compelling testimony that he had "controlled every aspect of my life from where I went to what I wore, to what possessions he allowed me to own." Wolitter received a 4.5-year sentence.

It's the pattern of enforced subordination that is the problem here, not one or two incidents. Changing the domestic violence laws to include coercive control will draw attention to serious cases of controlling behavior and obligate law enforcement to examine them more closely.

According to the American nonprofit organization Everytown for Gun Safety, an average of 50 women in the U.S. are shot to death each month by a current or former intimate partner. While most domestic abusers will not become mass murderers, early, consistent and effective domestic violence intervention might keep us all safer.

44. Dealing with Terrorist Threats*

Sean Britton

Violence is a potential threat to every community—a threat that demands preparedness from local government administrators. Recent events in the United States, as well as around the world, highlight the need for valid strategies to prepare for—and respond to—violent actions affecting the public.

The intention of this article is to provide a fundamental understanding of active shooter incidents and complex coordinated attacks for managers, so they may better assess their own community's efforts to prepare for and respond to these events.

Methods of Attack

The criminal justice system mitigates violence within the community by arresting and prosecuting individuals involved with various criminal activities. This strategy of prevention may be effective in reducing violence associated with profit-motivated criminal enterprises, but it does not necessarily address the threats posed by an individual motivated by ideology or other factors.

The FBI defines terrorism as "the unlawful use of force or violence against persons or property to intimidate or coerce a government, the civilian population, or any segment thereof, in furtherance of political or social objectives." One example is the detonation of a pipe bomb by a 27-year-old male in the Port Authority Bus Terminal in New York City on December 11, 2017.

Another recent example is of a 29-year-old male who killed eight individuals, and injured eleven others, with a pickup truck in Manhattan in October 2017. Although both of these events occurred within New York City, it definitely is not the only local government at risk from a terrorist attack.

Methods for inflicting a terrorist action against the public include both an active shooter incident and a complex coordinated attack. The FBI also defines an active shooter as "an individual actively engaged in killing or attempting to kill people in a confined and populated area."[1]

While this article uses the term "active shooter," these incidents may also be identified as active-assailant or active-threat, since violence is not limited to the use of firearms given that such other handheld weapons as knives or even motor vehicles can be used.

*Originally published as Sean 4, "Dealing with Terrorist Threats," *PM Magazine*, August 2018. Reprinted with permission of the publisher.

While an active shooter may be terrorism-inspired, terrorism may not be the sole trigger of these incidents. Other factors, including severe psychiatric illness or an unexpected life event like job loss, divorce, or death of a loved one, may be a contributor.

According to research performed by Texas State University in partnership with the FBI, 160 active shooter incidents occurred in the United States between 2000 and 2013, with an increasing frequency in more recent years.[2]

Among the incidents in which duration could be ascertained, 69 percent ended within five minutes, and of those, 52 percent ended within two minutes. Approximately 60 percent of all incidents during this time period ended prior to the arrival of law enforcement, sometimes as a result of unarmed residents restraining the shooter.

In 40 percent of these incidents, the event ended by the shooter committing suicide. The most frequent locations for these events were commerce centers (46 percent), followed by educational environments (24 percent), followed by government properties (10 percent). Of the government properties, 50 percent were local government facilities.

Complex coordinated attacks are described as several terrorist actions occurring in close succession. Firearms, explosive devices, and vehicles are all methods that can be used in this type of attack.

The largest complex coordinated attack to date was perpetrated by 10 men associated with the Lashkar-e-Tayyiba terrorist group and involved four separate sites within Mumbai, India, in November 2008.

In another instance, Islamic State terrorists killed 130 and injured hundreds more by conducting a series of attacks within a 20-minute period in Paris in 2015. A complex coordinated attack involving suicide bombers killed 31 and injured 300 at two sites in Brussels in 2016.

Taking Preparedness Measures

All emergencies start and end on the local government level. Local government typically provides or ensures the provision of such emergency services as law enforcement, fire suppression, and emergency medical services.

Responses to these events are multi-disciplinary and require coordination and collaboration among various emergency services disciplines. Managers have a duty to residents to ensure effective preparedness actions have been taken.

The first action to take is to engage emergency management and emergency services leadership to determine what preparedness actions have already been accomplished. The Federal Emergency Management Agency outlines several components to ensure effective preparedness for a threat or hazard: planning, organizing and equipping, training, conducting exercises, and evaluating/improving procedures.[3]

Planning involves stakeholders coming together to develop a written plan of how a hazard or threat will be managed. For a plan to be effective, it must have the support of any unit or individual assigned a role within the plan.

Plans alone don't control emergencies; however, they do provide a shared understanding of roles and anticipated actions to be performed. Local government staff should verify the agency or individual(s) assigned with plan development.

While the planning process may involve agency representatives, the person in charge needs to verify that the final plan has the official support of each agency's chief officer.

It is critical to ensure there are individuals with varied skillsets and organizations represented during the planning process. Events causing mass casualties and fatalities will require emergency response from organizations beyond police, fire, and EMS.

Examples of response actions performed by nontraditional response agencies include performing crisis counseling for survivors and managing the mortuary needs of decedents. Often the planning process will require the inclusion of nongovernmental agencies.

Beginning in 2013, the American College of Surgeons (ACS) formed the Joint Committee to Create a National Policy to Enhance Survivability from Intentional Mass Casualty and Active Shooter Events to develop a protocol for national policy to enhance survivability from active shooter and intentional mass casualty events.

This committee compiled its recommendations into the Hartford Consensus, which now has three subsequent updates. These four reports can serve as a tool for emergency planners to develop effective preparedness plans for these events.[4]

Planning efforts can also be guided by the U.S. Department of Homeland Security, Interagency Security Committee's (ISC) document Planning and Response to an Active Shooter: An Interagency Security Committee Policy and Best Practices Guide.[5]

Organizing and equipping involves the equipment and supplies necessary for response to the event. While the identification of necessary equipment and supplies is accomplished during the planning process, the procurement occurs during this phase.

Fire departments and emergency medical services agencies have been increasingly purchasing ballistic vests for personnel in recent years. These capital acquisitions may have significant impact upon agency budgets.

This phase can also involve making the strategic decision to purchase and locate bleeding-control items, including dressings and tourniquets, in public places and government facilities. Increasingly, bleeding-control supplies are being located with automated external defibrillators (AEDs).

Local government managers should remain informed on the personal protective equipment being selected by response agencies within their jurisdiction and if public access bleeding-control initiatives are underway.

Training involves providing instruction to both responders and the community at large. Responder training is discipline-specific and can include emergency medical services practitioners completing the National Association of Emergency Medical Technician's Tactical Emergency Casualty Care (TECC).[6]

Civilian training can include the American College of Surgeons "Stop the Bleed" course, which is a brief course (less than two hours) on bleeding control for injured patients.[7]

Recent active shooter incidents have demonstrated that actions taken by bystanders prior to the arrival of emergency responders may decrease morbidity and mortality. Managers should assess what training is being taken by responders or offered to the public as community education.

Exercises, often known outside of the emergency management community as drills, test whether organizations have the capabilities for which they have planned, equipped, and trained. Until an organization exercises a plan, it has no way of knowing how well personnel will execute a mission.

Exercises take resources—time, money, and supplies—to both plan and conduct. Managers should verify that response organizations within their jurisdiction are conducting exercises and then support these exercises by allocating needed resources.

Critical evaluation drives improvement in performance. Exercises need to be objectively evaluated to ensure response organizations are able to perform mission-essential functions. Organizations do not grow and develop without acknowledgment of well-performed exercise elements and constructive criticism of areas requiring performance improvement.

Managers should challenge response organizations to identify both strengths and weaknesses in current capability levels. The identification of weaknesses is then able to drive future planning efforts, equipment and supply purchases, and training offerings.

An Unfortunate Reality

Active shooter incidents and complex coordinated attacks will continue, unfortunately, to pose a threat to public health and safety for the foreseeable future. Bottom line, the research I've conducted shows that managers should work to ensure their communities have followed the preparedness actions necessary to improve the response to these types of events.

NOTES

1. Blair JP, Schweit, KW. A Study of Active Shooter Incidents, 2000–2013. Texas State University and Federal Bureau of Investigation, U.S. Department of Justice, Washington, D.C., 2014.

2. *Ibid.*

3. U.S. Department of Homeland Security. Plan and Prepare for Disasters. Retrieved from https:// www. dhs.gov/topic/plan-and-prepare-disasters on April 26, 2018.

4. American College of Surgeons. The Hartford Consensus. Retrieved from https://www.facs.org/ about-acs/hartford-consensus on April 26, 2018.

5. Interagency Security Committee. Planning and Response to an Active Shooter: An Interagency Security Committee Policy and Best Practices Guide. November 2015.

6. National Association of Emergency Medical Technicians. Tactical Emergency Casualty Care course. Retrieved from http://www.naemt.org/ education/tecc on April 26, 2018.

7. American College of Surgeons. BleedingControl.org. Retrieved from https://www.bleedingcontrol.org on April 26, 2018.

45. Orlando Paramedics Didn't Go In to Save Victims of the Pulse Shooting*

Abe Aboraya

"I need the hospital! Please, why does someone not want to help?"

The man's screams inside the Pulse nightclub pierced the chaos in the minutes after the shooting stopped on June 12, 2016. With the shooter barricaded in a bathroom and victims piled on top of one another, Orlando police commanders began asking the Fire Department for help getting dozens of shooting victims out of the club and to the hospital.

"We need to get these people out," a command officer said over the police radio.

"We gotta get 'em out," another officer responded. "We got him [the shooter] contained in the bathroom. We have several long guns on the bathroom right now."

A few minutes later, the Orlando Police Department's dispatch log shows the police formally requested the Fire Department to come into the club. "We're pulling victims out the front. Have FD come up and help us out with that," one officer said.

The Orlando Fire Department had been working on a plan for just such a situation for three years. Like many fire departments at the time, Orlando had long relied on a traditional protocol for mass shootings, in which paramedics stayed at a distance until an all-clear was given. The department had tasked Anibal Saez, Jr., an assistant chief, with developing a new approach being adopted across the country: Specialized teams of medics, guarded by police officers and wearing specially designed bulletproof vests, would pull out victims before a shooter is caught or killed.

After a recommendation from Saez in 2015, the department bought about 20 of the bulletproof vests and helmets. The vests had pouches filled with tourniquets, special needles to relieve air in the chest, and quick-clotting trauma bandages.

None of that equipment was used at Pulse. Emergency medical professionals stayed across the street from the club. And the bulletproof vests filled with life-saving equipment sat at headquarters.

In the three and a half years before the shooting, bureaucratic inertia had taken hold. Emails obtained by WMFE and ProPublica lay out a record of opportunities

---

*This story was originally published by ProPublica as Abe Aboraya, "Orlando Paramedics Didn't Go In to Save Victims of the Pulse Shooting," https://www.propublica.org/article/pulse-shooting-orlando-tragedy-response-plan (September 26, 2018). Reprinted with permission of the publisher.

missed. It's not clear whether paramedics could have entered and saved lives. But what is clear is Saez's plan to prepare for such a scenario sat unused, like the vests.

His effort had sputtered and was ultimately abandoned after a new fire chief, Roderick Williams, took over the department in April 2015. Williams named another administrator to finalize and implement the new policy. That administrator declined multiple requests to comment for this story. Saez said he offered to help but never heard back.

"There was a committee that was responsible for the [policy], however, I am not sure whether one was created and approved," one fire official emailed another on March 30, 2016.

In April 2016, two months before Pulse, Williams emailed his deputy chiefs asking for a progress report: "Update on Active Shooter?"

The only response was an email asking if anyone had responded. No one did.

Ultimately 49 people died during the Pulse attack, one of the worst mass shootings in modern history.

Saez, a 30-year veteran of the Orlando Fire Department, a paramedic and a member of the bomb squad, has been haunted by the possibility that things didn't have to turn out the way they did. "I wonder sometimes if I should've done something else," he said in an interview.

"In my mind I'm thinking, 'Man, if I would have had that policy, if I could have got it done, if I could have pushed it, maybe it wouldn't be 49 dead…. Maybe it would be 40. Maybe it would be 48. Anything but the end result here,'" he said.

A study published this year in the journal Prehospital Emergency Care concluded that 16 of the victims might have lived if they had gotten basic EMS care within 10 minutes and made it to a trauma hospital within an hour, the national standard. That's nearly one third of victims that died that night.

"Those 16, they had injuries that were, potentially were survivable," said Dr. Edward Reed Smith, the operational medical director for the Arlington County, Virginia, Fire Department, who reviewed autopsies of those who died with two colleagues. Smith, whose department was one of the first in the country to allow paramedics into violent scenes with a police escort, has reviewed more than a dozen civilian mass shootings using the same criteria. "How would they be survivable? With rapid intervention and treatment of their injuries."

A separate Justice Department review last year concluded "it would have been reasonable" for paramedics to enter after 20 minutes, a different time frame from the one Smith analyzed.

Orlando's mayor, as well as the Police and Fire chiefs, dispute that they could have done anything differently. They say it was impossible to know at the time that there was only one shooter at Pulse or that he wouldn't resume shooting after he barricaded himself in the bathroom. It was also impossible to know whether a bomb threat he later made was real. All of that, they say, would have kept victims from getting care in time.

Williams, the fire chief, said he still believes the inside of Pulse nightclub was a "hot zone," or a place of direct threat, which would have stopped first responders from going in.

"We're not prepared to go in hot-zone extraction. That's just not what we do as a fire department," Williams said. "It was active fire, active shooting."

But not everyone who responded that night is sure the Fire Department had done all it could. They say some victims might have had a chance had Orlando finished what it started.

Orlando Fire District Chief Bryan Davis was in charge of his agency's response the night of the Pulse shooting. In an interview, he said his department had done active shooter drills, but it wasn't enough.

"We didn't have formalized training," Davis said. "We didn't have a policy. We didn't have a procedure. We had the equipment [bulletproof vests]. But it was locked up in EMS in a storage closet.... And unfortunately, we were a day and a dollar too late."

"A Wake-Up Call That, for Us, It Can Happen Anywhere"

Just after midnight on March 18, 2013, a former University of Central Florida student pulled a fire alarm in a building that housed 500 students.

He was armed with a rifle, a handgun, hundreds of rounds of ammunition and four Molotov cocktails. Three minutes later, a person in Room 308 called 911: His roommate had pointed a rifle at him.

When police entered the room, the would-be shooter was dead. After his rifle had jammed, he killed himself with his handgun.

Police found handwritten notes about his planned rampage.

"That was a near miss and that was certainly a wake-up call that, for us, it could happen anywhere," said Orange County Fire Rescue Chief Otto Drozd, whose agency helped respond to the scene. "Everybody is susceptible."

That year, Orange County, where Orlando is located, started holding department-wide training sessions on how to respond to such situations. It also wrote a new policy that said paramedics, guarded by sheriff's deputies, should provide aid to victims after a shooting ends, but before a perpetrator is caught or killed.

Also in 2013, the city of Orlando Fire Department assigned Saez, an assistant chief, to create its active shooter policy.

Saez said he began by using the policy adopted by Arlington County as the backbone of his draft but stopped when he learned that another group within the Fire Department also was working on the project. When he tried to merge the two groups together, he was instead told that the other group would handle the policy.

"They were, for lack of a better term, a little gun-shy about how aggressive we were gonna get," said Saez, who goes by JR, drinking a pint of craft beer through a grey goatee and wearing a Five Finger Death Punch T-shirt. "They started saying 'Hey, JR's crazy.'"

Then, in 2015, as the FBI was planning a major drill with public safety agencies, Saez said he was again asked to take the lead on the policy. At the time, Fire Chief John Miller was in the process of retiring and Williams, a longtime veteran of the department, had been named to succeed him.

"The whole active shooter thing, it wasn't rocket science, it was common sense," said Saez, who had a reputation for being blunt.

In March, Saez wrote an email to a group of firefighters, including the incoming chief and other high-level administrators as well as medics, "Looks Like I got a Dream Team for this Active Shooter Exercise." In the email, he laid out a timeline for getting the policy finalized and an active shooter exercise done in April. He said he was choosing which bulletproof vests and equipment to buy and hoped to train the entire department by the end of the year.

But within a month, Williams was sworn in as fire chief and Saez was sent back to work in a fire station. (Such personnel changes are common when a new chief takes over.) The active shooter policy was given to another administrator.

Two months later, the city of Orlando's emergency manager sent an email to Williams and other members of the Fire Department's administration calling their attention to a Department of Homeland Security guide for responding to an active shooter. It recommended that fire personnel in bulletproof vests go into "warm zones," places where victims may be but where a shooter is not believed to be, guarded by the police.

"It echoes our lessons learned and fixes," the official, Manny Soto, wrote, referring to the Fire Department's previous active shooter drills, which included practices involving rescue task forces.

In July 2015, the city of Orlando spent $33,000 on about 20 bulletproof vests, according to purchase orders obtained by WMFE. Each vest could hold enough supplies to treat 10 to 15 patients. That was enough for each of the five district chiefs working on any given shift to equip a rescue task force.

The policy was never finished, though, and on June 12, 2016, the night of the Pulse massacre, the Orlando Fire Department policy told paramedics to stay three blocks away if they felt "uncomfortable with the situation."

"To Know That He Could Have Survived Would Be Horrific"

The gunfire started at 2:02 a.m. on Sunday, June 12, just after last call. A request for immediate assistance brought hundreds of officers from 15 police agencies across Central Florida. When the shooting stopped eight minutes later, Officer Brandon Cornwell of the Belle Isle Police Department and three other officers went inside the Pulse nightclub to kill or arrest the shooter.

They entered through a broken window in the front of the club. The club was dark, lit by pink and blue video screens and disco balls. There was no music playing. Unfinished drinks and unpaid bar tabs littered the tables.

As they got farther inside, a woman could be heard screaming over and over again, according to police body camera video of the scene reviewed by WMFE. Sometimes she screamed for help. Sometimes she just screamed.

The scene was so chaotic, police couldn't figure out who was screaming.

"Who the fuck is this coming from!" one of the officers shouted.

The team walked toward the gunfire and believed it had the shooter cornered in one of the club's bathrooms. They pointed assault rifles and handguns at the doors and hallways to keep the shooter contained.

Officers then started bringing 14 incapacitated victims out of the club. Victims grabbed police officers' ankles as they walked by, according to first responder recollections in the Justice Department report.

People—some dead, some alive—fell stacked on top of one another "like matchsticks." Some victims played dead. Phones rang and rang.

In the ensuing minutes, body camera footage captured the discussion between officers and commanders about getting help.

At 2:23 a.m., a police command officer tried to come up with a way to get paramedics inside. He asked if the shooter's rounds could get into the main area "if we start bringing FD to try to get some of these guys out of here?"

The officer inside responded: "He's got a long gun, so yes, can penetrate," but then said that he was contained in the bathroom and that they had to get the victims out.

A few minutes later, the Orlando Police Department's dispatch logs show the police asked for the Fire Department "to go in scene secure," meaning dispatchers were asking the Fire Department to come into the club.

This is about the time the Justice Department concluded a rescue task force could have entered the Pulse nightclub.

Still, the Fire Department did not enter.

Orlando city officials downplayed the significance of the log, saying in a written statement that it only reflected the judgment of a "single officer."

"In this type of changing situation, this was an isolated perspective and 'secure' did not mean the scene was 'clear,' which is very important to distinguish," the statement said. "This was still an active scene with an armed shooter and many unknown threats, like were there additional shooters or were there explosives."

"And in fact, within moments, the suspect made the threat of explosives and pledged allegiance to ISIS. Shortly after this, there were also reports of a second shooting at Orlando Health and the hospital was locked down for approximately an hour."

At 2:50 a.m., the shooter threatened to blow up a city block with explosives in his car. Around the same time, the Orange County Fire Rescue Department, which had trained with the Sheriff's Office beginning in 2013, brought 12 ballistic vests to Orlando Fire Department commanders on the scene.

Davis, the Orlando Fire Department district chief in charge of his agency's response that night, said he told Orange County commanders that city firefighters and paramedics hadn't been trained on how to use the vests—and wouldn't use them. Davis's account was confirmed by an after-action report by the county.

In an interview, Davis said that while his department had done active shooter drills, those hadn't been enough. In retrospect, he said he wishes he had asked the county firefighters to send a rescue crew into the club.

"When that Orange County chief arrived, I would have looked at him and said, 'Hey Chief, my guys are not properly trained in the use of those vests. Do you have individuals here that are?'" he said. "And if so, then we utilize those resources that were properly trained ... and we assemble them into the rescue task force and move them forward into the scene."

Orlando Mayor Buddy Dyer said vests or no vests, commanders on the ground would not have told firefighters to go inside Pulse.

"I don't think that scene was the appropriate place to do it," Dyer said. "Whether we had the policy strictly or not, I don't think it affected the outcome at all."

While paramedics didn't enter Pulse, some victims who had left the club managed to go back in to help friends.

Jean Carlos Mendez Perez made it outside the club after the shooting, but he realized his boyfriend was still back inside. He went back in to get Luis Daniel Wilson-Leon, who everyone called Dani.

The couple was found by the entrance in the club. Wilson-Leon had wounds to his back, while Perez had wounds to his front. They both died.

"I think (Dani) was protecting Jean," Laly Santiago-Leon, Dani's cousin, said.

Santiago-Leon says it's heartbreaking to learn that the Fire Department put the policy on the backburner. She said she hopes to never learn who the 16 victims with survivable wounds were.

"I'm still, as I said, I'm still angry that he's gone," she said through quiet tears. "But to know that he could have survived would be horrific."

Orlando Fire Department's Leadership Didn't Show Up During Attack

Fire and police agencies from across the Orlando region swarmed to the scene as word of the Pulse shooting spread. Initially, they each responded independently, but sometime in the first hour they established a mobile command center to coordinate their responses. The Orlando Police Department took the lead, but it was joined by two sheriff's offices, as well as the Florida Department of Law Enforcement and the FBI.

The Orlando Fire Department leadership wasn't part of it.

According to department protocol, the fire chief was paged at 2:14 a.m. But the Justice Department's report on how the police responded to Pulse said the fire chief didn't arrive at the scene until after the shooter was dead. There was no follow-up call to make sure the page was received, the report said.

Williams declined multiple requests to explain why he didn't show up that night, but city officials have blamed it on a faulty paging system. The policy has changed since Pulse: Now, if the fire chief doesn't answer a page in three minutes, he or she will get a phone call.

Dyer said he views what happened as a breakdown in communication, not a lack of leadership.

"Operationally, it didn't affect it," Dyer said, referring to the Pulse response. "It just would have been better for the morale of the organization if the chief would have been on site."

Firefighters had their own command system, separate from the Police Department, whose chief was present. The two sister agencies didn't even operate on the same radio channel, the type of challenge identified more than a decade earlier after the September 11 terrorist attacks. The Justice Department report said the setup outside Pulse "negatively impacted information and resource sharing, coordination, and overall situational awareness."

Davis, the firefighter in charge of the department's response, was four ranks below chief. Looking back, he said, he wishes that he or someone else in his department's leadership had gone to the police command post.

Williams disputed the notion that being in the command center would have changed the department's response or prompted officials to send in a rescue crew earlier. In a recent interview with WMFE, he said that training had been in place and that a rescue task force could have gone in if asked for.

"Those commanders on the scene made those choices," Williams said. "We did exactly what was appropriate based on the resources that was required at the time."

But a month after the Pulse shooting, Williams gave a different response in an interview with WMFE. He said that his department was looking at active shooter protocols and vests, but that "we haven't trained to that level."

Smith, operational medical director for the Arlington County Fire Department, said if the Pulse nightclub shooting happened in his community, the response would have been different. With the shooter barricaded in a back bathroom, paramedics and EMTs would have put on ballistic vests and gone inside the club to pull victims out with a police escort.

While conceding that his assessment had the benefit of hindsight, Smith said the story of how Orlando responded to Pulse nightclub isn't just about the lack of a rescue task force. It's about the lack of communication between the Orlando Police and Fire departments.

"They had two separate command centers that were, by the way, were on opposite sides of the club" for part of the event, Smith said. "The police commander couldn't walk outside and walk over to the fire command because they had the club in between the two of them. So there's no integration there."

According to Smith's study of Pulse victims, out of the 16 victims who possibly could have lived, four died at the hospital. That leaves 12 who died either inside the club or in the triage area outside. It's not possible to know how many of those died on the dance floor, where rescuers could potentially have reached them and provided aid, or inside the bathroom, where the shooter had barricaded himself and held them as hostages. It's also not clear who would have survived if they had gotten help within 10 minutes of being shot. And for those who could have survived, it's not clear how debilitating their injuries would have been.

Smith and his team previously studied 12 mass shooting events, including one at a San Diego McDonald's in 1984 and one at the Washington Navy Yard in 2013. In those 12 incidents, an average of 7 percent of victims died with potentially survivable wounds. According to Smith's analysis, nearly a third of victims had survivable wounds at Pulse.

Both the fire chief, Williams, and the police chief, John Mina, have a simple response to those who criticize how the Pulse nightclub shooting was handled.

"The fact of the matter is those people weren't there," Mina said of Smith and others who criticize the response. "So they can't say, 'I would have done this' or 'I could have done this' or 'I should have done this' because they weren't there."

The city said the Police and Fire departments had nine joint training exercises between 2005 and 2016 on how to respond to an active shooter.

"If we had needed the Fire Department in there, we would have called them," Mina said. "Many officers were inside the club transporting the wounded directly to the fire department feet away to their triage center."

Mina later declined to comment further when asked about the dispatch logs showing that the that the police asked for the Fire Department to come to come inside the nightclub. Dyer described those logs as a "random individual talking about that," which didn't reflect the views of police.

Pulse is no longer the worst mass shooting in the U.S. history. Las Vegas took the mantle last year. Just this year, Florida saw mass shootings at Marjory Stoneman Douglas High School in Parkland and at a video game tournament in Jacksonville.

But Pulse changed the way many law enforcement agencies view the need for a rescue task force. Drozd, the Orange County Fire Rescue chief whose department brought vests to the scene, began working with the National Fire Protection Association to create a blueprint for how police and fire departments should work together to respond to active shooter incidents, which came out this year. He said he hopes fire agencies become more willing to enter "warm zones."

"That's where as an industry we can do the most good."

"I Pray She Made It"

Two weeks after the Pulse nightclub shooting, the upper echelons of the Orlando Fire Department called a meeting. The topic? "Active shooter project discussion."

Within 10 months, more vests were purchased, and all firefighters had gone through a mandatory 16-hour rescue training course modeled off of the military's approach to field medicine, reworked for civilians. In April 2017, the mayor stood in front of a fire engine and donned a bulletproof vest with "Fire-Rescue" written in big red letters on the front and "Orlando Fire Department" on the back.

The point of the April 2017 press conference was to show off new equipment the city had purchased to help respond to future disasters like the Pulse shooting. Like the vests that had been sitting in the department's headquarters on the night of the shooting, the vest Dyer modeled had pouches filled with tourniquets, special needles to relieve air in the chest, and bandages.

Dyer and Williams also unveiled their new rescue task force policy.

"Since Columbine, all these different events happened," Williams said at the press conference. "We realize a new norm somewhat, but our goal is to make sure our personnel is equipped to handle that new norm."

Dyer said vests and helmets, which cost about $118,000 would add a layer of protection if firefighters came in the line of fire. The city now has about 150 vests, enough for each firefighter working on a shift to have one.

Those vests could have been helpful in past events, he acknowledged: "Certainly Pulse."

Neither Williams nor Dyer mentioned the vests and helmets sitting at the agency's headquarters untouched at the time of the Pulse shooting. Nor did they mention the years of work on an active shooter policy that hadn't been completed.

The active shooter policy adopted in April 2017 is just two pages long. It says that firefighters working at certain stations will be called into risky situations, operating as a rescue task force, and that all firefighters may be required to do the same.

Ron Glass, president of the union representing the Orlando Fire Department, said the new policy doesn't have enough details for emergency medical professionals treating patients. He said if another Pulse happens tomorrow, "we're gonna do the exact same thing again."

"We have a three-inch notebook … on every type of house fire, every type of specialty, high angle call, below-grade call, extrication call, elevator extrication call," Glass said. "The only thing that's not in the book is … active shooters."

The Justice Department's Community Oriented Policing Services office, which critiqued the police response to Pulse, has been commissioned by the Fire Department to evaluate its response.

That report is due out soon, and it could give needed closure about the department's response to the Pulse shooting.

Saez, the assistant chief who had been charged with modernizing the department's active shooter policy, was not on duty the night of Pulse. But when his wife, who worked for the Orlando Police Department, texted him that the shooting was the "for deal," Saez remembers driving his hybrid Toyota more than 100 mph to get to the scene.

After the arson squad used explosives to breach the outer wall of the club and the shooter was killed, the police dragged a woman to Saez. She had been shot multiple times.

"All I could do was put my hand on her chest to hold pressure and pray, hope, fuck, I hope I did something," Saez said.

An ambulance finally did come and bring the shooting victim to the hospital. Saez doesn't know what happened to her.

"I pray she made it," Saez said.

Saez has filed a hostile work environment complaint with the city of Orlando's human resources department against his immediate supervisor and the fire chief. The city of Orlando said it is "currently reviewing the facts of this case as it is active and ongoing."

Saez said he thinks about the Pulse nightclub shooting every day, and feels responsible for not getting the active shooter protocol pushed through. He has a "sick feeling in the gut."

Correction, October 3, 2018: This story originally misidentified the function of special needles carried in the pouch of bulletproof vests. They relieve air pressure in the chest, not bleeding. It also misidentified the role of Anibal Saez, Jr., on the night of the Pulse shooting. He did not work on the explosive breach of the club.

• *G. Mental Health and Suicide* •

46. Myth vs. Fact

*Violence and Mental Health**

Lois Beckett

After mass shootings, like the ones these past weeks in Las Vegas, Seattle and Santa Barbara, the national conversation often focuses on mental illness. So what do we actually know about the connections between mental illness, mass shootings and gun violence overall?

To separate the facts from the media hype, we talked to Dr. Jeffrey Swanson, a professor in psychiatry and behavioral sciences at the Duke University School of Medicine, and one of the leading researchers on mental health and violence. Swanson talked about the dangers of passing laws in the wake of tragedy—and which new violence-prevention strategies might actually work.

Here is a condensed version of our conversation, edited for length and clarity.

Mass shootings are relatively rare events that account for only a tiny fraction of American gun deaths each year. But when you look specifically at mass shootings—how big a factor is mental illness?

On the face of it, a mass shooting is the product of a disordered mental process. You don't have to be a psychiatrist: what normal person would go out and shoot a bunch of strangers?

But the risk factors for a mass shooting are shared by a lot of people who aren't going to do it. If you paint the picture of a young, isolated, delusional young man—that probably describes thousands of other young men.

A 2001 study looked specifically at 34 adolescent mass murderers, all male. 70 percent were described as a loner. 61.5 percent had problems with substance abuse. 48 percent had preoccupations with weapons. 43.5 percent had been victims of bullying. Only 23 percent had a documented psychiatric history of any kind—which means 3 out of 4 did not.

---

*This story was originally published by ProPublica as Lois Beckett, "Myth vs. Fact: Violence and Mental Health," https://www.propublica.org/article/myth-vs-fact-violence-and-mental-health (June 18, 2015). Reprinted with permission of the publisher.

People with serious mental illnesses, like schizophrenia, do have a slightly higher risk of committing violence than members of the general population. Yet most violence is not attributable to mental illness. Can you walk us through the numbers?

People with serious mental illness are 3 to 4 times more likely to be violent than those who aren't. But the vast majority of people with mental illness are not violent and never will be.

Most violence in society is caused by other things.

Even if we had a perfect mental health care system, that is not going to solve our gun violence problem. If we were able to magically cure schizophrenia, bipolar disorder and major depression, that would be wonderful, but overall violence would go down by only about 4 percent.

Federal law prohibits people who have been involuntarily committed to a mental institution from owning guns. Is that targeting the right people?

The criteria we have are both over-inclusive and under-inclusive at the same time. They capture a lot of people who are not really at risk, at least not anymore. For instance, think about someone who had a suicidal mental health crisis 25 years ago, was involuntarily hospitalized, but now they're recovered and fine, they haven't had problems in years. They want to get a job as a security guard and they can't because they can't possess firearms.

Under-inclusive, because think about someone who's in the middle of their first episode of psychosis, but hasn't been treated. This might be a serious, dangerous mental health crisis—a person with paranoid delusions, believing that everyone else is out to get him, isolated, maybe drinking heavily—but he is not disqualified from going and purchasing any number of guns.

Then there's another problem: Even if someone has a record of serious mental illness, these records might not actually make it into the background check system.

Reporting [of mental health records] is spotty. Mayors Against Illegal Guns put out this report [which found that, as of 2014, 12 states have still reported fewer than 100 mental health records to the national background check system.]

In one recent study, you found that adding more mental health records to the background check system can prevent some violence—but only a very small amount. Can you explain what you found?

The state of Connecticut provided a natural experiment. Prior to 2007, they didn't report mental health records to the National Instant Criminal Background Check System, and after that they did.

We compared two groups of people over eight years. Everyone had been hospitalized and had a major diagnosable psychiatric disorder, such as schizophrenia. One group had been hospitalized involuntarily, and was disqualified from buying guns. One group had been voluntarily hospitalized.

The criteria for involuntary commitment are intertwined with dangerousness and violence. Before Connecticut began reporting mental health records [to the background check system], people who had been involuntarily committed had a higher likelihood, month by month, of committing violence. After the period when the gun provisions were enforced, the difference went away—a 53 percent drop in their likelihood of committing a violent crime.

So blocking people with serious mental illnesses from buying guns worked—but it didn't have a huge impact. Adding the mental health records only prevented an estimated 14 violent crimes a year, or less than one half of 1 percent of the state's overall violent crime. Why is that?

The people who were [actually disqualified from buying guns] were only 7 percent of the study population of people with serious mental illness—and only a very, very small proportion of people at risk of engaging in violent crime.

It's like if you had a vaccine that was going to work against a particular public health epidemic, but only 7 percent of the people got the vaccine. It might work great for them, but it's not going to affect the epidemic.

After the Santa Barbara shootings, the House of Representatives approved an additional $19.5 million to help states add more mental health records to the background checks system—a rare bipartisan move. Do we know if adding more records nationwide will have a big impact on violence?

[There's an idea that] once we do that, it's going to have a big effect. We haven't done a lot of research on it.

When one of these mass shootings has occurred, there's immediately a lot of attention and finger-pointing. Mental health becomes the one square inch of common real estate between people who want to reform the mental health care system, and gun rights people.

So, if our current standards for denying people gun rights based on mental illness doesn't work very well, what would a better policy look like?

We want to focus more on behavioral indicators of risk, and not so much on "mental health" and "mental illness" as a category.

Even though the large majority of people with mental illnesses are never violent, there may be times in the course of illness and treatment when we do know that risk is elevated. One of those times is the period surrounding involuntary hospitalization. We think that if there are indicators of risk, that should be a time when firearms are removed—at least temporarily—with an opportunity for restoration of gun rights when the person no longer poses a public safety risk

There are lots of states when people are involuntarily detained for a 72-hour hold, never have a commitment hearing, and are not prohibited from firearms. People in that time frame, if guns were temporarily removed from them, that might have a big impact, particularly on suicide.

California Democrats are pushing a new state law that would create a "gun violence restraining order," based on the model of a domestic violence restraining order. [Update: Governor Jerry Brown signed the bill into law in September 2014. It will go into effect on January 1, 2016.] With a judge's order, law enforcement would be allowed to temporarily take away someone's guns. Is this a better model?

Yes. There are times when a family member, or people who know someone, can be legitimately concerned that person poses a threat. They might not have committed a crime. They might not even be having a mental health crisis. But if there were a way for family members to get law enforcement involved, that might actually save some lives.

In the Santa Barbara shooting, for example, the police were called. His family was concerned for him. But he didn't meet the criteria to be involuntarily detained.

Gun violence restraining orders would allow people to say that someone seems dangerous, and have their guns temporarily taken away. How do you protect against someone abusing this law?

Connecticut, Indiana, and Texas already have a dangerous person gun seizure law. With the gun violence restraining order idea, a judge would make that decision. There has to be evidence there. There is a constitutional right at stake.

You talk a lot about the tension between the way the media portrays mental health and violence, and the reality of the problem. If "mental health" isn't the key to violence in America, what is?

Violence is not distributed at random. If you look at the victims of homicide, for example—young African American men are far more likely to be victims of homicide.

We need to think of violence itself as a communicable disease. We have kids growing up exposed to terrible trauma. We did a study some years ago, looking at [violence risk] among people with serious mental illness. The three risk factors we found were most important: first, a history of violent victimization early in life, second, substance abuse, and the third is exposure to violence in the environment around you. People who had none of those risk factors—even with bipolar disorder and schizophrenia—had very low rates of violent behavior.

Abuse, violence in the environment around you—those are the kinds of things you're not going to solve by having someone take a mood stabilizer.

What are the best ways of figuring out who is likely to become violent?

If someone has a history of any kind of violent or assaultive behavior, that's actually a better predictor of future violence than having a mental health diagnosis. If someone has a conviction for a violent misdemeanor, we think there's evidence, they ought to be prohibited [from owning guns.] Things like a history of two DUI or DWI convictions, being subject to a temporary domestic violence restraining order, or convicted of two or more misdemeanor crimes involving a controlled substance in a five-year period.

Those are the evidence-based recommendations of the Consortium for Risk-Based Firearms Policy [a group of mental health, gun violence, and legal experts who came together after the Sandy Hook shootings. You can also read their full federal policy recommendations and state policy recommendations.]

Most of our peer high-income countries can take a different approach. They can say, it's just too dangerous for someone to have a personal handgun for their own protection. They broadly limit legal access to guns. That's why they have lower homicide rates. What we try to do is keep the guns out of the hands of dangerous people, and that's hard, because it's hard to predict, and we have almost more guns than people.

What do we know about the risk factors for school shootings, in particular?

Katherine Newman's book Rampage, which looks at school shootings, identifies five common factors. Every shooter in her study had some kind of "psychosocial problems," which may include mental illness.

The other factors: Shootings tend to happen in smaller communities, where everybody knows everybody, and the person who does the shooting perceives himself as purely marginal. And there are cultural scripts that give them a model: the idea that if you go out and shoot people, you're going to become this notorious anti-hero, on the front pages of every newspaper.

Then there's the failure of surveillance systems—a teacher might have seen that the shooter was troubled, or it might be another kid. If everybody had been able to sit down together and connect the dots, they might have realized what was happening.

And the fifth factor is the availability of the weapons.

You've written a lot about the danger of making policy in the wake of high-profile tragedies. From the mental health perspective, what are the one or two worst laws pushed through in the wake of the Sandy Hook shootings?

One was the particular feature of the New York SAFE Act, that put in place mandated reporting by mental health professionals of clients who disclosed a risk of harming themselves or others. They were required to report the names of individuals to the police, so that the names could be matched to the gun permit database and their guns taken away. A lot of mental health professionals in New York [did not support this] because of the potential chilling effect. It might keep people away from help-seeking and inhibit their disclosures in therapy.

You've estimated that preventing mental health-related gun deaths could save 100,000 lives over a decade—but most of these would not be mass shooting victims, or even gun homicides.

Everyone has been through our National Mall and seen the Vietnam Memorial—what a sobering sight it is to look at 58,000 names, over a 10-year period of time, U.S. military deaths. But if we were to build a monument to commemorate all the people who died as a result of a gunshot in the last 10 years, we would need a monument five times bigger than the Vietnam Memorial.

I've done these back-of-the envelope calculations. If you were to back out all the risk associated with mental illness that's contributing to the 300,000 people killed by gunshot wounds in the last ten years, you could probably reduce deaths by about 100,000 people. Ninety-five percent of the reduction would be from suicide. Only 5 percent would be from reducing homicide.

Mental illness is a strong risk factor for suicide. It's not a strong risk factor for homicide.

So if what matters is preventing suicides, why are we talking about guns?

Suicide is a permanent solution to a temporary problem. Lots of times, it's the impulsive action of a young person who's intoxicated. There's a huge possibility to prevent it. If a person survives a suicide attempt, there's good evidence they're unlikely to go and die from another suicide.

But the fatality rate for gun suicide attempts is just huge. You might survive an overdose. You're not going to survive a shot to the brain at close range. At the time that someone is inclined to harm themselves, you don't want them to have a gun. I'm all for improved access to mental health care. But part of the suicide prevention puzzle has to do with limiting access to lethal means.

I don't think we're ever going to live in a world where we're not going to have troubled, confused, isolated young men. But we shouldn't live in a world where men like that have very easy access to semi-automatic handguns.

So what are some of the ways to limit access to lethal means?

We're not a country like the UK or like Australia, where we can say, "Let's just limit legal access to handguns." Guns are here to stay. Universal background checks, I would support. That, all by itself, wouldn't be sufficient. We need to do something about limiting access to the guns people already have when they are inclined to harm others or themselves. In some states, 50 percent of people live in homes where they have guns already.

I have colleagues who are psychiatrists. When they see patients with serious depression, they counsel them about the danger of having a gun in the house. They have a conversation with family members. You can do a lot without invoking law, by talking to people about harm reduction and locking up guns. Getting family members to voluntarily store guns somewhere else.

In Switzerland, an army policy reform in the mid–2000s effectively cut in half the number of soldiers with guns stored in their homes. Researchers were able to show that this change in gun access resulted in a very significant decrease in the overall suicide rate.

We talked about why the current standards for disqualifying someone from owning a gun don't work very well. But there's also an interesting historical angle here. Why is the bar having been "committed to a mental institution"? Where does this standard come from?

The 1968 Gun Control Act—passed the year that Sen. Robert F. Kennedy and Martin Luther King, Jr., were assassinated.

When the law was enacted, the mental health system was very, very different. We had massive numbers of people locked up involuntarily in psychiatric hospitals, often for long periods of time. In 1950, there were about 500,000 people in these institutions. Now, after deinstitutionalization, there are probably 50,000.

Fewer people now are disqualified on the basis of a mental health record. That's not to say that the overall number of people disqualified from owning guns is lower. Some of the people who, in the old days, would have been disqualified because they were involuntarily committed—now some of them may have been disqualified due to a criminal record, and some would be incarcerated.

In Connecticut, we looked at 23,292 people with a history of serious mental illness. Only 7 percent of them were disqualified from owning guns because of mental health records. But 35 percent of them had a disqualifying criminal record.

But just because someone has a mental illness and they committed a crime—the illness isn't necessarily why they did it. Among these people with serious mental illness, the risk factors for committing a violent crime appeared to have more to do with the overall risk factors for violence: being young, male, socially disadvantaged, and involved with substance misuse.

Correction, June 10, 2014: A sub-headline for this article incorrectly identified Dr. Swanson as a psychiatrist. Dr. Swanson, a professor in psychiatry and behavioral sciences at the Duke University School of Medicine, is a medical sociologist.

Correction, June 10, 2014: An earlier version of this story misstated one of the findings of a gun study. After Connecticut added mental health records to its background check system, people who had been disqualified from owning a gun showed a 53 drop, not a 6 percent drop, in their likelihood of committing a violent crime.

47. More Mental Health Care Won't Stop the Gun Epidemic, New Study Suggests*

Tom Wickizer, Evan V. Goldstein, *and* Laura Prater

Guns exact a heavy toll on the American public every day. On the average day, around 100 people die from a gun death. Because of the rise in gun deaths in recent years, the nation now faces a serious man-made epidemic.

When people think of firearm death, they tend to focus on mass shootings such as the massacre at Sandy Hook Elementary School in Newtown, Connecticut; the shooting at Marjory Stoneman Douglas High School in Parkland, Florida; and the very recent mass shootings in El Paso, Texas. and Dayton, Ohio. Although mass shootings happen frequently, research suggests that they account for less than 0.2 percent of all homicides in the U.S.

Suicide by guns accounts for a much greater loss of life than murder. In 2017, 39,773 people died from firearms. Murder accounted for 37 percent of these deaths. Law enforcement and accidental shootings accounted for about for 3 percent of the deaths. The remaining 60 percent of firearm deaths resulted from suicide.

Suicide is the 10th leading cause of death among U.S. adults and the second leading cause of death among teens. The majority of suicides are completed using a firearm.

There's been a lot of discussion recently about the role that mental illness plays in shooting deaths, especially firearm suicide. As health services researchers from The Ohio State University College of Public Health, we analyzed firearm suicide and the capacity of states to provide behavioral health care services: that is, mental health services and substance disorder services. We wanted to know if suicide deaths by guns were lower in states that offered more expansive behavioral health care.

Deaths by Suicide on the Rise

Since 2005, the firearm suicide rate has increased by 22.6 percent, compared to a 10.3 percent rise in the firearm homicide rate. Without question, the U.S. has the most firearm deaths and firearm suicides compared to all other high-income, developed

---

*Originally published as Tom Wickizer, Evan V. Goldstein, and Laura Prater, "More Mental Health Care Won't Stop the Gun Epidemic, New Study Suggests," *The Conversation*, https://theconversation.com/more-mental-health-care-wont-stop-the-gun-epidemic-new-study-suggests-124253 (October 7, 2019). Reprinted with permission of the publisher.

countries. The U.S. firearm homicide rate is more than 25 times higher than other high-income developed countries, while the firearm suicide rate is eight times higher.

A number of factors contribute to America's high firearm death rate, but one factor unique to America stands out—the widespread availability of guns.

The high prevalence of gun ownership in the U.S. contributes to the burden of firearm-related injury. Estimates indicate over 390 million guns are owned in the U.S. by approximately one-third of the nation's population, which amounts to 120.5 guns owned for every 100 persons in the country. In contrast, there are 34.7 guns owned per 100 persons in Canada. There are comparatively far fewer firearm homicides in Canada than in the U.S.

Firearm Suicide and Behavioral Health Care

Having a mental health professional involved with a person who is experiencing suicidal thoughts may help prevent suicide. Monkey Business Images/Shutterstock.com

Using data provided by the Centers for Disease Control and Prevention and other government agencies, we performed a detailed statistical analysis to examine firearm suicide rates from 2005 to 2015 in each state in relation to the size of behavioral health care workforce and the number of substance disorder treatment facilities.

In a study published in Health Affairs October 7, we found a statistically significant 10 percent increase in the behavioral health care workforce was associated with a 1.2 percent decrease in the firearm suicide rate. We controlled for variables such as the unemployment rate, race, gender and population size, among others. Increasing the workforce by 40 percent, a change that could potentially take significant time and resources, would perhaps lead to a reduction in the firearm suicide rate of only 4.8 percent.

Increasing the capacity to provide needed behavioral health care could be a costly approach to reducing firearm suicides.

Based on our statistical analysis, and taking account of the salaries for mental health professionals, it could cost as much as US$15 million to increase the size of Ohio's behavioral health care workforce enough to prevent one firearm suicide.

Policy Implications and a Path Forward

Our study reinforces what many in public health recognize: There is no single solution to the complex problems of firearm death and firearm suicide. If expanding the mental health workforce and identifying people at risk are not sufficient solutions, then broader action is required.

Based on our research, we believe that several concrete steps could be taken to foster preventive measures.

First, although increasing access to mental health care is necessary for a variety of compelling reasons, our findings suggest that strengthening mental health services won't reduce firearm violence. Rather, action may be needed at the federal, state and local levels to strengthen laws and regulations shown to promote gun safety and prevent firearm deaths. Other countries, in particular Australia and New Zealand, responded forcefully to mass shooting events when they occurred and adopted regulatory measures to protect their citizens against gun violence.

Second, the medical and public health communities do more to prevent firearm suicide and deaths. Individual physicians working in their clinical roles could perform screenings to identify persons with mood disorders who are at risk for suicide. The medical community and public health community, acting through their professional associations, could advocate firearm safety.

Third, the Dickey Amendment, which was passed in 1996, and related policies have stifled federal funding for gun violence research. We believe that Congress should repeal the law and related policies. There is a critical need to conduct research to improve understanding about the risk factors for firearm suicide and gun violence and about the measures that could be taken to combat the firearm death epidemic afflicting our communities.

The substantial majority of the public, both gun owners and non-gun owners, favor stronger regulation for the purchase of guns and for their use and storage. Research shows having firearms available and keeping them in the home are strong risk factors for completed suicide, especially among adolescents.

So far the country has made little meaningful progress in combating the epidemic of firearm suicide and firearm deaths.

Data show the problem is getting worse, not better. Finding effective approaches to reducing the problem of firearm suicide and gun violence will require that the country become more politically unified in its willingness to recognize the scope and nature of the problem. There seems little excuse for continued inaction.

48. Among U.S. States, New York's Suicide Rate Is the Lowest. How's That?*

MICHELLE ANDREWS

"I just snapped" is how Jessica Lioy describes her attempt in April to kill herself.

After a tough year in which she'd moved back to her parents' Syracuse, New York, home and changed colleges, the crumbling of her relationship with her boyfriend pushed the 22-year-old over the edge. She impulsively swallowed a handful of sleeping pills. Her mom happened to walk into her bedroom, saw the pills scattered on the floor and called 911.

In 2017, 1.4 million adults attempted suicide, while more than 47,000 others did kill themselves, making suicide the 10th-leading cause of death in the United States, according to the federal Centers for Disease Control and Prevention. And the rate has been rising for 20 years.

Like other states, Jessica Lioy's home state of New York has seen its rate increase. But New York has consistently reported rates well below those of the U.S. overall. Compared with the national rate of 14 suicides per 100,000 people in 2017, New York's was just 8.1, the lowest suicide rate in the nation.

What gives? At first glance, the state doesn't seem like an obvious candidate for the lowest rank. There's New York City, all hustle and stress, tiny apartments and crowds of strangers. And upstate New York, often portrayed as bleak and cold, is famously disparaged in the Broadway musical "A Chorus Line" with the comment that "to commit suicide in Buffalo is redundant."

Experts say there's no easy explanation for the state's lowest-in-the-nation rate. "I can't tell you why," said Dr. Jay Carruthers, a psychiatrist who is the director of suicide prevention at the New York State Office of Mental Health.

Guns and Urbanization Are Likely Factors

There's no single answer, but a number of factors probably play a role, according to Carruthers and other experts on suicide.

Low rates of gun ownership are likely key. Guns are used in about half of suicide deaths, and having access to a gun triples the risk that someone will die by suicide,

*Originally published as Michelle Andrews, "'Among U.S. States, New York's Suicide Rate Is the Lowest. How's That?," *Kaiser Health News*, December 11, 2019. Reprinted with permission of the publisher. *Kaiser Health News* is a nonprofit news service covering health issues. It is an editorially independent program of the Kaiser Family Foundation that is not affiliated with Kaiser Permanente.

according to a study in the Annals of Internal Medicine. Because guns are so deadly, someone who attempts suicide with a gun will succeed about 85 percent of the time, compared with a 2 percent fatality rate if someone opts for pills, according to a study by researchers at the Harvard Injury Control Research Center.

"The scientific evidence is pretty darn good that having easy access to guns makes the difference whether a suicidal crisis ends up being a fatal or a nonfatal event," said Catherine Barber, who co-authored the study and is a senior researcher at the Harvard center.

New York has some of the strongest gun laws in the country. In 2013—after the mass shooting at Sandy Hook Elementary School in Newtown, Connecticut—the state broadened its ban on assault weapons, required recertification of pistols and assault weapons every five years, closed a private sale loophole on background checks and increased criminal penalties for the use of illegal guns.

This year, the state enacted laws that, among other things, established a 30-day waiting period for gun purchases for people who don't immediately pass a background check, and prevented people who show signs of being a threat to themselves or others from buying guns, sometimes referred to as a "red flag" or "extreme risk" law.

The population is also heavily concentrated in urban areas, including more than 8 million people living in New York City. According to the Census Bureau, nearly 88 percent of the state's population lived in urban areas in the 2010 census, while the national figure is about 81 percent.

Suicide rates are typically lower in cities. In 2017, the suicide rate nationwide for the most rural counties—20 per 100,000 people—was almost twice as high as the 11.1 rate for the most urban counties, according to the CDC. The trend is accelerating. While the suicide rate in the most urban counties increased by 16 percent from 1999 to 2017, it grew by a whopping 53 percent in the most rural counties.

Loneliness, isolation and access to lethal weapons can be a potent combination that leads to suicide, said Jerry Reed, who directs the suicide, violence and injury prevention efforts at the Education Development Center. The center runs the federally funded Suicide Prevention Resource Center, among other suicide prevention projects.

People in rural areas may live many miles from the nearest mental health facility, therapist or even their own neighbors.

"If your spouse passes away or you come down with a chronic condition and no one is checking on you and you have access to firearms," Reed said, "life may not seem like worth living."

Intervention Helps "Force You" to Move Forward

New York's efforts to prevent suicides include conducting a randomized controlled trial to test the effectiveness of a brief intervention program developed in Switzerland for people who have attempted suicide—because they are at risk for trying again.

The trial has yet to get underway, but clinicians at the Hutchings Psychiatric Center in Syracuse were trained in the Attempted Suicide Short Intervention Program, as it's called. They began testing it with some patients last year.

Jessica Lioy was one of them. After her suicide attempt, she spent a week at the inpatient psychiatric unit at Upstate University Hospital in Syracuse. A social worker approached her about signing up for that outpatient therapy program.

The program is simple. It has just four elements:

In the first session, patients sit down with a therapist for an hourlong videotaped discussion about why they tried to kill themselves.

At their second meeting, they watch the video to reconstruct how the patient moved from experiencing something painful to attempting suicide.

During the third session, the therapist helps the patient list long-term goals, warning signs and safety strategies, along with the phone numbers of people to call during a crisis. The patient carries the information with them at all times.

Finally, during the next two years, the therapist writes periodic "caring letters" to the patient to check in and remind them about their risks and safety strategies.

In the Swiss trial, about 27 percent of the patients in the control group attempted suicide again during the next two years. Only 8 percent of those who went through the intervention program re-attempted suicide during that time.

"The difference with ASSIP is the patient involvement. It's very patient-centered," said Dr. Seetha Ramanathan, the Hutchings psychiatrist overseeing the program. It's also very focused on the suicide attempt, not on other issues like depression or PTSD, she said.

Lioy said that, at the beginning, she didn't have high hopes for the program. She had already told her story to many doctors and mental health therapists. But this felt different, she recalled.

"They steal you for an hour from the universe and make you focus on the worst thing in your life and then coach you through it," Lioy said. "They force you to feel something, and they force you to just reflect on that one situation and how to move forward to not end up back in that place. It's very immediate."

It hasn't all been smooth sailing. Shortly after returning home, Lioy felt depressed and couldn't get out of bed. But she had learned the importance of asking for help, and she reached out to her parents.

"I was able to talk with them, and it felt amazing," she said. "I'd never done that before."

There have been other changes. Since returning home, Lioy finished her bachelor's degree in molecular genetics and is working as a pharmacy technician. She's applying to doctoral programs and she has a new boyfriend, although she said she no longer needs a boyfriend to feel OK about herself.

"It's been a really big journey," Lioy said.

49. What Happens After a Campus Suicide Is a Form of Prevention, Too*

Aneri Pattani

CHAPEL HILL, North Carolina—Ethan Phillips was 13 years old when he first heard the term "suicide contagion."

It's the scientific concept that after one person dies by suicide, others in the community may be at higher risk.

Phillips learned the phrase growing up in Fairfax County, Virginia, where more than a dozen teens and preteens died by suicide while he was in middle school. It came up again when a high school classmate killed himself. By the time Phillips entered college at the University of North Carolina–Chapel Hill in 2019, he'd developed "an unfortunate level of experience" in dealing with the topic, he said.

So this fall, when Phillips—now a junior and head of the student government's wellness and safety division—heard that two students had died by suicide on campus within 48 hours, he knew what to do. Along with his peers in student government, Phillips shared mental health resources on social media, developed email templates for students to request accommodations from professors and held a meeting of various mental health clubs on campus to coordinate their response. His focus was first on communicating quickly and clearly, and second on informing students about mental health resources available to help them deal with their grief.

Those are two crucial steps in a growing area of study known as "suicide postvention." Just as there's research on the prevention of mental health crises and interventions for people who are actively suicidal, research is also developing around the steps that can be taken after a suicide to help communities grieve, restore a sense of stability and limit the risk of more deaths.

How Does "Postvention" Work? According to emerging best practices, a postvention plan—ideally developed in advance and deployed immediately after any death by suicide—should include:

- A defined team to handle the response. Members may include university leaders, counselors, campus security staffers, residence hall management, the school's communications team and legal advisers.

*Originally published as Aneri Pattani, "What Happens After a Campus Suicide Is a Form of Prevention, Too," *Kaiser Health News*, November 19, 2021. Reprinted with permission of the publisher. *Kaiser Health News* is a nonprofit news service covering health issues. It is an editorially independent program of the Kaiser Family Foundation that is not affiliated with Kaiser Permanente.

- A way to communicate the news to students, staffers and the wider community. Acknowledging the death was a suicide, rather than referring to it as an accident or unexpected passing, is important, but so is avoiding sharing details about the suicide that someone could replicate.
- Counseling and other mental health resources to help people affected by the suicide deal with trauma and grief.
- Guidelines on funerals or memorials. To reduce the risk of suicide contagion, any memorial sites or activities should not glorify, vilify or stigmatize deceased students or their deaths.
- A clear vision of future prevention efforts. Many suicide researchers say postvention is a form of prevention. It can provide an opportunity to recognize risk factors such as depression and to implement ongoing mental health support for the community.

It's an area of particular interest for colleges, as suicide is the second-leading cause of death for U.S. teenagers and young adults, and these are the groups most likely to experience contagion. With the Covid-19 pandemic exacerbating depression and thoughts of suicide, several universities have needed postvention strategies over the past year and a half.

Saint Louis University, Dartmouth College and West Virginia University have lost multiple students to suicide during the pandemic. At UNC, the two deaths in October came after a suicide death and suicide attempt in September, according to the campus police log. A national survey in the spring by the American College Health Association found 1 in 4 students had screened positive for suicidal thoughts and 2 percent had attempted suicide in the past 12 months.

"Knowing this, we have to be even more alert," said John Dunkle, former director of counseling services at Northwestern University and a senior director with the non-profit Jed Foundation, which works to prevent youth suicide. "Getting that postvention plan in place before a tragedy occurs is really critical."

Schools should know how they will communicate the news, identify students at greatest risk of harming themselves, deploy counseling resources and determine whether to hold memorials, he said.

Julie Cerel, director of the Suicide Prevention and Exposure Lab at the University of Kentucky, said her research shows that, on average, 135 people are affected by each suicide. Postvention strategies can prevent suicides among that group, she said.

Yet creating a postvention plan is a challenging task, involving the uncomfortable topic of death, thorny legal questions of liability and the sometimes conflicting desires of the deceased student's family and the campus population.

Phillips saw these complexities when he was in middle and high school. So when UNC leaders took a day and a half to release a statement on the October suicides, he understood why.

Still, he saw the repercussions of that delay in the college community. Rumors swirled on social media and people wondered if the university was ignoring the issue. "Where it showed its negative effects most acutely were in faculty who did not know what was occurring on campus," Phillips said. Some were caught off guard by students' grief and anger at the university or requests for extensions on assignments.

UNC declined to answer questions about its response to the suicides and whether it has a postvention plan. On November 15, the university did hold a one-day mental health summit "for faculty, staff and student leaders" to address campus culture, crisis services and prevention. In a written statement, the university said it also plans to launch a campus-wide mental health campaign to make students and other community members aware of the signs and symptoms of mental health distress, and inform them of the different ways they can reach out to each other and to university services for support.

Dunkle said communication is among the trickiest pieces of postvention. While students want information immediately, universities can be hamstrung by pending death investigations or a family's wishes for privacy. Officials also must avoid sharing details, like the manner of suicide, as that can increase contagion.

What's most important, Dunkle said, is to provide mental health resources.

After the suicides, UNC's communication to students listed the campus counseling center, the dean of students office, peer support services and national hotlines. The school also created temporary support centers with counselors throughout campus.

But since the centers were open only during the daytime, Phillips said, some students found it difficult to go between classes.

Christopher Grohs, a student in occupational therapy and director of health and wellness for the graduate and professional student government, echoed that concern. Many graduate students have told him they don't know where the counseling center is on UNC's 729-acre campus or how to use it. "A big barrier to using a resource is being able to locate it," Grohs said.

This on-the-ground understanding is why students should be consulted when universities develop postvention plans, said Amy Gatto, a senior manager at Active Minds, a nonprofit focused on mental health for young adults. "They're going to be able to give more valuable feedback than just a committee of staff members."

At Johnson C. Smith University—a small, historically Black college in Charlotte, North Carolina—counseling services director Tierra Parsons said she looks for opportunities to survey students and adjust services accordingly. Over the years, students have suggested they'd like more virtual and text-based options, she said. In fall 2020, the school brought on telehealth provider TimelyMD. This year, it asked social work graduate students to spend their internship hours in undergraduate residence halls to be available to students where they live.

"We want to be where students need us, and sometimes that requires coming out from behind the desk," Parsons said.

Equally important as campus-wide outreach is directly contacting those who were closest to the student who died, mental health experts say.

At the University at Albany in New York, the counseling center creates a list of these students and fast-tracks them to an urgent consult if they reach out, said center director Karen Sokolowski. If the students don't reach out, counselors contact them to talk about grief and ask whether they need extensions on homework or time away from school.

Students should also be asked about their access to lethal means, said Qwynn Galloway-Salazar, student division chair for the American Association of Suicidology. Depending on their answers, the university could distribute gun locks, talk about safe storage of medications or, more generally, limit access to the top floors of tall buildings. After a series of suicides at Cornell, the university added safety nets to local bridges.

Another important postvention step can be limiting memorials. Although students need opportunities to grieve, experts say memorials sometimes glamorize suicide and lead others with suicidal thoughts to see death as a way to receive love and attention. Instead, they suggest directing students to volunteer or donate to a cause they care about in their classmate's memory.

At UNC, in the days after the two suicides, members of the campus Active Minds chapter wrote more than 150 notes of affirmation and distributed them with lists of mental health resources, said club co-president Evan Aldridge. Other students wrote messages in chalk outside the student union reminding peers "it's OK to rest" and "you are so loved."

Although those messages have faded in the weeks since, the students' postvention efforts have not.

Phillips said they should continue for years, just as they have where he grew up. "I don't know that we're ever out of postvention."

50. Five First Responders to the Pulse Massacre. One Diagnosis: PTSD*

Abe Aboraya

On the morning of June 12, 2016, police officer Omar Delgado pulled his cruiser up to his two-story townhome in Sanford, Florida, and sat in silence for 15 minutes, trying to process what he had seen during 3½ hours inside the Pulse nightclub.

He stripped his bloody uniform and gear off, put them in a trash bag, and took a shower. Then, he shut the door to his bedroom, locked it and tried to sleep.

That same morning, firefighter EMT Brian Stilwell walked back to Orlando Fire Department Station 5. Working at the station just 300 feet from Pulse nightclub, Stilwell was one of the first on scene hours earlier.

In the dawn's light, he saw a pool of coagulated blood in front of the station. It was from a Pulse patron who had been shot in the stomach and dragged to that spot. Stilwell wondered if the man survived the night. Then, with a bucket of bleach and water, he helped clean the blood off the concrete.

Down Orange Avenue, Alison Clarke and a fellow Orlando Police officer walked into a McDonald's to use the bathroom. The restaurant had a TV with the news on, streaming live video of the scene she had just come from. People looked up from their coffee and breakfast, glanced at her and her partner, then back to the food. She used the restroom, washed up and bought two coffees. No one said anything. It was surreal.

Josh Granada and his partner drove their ambulance back across town to their Orlando Fire station. They spent the night ferrying 13 people who had been shot at Pulse to the hospital. Before showering, they threw away their uniforms.

"We were covered in just sticky, nasty—just covered in blood," Granada said. "I'm not gonna put that much blood in the washer."

Orlando Police officer Gerry Realin was called in from vacation on June 12 to work a 16-hour shift the morning after the shooting. He spent four or five hours of that inside the nightclub, preparing bodies to be taken to the morgue, and it wasn't until 2:30 a.m. the following day that he came back to his home in New Smyrna Beach, an hour northeast of Orlando. He looked in on his two sleeping children. In the shower, he started wailing. Outside the bathroom, his wife heard him saying, over and over again, how sorry he was for the victims.

*This story was originally published by ProPublica as Abe Aboraya, "Five First Responders to the Pulse Massacre. One Diagnosis: PTSD," WMFE https://www.propublica.org/article/pulse-shooting-first-responders-ptsd-diagnosis (June 11, 2018). Reprinted with permission of the publisher.

"I never saw myself in this position," he would later say. "I've never been the same since, and I can't go back."

Pulse was one of the nation's largest mass shootings, where 49 people died and at least 53 others were wounded. The invisible injuries to first responders represent another toll of the catastrophe.

For these five first responders—and many others—June 12 was the first day of their new lives, one in which they would confront post-traumatic stress disorder. Even though most had responded to gruesome scenes of murder, suicide and car accidents, that didn't prepare them for the psychological injury of PTSD. Going forward, they would relive that day in flashbacks and nightmares, see danger behind every closed door, and become irritable and impatient with spouses and coworkers.

"There are just some events that are so horrific that no human being should be able to just process that and put it away," said Deborah Beidel, a University of Central Florida professor who runs a clinic called UCF Restores that treats first responders with PTSD.

Some of the five also would face indifference, resistance and harassment from the departments they served. One said he was fired because of PTSD, another was fired for a mistake on the job, and a third was never cleared to return to work. They said they were subjected to retaliation for speaking up. Those three have each filed lawsuits asserting they've been mistreated.

The other two were offered work reassignments to seek treatment and reduce stress, and said they were satisfied with their agencies' responses.

Orlando Police Department Chief John Mina said he's been through counseling himself, and that officers dealing with PTSD can come forward to get treatment and request a change of assignment without affecting future promotions and transfers. Orlando Fire Department Chief Roderick Williams likewise said his department provides resources to help firefighters confronting PTSD.

But if employees disclose that they're dealing with PTSD or mental health issues, they can be given a "fit for duty" test, both Mina and Williams said.

"We wouldn't want someone out on the street who was having issues," Mina said. "We may be held liable because of that, because we knew about that. But again, I'll go back to the fact that they don't have to come forward. They can receive treatment anonymously."

The Nightmares Began Immediately

In his bedroom alone the morning after the shooting, Eatonville Police Officer Omar Delgado had his first nightmare: He's back inside Pulse, bodies stacked on each other on the dance floor. He's dragging one of the victims out when the rapid gunfire starts again.

"And I'm yelling, get down, get down, get down!" Delgado said. "Not knowing if he's shooting at us because we're pulling bodies out, he's maybe upset or whatever. Not knowing where the bullets were making their way. When you're trying to pull somebody and you slip and fall and now you're on the ground, trying to take cover because you don't know where the shooting is coming from."

Even though two years have passed, Delgado says he often has that same nightmare. Delgado stayed inside Pulse for more than three hours while the shooter was barricaded in a bathroom. When the smell of gunpowder, blood, death and liquor got to be too much, he tried to breathe through his mouth. Then he tasted it.

He now has flashbacks. One of his triggers: The default iPhone marimba ringtone. While Delgado was inside Pulse, phones rang and rang and rang. Sometimes he could see the caller ID. Mom, sister, friend. He saw one phone vibrate and slide away in a pool of blood.

"I hear an iPhone ring and I freeze. I pause. I'm back there a quick second," Delgado said. "Then I realize, OK, I'm not there, I'm here, I'm OK."

In August of 2016, Delgado told his department that he couldn't keep working as a patrol officer. His bosses ordered him to report to the University of Central Florida's Restores clinic.

The clinic was originally funded by the U.S. Department of Defense for post–9/11 combat veterans with PTSD. It uses virtual reality, sounds and smells to recreate the scenes of war—exposure therapy in which participants relive the events that caused their PTSD and the triggers that provoke flashbacks and nightmares. Such therapy has been shown to reduce symptoms for some, and is combined with group therapy for anger, depression, guilt and social isolation.

After Pulse, UCF Restores opened its doors to first responders. So for three weeks, Delgado sat and recounted, in vivid detail, everything that happened inside Pulse.

Near the end of the third week, his counselor took him on a field trip back to Pulse. They pulled into the Einstein Bros. Bagels parking lot across the street from the nightclub, which was used as a triage site the night of the shooting. Delgado didn't want to get out of the car.

"I got angry," Delgado said. "Where you're standing, there were nothing but bodies laying around here."

The counselor wanted him to start at the intersection of Orange Avenue and Kaley Street, where he first pulled up to the scene, and recount what happened. To walk across the street and get close to the club.

"The icing on the cake was when I heard an ambulance or a fire truck with their sirens going off, and I couldn't take it anymore," Delgado said. "I dropped to my knees and started crying like a little 5-year-old on the corner of Orange and Kaley. A hundred plus degrees outside, I didn't care. I just got overtaken. It was just way, way too much for me."

The UCF Restores program typically lasts three weeks. Delgado spent 10 weeks going through the program. He said it was hell repeatedly reliving Pulse.

"Did it help? I don't know. Did it make it worse? I don't know," Delgado said. "But I'm not well. And when you're not well, is something working?"

In total, 26 Pulse first responders have been evaluated by or treated at the UCF Restores clinic, including the five interviewed for this story. Another 96 first responders have gone through the program for events not related to Pulse.

The clinic says that 60 to 70 percent of the people who complete the program no longer meet the diagnostic criteria for PTSD, meaning their symptoms are no longer disabling. Police and fire departments like the clinic because it's nearby, effective and free—funded by state and federal governments. Many first responders say they like the program because it's a neutral place to get treatment without tipping off their departments.

But some first responders like Delgado worry the clinic isn't enough. Until this year, the UCF Restores clinic didn't have a psychiatrist available to see patients and write prescriptions. In the first year after the shooting, the therapy was provided by a psychologist leading a team of doctoral students. With more state funding, the therapy is now done entirely by licensed, full-time clinicians.

Moreover, exposure therapy can worsen symptoms if it's done too soon, said Beidel, who runs the clinic.

"We don't want to do treatment in the first couple months," Beidel said. "That can make people worse in some cases. Three to six months is the sweet spot. We want to get people into treatment before patterns of avoidance set in, before patterns of using too much alcohol to sleep set in."

After Delgado's 10 weeks in the UCF Restores program, the Eatonville Police Department gave him a "fit for duty" test and put him back on the road. Afterward, a citizen complained that when Delgado and his partner arrested her, Delgado told her, "I'm emotionally disturbed right now."

In December 2017, Eatonville terminated Delgado. During a press conference that month, city officials said Delgado was terminated because of his behavior during the arrest. But in his personnel file, obtained by WMFE under Florida's public records laws, officials cite medical reasons. Delgado says department leaders told him it was because of his PTSD. Eatonville's mayor, chief administrative officer and the police chief at the time declined to comment for this story through the town clerk.

"I believe they [the city of Eatonville] should have stepped up and found more therapy for me," Delgado said. "There are so many programs out there now. They looked at one and that was the end of it and they thought it was gonna be the cure for all, and it wasn't."

Struggling at Home, and On the Job

As the first anniversary of the nightclub shooting approached, Amber Granada woke up at 5 a.m. to her husband Josh searching, angrily, for a bloodstone bracelet.

He was slamming drawers. He asked if the dogs took it. He asked if Amber took it.

Then, Josh walked out of the bedroom and kicked the couch. It slid into the coffee table, knocking the glass coasters to the ground and shattering them. The couple's two dogs scattered. Amber started crying. She handed Josh a different bracelet and told him to leave the house.

His face was red. His eyes were bulging. He screamed: "It's not the bloodstone!"

"And I'm looking at him like, I have no idea who this is," Amber said. "He ends up just leaving, slams the door. He leaves and I'm sitting there on my hands and knees like mopping up this shattered glass that's all over the floor in tears because I have no idea what that was."

This was the first time Amber realized something was wrong. Right after Pulse, Josh Granada had trouble sleeping and nightmares. His coworkers at the Orlando Fire Department also noticed his temper flare in ways they hadn't seen before. That didn't stop him from putting in for a promotion and being elevated to an engineer. Granada and his partner Carlos Tavares were among Florida's firefighters of the year in 2017 for their response to Pulse.

But as the first anniversary approached, journalists sought out Granada and Tavares to ask about what they saw that night. The anxiousness he had right after the shooting returned, along with the nightmares.

Around the same time, Granada drove his ambulance by Pulse for the first time since the shooting. He looked over at the nightclub, which had become a makeshift memorial of flowers and mementos to the dead. Then he looked across the street, at the Einstein Bros. Bagels.

In his mind, he saw blood running down the driveway and into the storm drain.

"And I knew it wasn't there, but I saw it plain as day," Granada said. "And that's what it was that night. The night we were there, that's exactly what it looked like. There were so many people dying and bleeding behind Einstein that it was literally a pool that was coming down the driveway … and running into the gutters … and I just remember that image. And it still sticks with me. I can still see it."

That night, survivors grabbed Granada, begging for help, and slapped the windshield of his ambulance when it was full. There were so many patients, Granada used a penlight and gauze to make tourniquets when the supplies ran out. Two patients died at the triage site and had to be placed off to the side with a makeshift curtain around them.

"I saw a guy crawling and take his last breath," Granada said. "It was horrible."

Granada's home life and professional life suffered as his PTSD symptoms grew worse. The other responders interviewed for this story described similar problems.

Granada's wife Amber told him to ask the department for help. Granada decided his family life was worth more than his pride. In June 2017, he told his lieutenant at the fire department about the flashback when he drove by Pulse.

On July 19, 2017, Lt. Gregg McLay wrote an email to the district chief in charge of health and safety at the Orlando Fire Department, recommending that Granada be given an excused absence with pay to go into the UCF Restores program.

Then, Granada waited. And waited.

Finally, in August, McLay told Granada that he had been told that a top Fire Department official had said, "PTSD is bullshit. These pussies need to man up," Granada said.

"And the second I [was] told that, I got really depressed and stressed. I didn't really tell anybody … but that's when I started having suicidal thoughts."

On August 17, Granada broke the chain of command and wrote an email directly to deputy fire chief Gary Fussell, the man he believed was blocking his access to care.

"It has been well over 2 months since I reached out to the department for help," Granada wrote. "Two long months of waiting for something to happen while our administration has no sense of urgency or care."

Three hours after Granada sent the email, McLay sent another email to the district chief in charge of health and safety, copying Granada. McLay seemed frustrated—both that Granada broke chain of command and at the administration's slow response to Granada's request.

"I will be totally honest with both of you," McLay wrote. "Our department [takes people off shift] all the time. If a person was to ask [for] help for a substance abuse problem, he is immediately taken off shift and offered help. In this case, Josh is seeking help and the licensed mental health professional that he is seeing is recommending a beautiful opportunity for him to be with fellow workers and military to share stories and coping skills."

But Granada wasn't taken off duty. Instead, 10 days after that email, he made a mistake that would cost him his job.

It was a routine medical call. A woman didn't check out of the penthouse suite at the Doubletree hotel near the theme parks, and she was unresponsive. When paramedics woke her up by rubbing her sternum with their knuckles, Granada says she started yelling. Granada pulled out his iPhone, started the audio recorder, and put it back in his pocket.

The patient refused treatment and everyone left. Back at the fire station, Granada played the recording for his coworkers at the dinner table before he deleted it, a possible violation of federal and state privacy laws.

The next day, an internal investigation was started. The patient he recorded was Orlando City Commissioner Regina Hill. Granada wrote an email admitting what happened and apologizing, saying it was "not a smart idea." Hill filed a complaint with the Orlando Police Department, alleging Granada violated her privacy.

Granada was put on light duty while internal affairs investigators spent three months looking into what happened. During that time, he was finally able to go to the UCF Restores program for PTSD therapy.

Ultimately, Granda was fired for violating two department policies and for violating state law by recording someone without consent. He is currently suing the Orlando Fire Department in the Ninth Judicial Circuit Court in Orange County for wrongful termination, and alleging that the city violated a state law that protects people who file worker's compensation claims from retaliation. The department has denied wrongdoing, saying in a pleading in response to Granada's lawsuit that the city "is not liable because it also had valid, legal reasons for taking the adverse employment action."

McLay, Granada's boss, told a reporter that he would not be able to speak without permission from the Orlando Fire Department. The department refused, citing the lawsuit. In court documents, the city denied that an official had said "PTSD is bullshit."

If Granada is unsuccessful in court, his firing will have very real consequences: He will not be eligible for any kind of pension.

"The second I raised my hand and said something's wrong with me in June, they should have pulled me off shift," Granada said. "I should have been getting help. I never should have been allowed to run those calls, day in and day out, my head was not right, I can admit. My head's still not right."

In a job evaluation less than a month before Granada was fired, obtained by WMFE under Florida's public records laws, McLay wrote that Granada was "without a doubt one of the department's sharpest medics." But he was having spontaneous outbursts, and McLay wrote that Granada "started to unravel" when there were delays getting into treatment.

"I do not think this is a true character of Josh," McLay wrote. "I believe he is struggling inside and needing some guidance to get past this hurdle."

"Get over it and move on"

Unlike Delgado and Granada, Gerry Realin didn't arrive at Pulse during the shooting or its immediate aftermath. He worked inside the club after the shooting ended, when many of those first on scene had gone home.

He was part of a small Hazmat team within the Orlando Police Department that placed bodies and body parts into bags to go to the medical examiner for autopsy and identification. The building had no air conditioning, and the smell was choking.

Wearing a white hazmat suit without a helmet, Realin spent four or five hours inside the nightclub, his boots turning yellow and then red from the blood and gore.

In the weeks that followed, Realin had nightmares, flashbacks and panic attacks. He tried to work but often called out sick or left early. After about two weeks, a doctor at a walk-in clinic diagnosed Realin with "acute post-traumatic stress disorder" and wrote that he couldn't even work a desk job. The doctor referred him to a psychiatrist.

Realin, burning through his sick time, filed a worker's compensation claim, and in August started doing interviews with the press about his struggles. He was relieved of duty with pay, meaning the department kept sending him a paycheck as long as he kept up with paperwork. (It didn't legally have to do this under Florida's worker's compensation system at the time.)

Going public, though, came with a price. His wife, Jessica Realin, said the rumor among police officers was that her husband was a faker trying to game the system. Two psychiatrists wrote in their reports that the department's treatment of Realin likely worsened his condition.

His union warned Realin that he could be put under surveillance, so he should be careful not to do anything that would appear to contradict his diagnosis. A union official wrote that he was worried Realin was getting bad advice that could cost him a disability pension.

The department got involved in Realin's clinical care as well. Realin's deputy chief, Orlando Rolon, met the Realins at a gas station in early September 2016. Rolon gave him a copy of a memo: It was a direct order to report to the Restores clinic for treatment.

"Gerry, as you know, the members of the law enforcement profession are exposed to horrible situations during their careers," Rolon wrote in the memo. "I am confident that this program, that has helped many, will address some of your needs and for this reason I'm ordering you to participate. Your wellbeing is our top priority!"

At the gas station, Realin said he told Rolon he had already been to the clinic and didn't want to go back. Things escalated. Rolon asked Realin if he was a threat to himself or others and, according to allegations in one of Realin's two civil lawsuits against the city, threatened to have Realin involuntarily admitted to the hospital on a psychiatric hold.

Rolon told him about responding to a scene in which a 12-year-old had hung himself in a closet. Realin "needed to get over it and move on," Realin said Rolon told him.

Rolon did not return phone calls or text messages for this story. Asked in an interview in September 2016 whether officers with PTSD should be eligible for worker's compensation, he said, "I think it's tough to be able to justify that when you are already expected to be exposed to so much that the average person may not be able to handle."

In March 2017, Realin was ordered to report back to work for the city of Orlando. He would monitor city cameras for drivers who drift into bike lanes. Realin's psychiatrist worried that Realin could witness fatal pedestrian accidents and recommended that he not report for the new job, so he did not.

That decision grabbed headlines: Orlando police officer with PTSD ordered back to work at City Hall—but he's not going.

Dr. Noel Figueroa, Realin's psychiatrist, wrote in his medical chart that, in his opinion, Realin was not able to work "at any job at this point. As far as I'm concerned, the patient is permanently unable to return to full duty."

He continued: "The patient has been feeling 'prosecuted' [sic] by his employer throughout this process. The behaviors by the employer in the last 72 hours only have enhance [sic] his perceptions."

Figueroa's notes were included in one of Realin's lawsuits against the city.

A year after the shooting, Realin said he hid from his children so they wouldn't be traumatized by his rage or depression.

"It's exhausting, physically and mentally," Realin said. "But then there's the moments you can't control. The images or flashbacks or the nightmares that you don't even know about, and your wife tells you the next day you were screaming or twitching all night."

Realin's fight with the city came to a head before Orlando's Police Pension Fund Board in July 2017. Realin was asking for a line-of-duty pension, which would entitle him to 80 percent of his salary for the rest of his life.

Dr. Herndon Harding, one of the doctors hired by the city to perform an independent exam of Realin, wrote that Realin had a "dramatic, perhaps histrionic element to his presentation" that could have been "an attempt to demonstrate his pathology." But he also wrote that one of the factors leading to Realin's inability to function was "how much the role of OPD has contaminated this treatment."

Steve McKillop, an outside attorney hired by the city of Orlando to fight the pension, argued that Realin never really wanted to get well. Getting a pension was his goal all along.

"Rather than accept the hand that has reached out to him, at every turn he's utilized all means necessary to suit his goal of obtaining permanent, in the line of duty benefits so that he does not have to return to work as a police officer," McKillop said to the board.

Ultimately, the board approved the disability pension, writing that Realin was permanently and totally disabled from police work in the line of duty because of PTSD. He was given 80 percent of his pay for the rest of his life: about $41,000 annually, after health insurance costs.

In one of Realin's lawsuits against the city, filed in December 2017, he alleges that the way the department treated him worsened his condition and that the city violated a state law protecting people from being fired or threatened because they file worker's compensation claims. In the other, he claims the city should cover his health insurance costs because he was disabled in the line of duty. The city is contesting the first lawsuit and hasn't yet responded to the second, which was filed in May. Both suits were filed in the Ninth Judicial Circuit Court in Orange County.

In an interview with WMFE, Orlando police chief Mina wouldn't comment on Realin's case because of the ongoing lawsuits. But he said when an officer is injured, officials never worry about the financial burden on the city.

"No, any time an officer is injured or can't perform, the financial aspect of that is never taken into consideration," said Mina, who is a candidate for Orange County Sheriff this year. "What's taken into consideration, by our pension board, which handles that, is was this an on-duty injury, did this happen in the line of duty, can this person go forward performing the job they were hired to do."

Keeping It Quiet, Trying to Get Better

In early 2017, firefighter EMT Brian Stilwell had requested a meeting with Orlando Fire Department Chief Williams to encourage him to commission an after-action review of the Pulse nightclub shooting and the department's response to it.

Stilwell, as well as leaders of the firefighters' union, thought the department needed an outside expert to come in and evaluate whether anything could have been done to reduce the death toll.

At the end of the conversation, Williams told Stilwell to take advantage of the city's employee assistance program for free counseling if he needed it, or to go through the UCF Restores clinic. Williams said that if Stilwell needed time on light duty to go to the clinic, the department would work with him.

Stilwell was already going to the clinic. Sometimes, he'd wake up in the middle of the night and couldn't get back to sleep because something would jar a memory of the shooting. At work, he would be shorter with patients. At home, he was curt with his wife, and would lose his temper.

"And I was like yeah, I've already been going to UCF, which he was kinda taken aback," Stilwell said.

On the night of the shooting, Stilwell was one of four men inside Station 5, about 300 feet from Pulse nightclub. On any given night, they were close enough to hear the music and see the club from the dinner table. On June 12, they heard the gunfire and saw a flood of survivors running for their lives down the street.

The gunfire was so loud, the lieutenant working that night wouldn't let them out to start treating patients until a few minutes passed and a police officer was out in front of the club with an assault rifle.

The firefighters and EMTs went to the triage area across the street, and helped the paramedics already there sort patients. Green tags meant a person was walking and stable. Yellow ones went to those who had serious injuries, but who were stable and could wait to go to the hospital. Red tags were for those people who needed to go to trauma surgery immediately or risked death. Black was reserved for those considered too far gone.

"Some of the people changed from being stable but serious to critical in front of us," Stilwell said.

Stilwell had been open with his coworkers about getting treatment for PTSD, but he hadn't formally told the department. In part, he says, that was because there's no clear protocol on what happens when a first responder comes out and says he or she needs help. He wondered: If you file an injury report for PTSD, are you taken off shift to go into treatment?

Stilwell also worried about how peers would view him. If someone in his department had a heart attack six months earlier, no one would worry about whether he or she was still physically able to do the job.

"No, you go in, you fight the fire, you do whatever you have to, never crosses your mind," Stilwell said. "But if you know a guy that had a mental breakdown or had some mental issues, the stigma is still like, 'Oh, this guy's weird.'"

Stilwell said the meeting with the chief was productive and didn't lead to any negative consequences at work. He completed the Restores program and says he's doing better.

Officer Alison Clarke with the Orlando Police Department is going through the Restores program now. She also was working the triage scene at Einstein Bros. Bagels. Clarke, an openly gay female who had previously worked at Pulse as an off-duty security officer, saw a flood of survivors knock down the fence outside the club.

"Of course, they were traumatized, screaming and crying, and not knowing where they were going," Clarke said. "At that point I started asking for ambulances, and there weren't any ambulances that were responding at that point. So we just started loading up patrol cars and [fellow officer] Jimmy Hyland's pickup truck and started running people to the hospital."

Clarke was able to work through her PTSD with a counselor provided by the city's Employee Assistance Program. She stopped working the night shift, and had gotten to the point where she was only seeing a counselor sporadically.

But then trauma hit again. In January of 2017, her boss Lt. Debra Clayton was tracking a man in an Orlando Walmart who was wanted for killing his pregnant ex-girlfriend.

Clarke heard the gunshots over the radio as her lieutenant was shot. When she got to the Walmart, she held Clayton's hand while others performed CPR. Clarke escorted the ambulance to the hospital, where Clayton was pronounced dead.

Afterward, the anxiety and agitation came back, with a new symptom—hypervigilance. Clarke would think the worst was going to happen on each call. Knocking on a door for a noise complaint, she'd worry that someone on the other side would shoot her through the door. She went to a psychiatrist, who prescribed Prozac.

"Now I've seen it twice," Clarke said. "My first look at evil was Pulse, and then my second look at evil was the day that Debra was killed. So I know it's there. I've seen it. I've experienced it. So now my brain thinks the worst thing's gonna happen when you're out on the street."

In February of this year, she responded to what she came to believe was a man who wanted an officer to shoot him, sometimes called "attempted suicide by cop." The man was holding his hands behind his back, acting like he had a weapon. Clarke drew her pistol. He kept yelling: "You know you want to shoot me, you know you want to shoot me."

Ultimately, the man was subdued with a Taser, and no one was seriously hurt. He was found to be unarmed.

"The moment the handcuffs went on and I was able to take a deep breath and realize that the situation was safe, my anxiety, I just full on had just a like a huge anxiety, panic attack. I couldn't get the adrenaline and my anxiety to calm down," Clarke said.

As she was walking to the patrol car, she thought: This was it. I can't be an initial responder. It was her last shift as a patrol officer.

Clarke asked to be put on light duty while she went through the Restores program, and the department agreed.

"It came to a choice where I could either keep suffering and ruin my home life or step forward and take the help being offered by the department," Clarke said. "Not just the department, the whole community."

How They Cope

Josh Granada has been teaching classes for paramedics and EMTs since he was fired from the Orlando Fire Department. He and his wife are having trouble making ends meet, so they're planning to sell their house and move in with Amber's father before they fall behind on the mortgage.

He leans on his therapy dog, Jack, which he got from the Pawsitive Action Foundation, a group that provides service dogs for veterans and people with disabilities.

Omar Delgado got a dog from the same group: Jediah.

On the days when Delgado has trouble getting out of bed, shaving or brushing his teeth, the dog gives him the motivation he needs, he said. Since he was terminated from the Eatonville Police Department, Delgado has been living off the proceeds of a GoFundMe campaign. He's stuck in limbo, waiting to see if his disability pension will be approved. Once that happens, he'll be able to decide what's next.

"We cut back on everything humanly possible," Delgado said. "It's rough. We gotta keep going. What else is there?"

Alison Clarke has accepted a position as a police department liaison to the LGBTQ community. She no longer works on patrol, and when she's ready to put a uniform back on, she plans to finish out her career at the Orlando Airport. To help cope, she drives her Mazda Miata with the top down, or takes an hour at the driving range, hitting golf balls with her headphones on.

After policing, she plans to work as a counselor to help other officers.

"I'll never be the same [as] before Pulse," Clarke said. "You can recover to a certain extent. At least for me, I can recover to a certain extent. But I know that I'll always have some type of small anxiety issue. It's just learning how to live with it and function with it."

To cope, Gerry Realin goes out paddleboarding and fishing. Walking ankle deep in saltwater in Webster Creek, north of Mosquito Lagoon and the Canaveral National Seashore, Realin casts out into the channel with a lure, hoping to catch redfish, jack and trout.

He sleeps better on the nights he fishes.

"I used to have pressure in my mind. I better hurry up and heal," Realin said. "But how? How do you hurry that up? With some physical injuries, you kinda know. Tear a hamstring, you're out six months. Sprain your ankle, couple weeks. But for this? I don't know."

Realin's wife has become a crusader. After realizing that Florida's workers' compensation law didn't cover lost wages for PTSD and mental conditions, Jessica Realin set out to change the law, and is running for local office. Under a law signed by Gov. Rick Scott in March, first responders will soon become eligible for these benefits.

Brian Stilwell has found healthy ways to cope. He rebuilds classic cars and plays drums. He still works for the Orlando Fire Department, but he's been transferred away from Station 5. Now, he's at a small station in an old Navy base, what he calls "the last stop on a trip to nowhere." He wants to go back to Station 5.

That station, so close to Pulse nightclub, feels like home to him.

"I feel a bigger connection to that area and that community now because of that," Stilwell said. "It feels like the station is a part of me now, not something I want to leave."

As the two-year mark for the shooting approaches, Stilwell says he may go back to UCF Restores for more treatment. The anniversary, he says, is bringing things back to the surface again.

This article was produced in partnership with WMFE, which is a member of the Pro-Publica Local Reporting Network.

• *H. Covid Pandemic* •

51. As Anxieties Rise, Californians Buy Hundreds of Thousands More Guns*

PHILLIP REESE

Handgun sales in California have risen to unprecedented levels during the Covid-19 pandemic, and experts say first-time buyers are driving the trend.

The FBI conducted 462,000 background checks related to handgun purchases in California from March through September, an increase of 209,000, or 83 percent, from the same period last year. That's more than in any other seven-month period on record.

People who study gun ownership think the increase means more people are buying guns for the first time. Handguns, as opposed to rifles and shotguns, are often the first firearm purchase made by someone looking for protection.

Background checks related to long gun or other gun sales also rose statewide, by 110,000, or 54 percent, from March through September compared with the same period in 2019. While that increase is steep, it does not match the rise in long gun sales seen in California during periods, often following mass shootings, when state leaders have considered legislation to sharply rein in access to military-style assault rifles.

In California, background checks for handguns and long guns correlate with gun sales, federal and state data show. Other states have purchasing systems that can result in a disconnect between background checks and sales.

Even so, the national numbers are startling: The FBI conducted about 7.7 million background checks related to handgun sales from March through September, an increase of 3.9 million, or 104 percent, from the same period in 2019.

Gun rights activists, gun control supporters and public health experts largely agree that the increase in gun sales is driven by fear, uncertainty and longing for a greater sense of protection.

Some Californians worry about dark fallout from pervasive unemployment and a faltering economy. Others are disconcerted by the angry and sometimes destructive protests over police shootings and pandemic lockdowns. The upcoming election has added to the unease.

---

*Originally published as Phillip Reese, "As Anxieties Rise, Californians Buy Hundreds of Thousands More Guns," *51*, October 28, 2020. Reprinted with permission of the publisher.

"Every dealer I know has a very low inventory of guns. They're backlogged for months in filling orders because of this run on guns," said Sam Paredes, executive director of Gun Owners of California, which advocates for fewer restrictions on gun purchases. "Every one of them, the first thing they say is, 'Sam, you will not believe how many new gun buyers we have.'"

With about 3,000 firearm-related deaths occurring each year in California and 40,000 nationwide, gun ownership is increasingly viewed through the lens of public health. Several studies have drawn a connection between gun ownership and gun-related deaths.

Researchers at UC-Davis' Violence Prevention Research Program said they are particularly concerned about the latest surge in sales, since many buyers appear to be introducing a gun into their home for the first time.

"There are obvious and well-documented risks associated with [going from] having no access to a firearm to having access to a firearm," said Julia Schleimer, a data analyst with the UC-Davis program. "That extends to all household members, not just the person who owns the gun. And that's for suicide, homicide, unintentional injury—basically for everyone, children included."

Schleimer and her colleagues recently published a study examining the effects of the rise in gun sales during the pandemic. Using national data from the Gun Violence Archive, the study estimated that additional gun sales accounted for nearly 800 excess firearm injuries and deaths during assaults from March through May.

Recent FBI statistics show a rise in homicides and aggravated assaults, crimes often committed with guns, in large California cities and across the nation in the first half of 2020.

Dr. Garen Wintemute, director of the UC-Davis violence prevention program, is among the experts concerned about the connection between gun sales and a rise in domestic violence incidents as families have been forced to shelter together amid pandemic-related quarantines and shutdowns.

"If a firearm is involved, risk that intimate partner violence will have a fatal outcome goes up by a factor of five," Wintemute said.

U.S. firearm suicide rates rose for several years leading up to 2020. Public health advocates fear that the mental strain of the pandemic combined with access to more guns will only exacerbate that trend.

"People have been cooped up and under tension with anxiety and depression," said Dr. Bill Durston, president of Americans Against Gun Violence. "Adding a gun to that is like adding gasoline to a fire."

For now, preliminary data does not show an increase in suicides in California during the pandemic. There were 1,621 suicides in California from March through July, down from 1,930 the year before, according to the California Department of Public Health.

It may be years before the full effects of the increase in gun sales during the pandemic are clear. In California, six of the top 10 months for background checks related to handgun sales have occurred during the pandemic. More than 60,000 handgun background checks were sold in September alone, double the number from September 2019.

Paredes said some dealers tell him more than 70 percent of their buyers are new customers. People "find themselves in a position where they're thinking, 'What might be the next step with the pandemic?' That they might have to protect themselves in their own homes," he said.

Even when the pandemic begins to taper off, Paredes expects the impact on gun sales to linger as first-time buyers become second- and third-time buyers.

"We will continue to see an increase," he said, "because you're going to have millions of people out there who are now going to experience guns."

This story was produced by KHN, which publishes California Healthline, an editorially independent service of the California Health Care Foundation.

52. Homicides Surge
in California Amid Covid Shutdowns
of Schools, Youth Programs*

Phillip Reese

After more than a decade of fairly steady decreases, California's homicide rate surged in 2020. The number of homicides per 100,000 California residents rose to its highest level since 2008.

Amid a pandemic that left law enforcement agencies stretched thin and forced shutdowns that left young men with little to do, California registered a devastating surge in homicides in 2020 that hit especially hard in Black and Latino communities.

The number of homicide victims in California jumped 27 percent from 2019 to 2020, to about 2,300, marking the largest year-over-year increase in three decades, according to preliminary death certificate data from the California Department of Public Health.

There were 5.8 homicides per 100,000 residents in 2020, the highest rate in California since 2008.

Similar increases were seen nationwide. The number of homicides in a sampling of large cities grew 32 percent from 2019 to 2020, according to preliminary FBI data. The data encompasses over 200 cities with more than 100,000 people but does not include some big cities, like New York, Chicago and Philadelphia, that did not report.

The California death certificate data reveals striking disparities in who fell victim to homicide in 2020.

The number of homicides that took the lives of Black Californians rose 36 percent from 2019 to 2020, while homicides that took Hispanic lives rose 30 percent. By comparison, the number of white homicide victims rose 15 percent and the number of Asian victims rose 10 percent.

Most victims of homicide in 2020 were young, between 15 and 34 years old; the number of homicide victims in this age group rose from about 900 in 2019 to 1,175 in 2020, a 31 percent rise.

Firearms were the most common instrument of death, and the number of homicides involving guns rose 35 percent last year, the state data shows. Extending another long-standing trend: Males were five times as likely to be the victims of homicide as

*Originally published as Phillip Reese, "Homicides Surge in California Amid Covid Shutdowns of Schools, Youth Programs," *Kaiser Health News*, May 17, 2021. Reprinted with permission of the publisher. *Kaiser Health News* is a nonprofit news service covering health issues. It is an editorially independent program of the Kaiser Family Foundation that is not affiliated with Kaiser Permanente.

females. The number of male victims rose 30 percent in 2020, compared with a 14 percent rise in female victims.

The increase in deadly violence played out across large swaths of the state, urban and rural, and was keenly felt in the San Francisco Bay Area. Among California's 10 most populous counties, the sharpest increases were reported in Alameda County, where homicides rose 57 percent, followed by Fresno (44%), Sacramento (36%) and Los Angeles (32%). Only one of the 10 most populous counties—Contra Costa—saw a decline in homicides last year.

Law enforcement officials and criminologists said an increase in conflict among young adults, particularly those in street gangs, was a significant factor in the violence. They noted that schools and sports programs shut down as Covid-19 surged, as did large numbers of community and nonprofit programs that provide support, recreational outlets and intervention services for at-risk youth.

"They were bored," said Reynaldo Reaser, executive director of Reclaiming America's Communities Through Empowerment (R.A.C.E.), which offers sports leagues, gang mediation and youth development in impoverished neighborhoods of South Los Angeles. "And so, having nothing to do—no programs, no sports, no facilities open—the only thing they could focus on is each other."

Reaser runs a dynamic youth softball league that typically would draw more than 600 players and spectators during Sunday play, he said, many of them young gang members. But those games and other programs were curtailed during the Covid pandemic.

Terrell Williams, an 18-year-old who lives in the West Athens area of South Los Angeles, said he spent many nights doing "delinquent stuff" before Reaser's program changed his life. He said many of his peers felt cooped up and restless during the pandemic lockdowns, which contributed to an increase in violence.

"Covid tended to, I guess, make people not want to stay inside the house, and drove them outside more towards each other," he said.

Jorja Leap, a UCLA anthropologist and expert in gangs, violence and trauma, echoed that theme, saying the restrictions on youth intervention programs and other healthy activities played "a huge role" in the rise in violence.

"The sports after school—football, basketball, whatever it might be—all that is stopped," said Leap, a faculty member at UCLA's Luskin School of Public Affairs. "So, frankly, you got a lot of adolescent and young adult energies out there."

Leap said young adults were particularly vulnerable to the mental toll of the pandemic. "They finally get programs; they have people interested in them. And then, it's all of a sudden withdrawn," she said.

Pandemic-fueled anxiety and isolation corresponded with a huge increase in gun sales, which Leap said may also explain some of the increase in homicides. "I am worried about how easy it has been to get a gun during such a crisis time in America," she said.

"It's not 'Pick one factor,'" she added. "All of these factors reinforce each other."

David Robinson is the sheriff in Kings County, a largely rural county in Southern California that registered 15 homicides in 2020, up from four in 2019. He is also president of the California State Sheriffs' Association, giving him a wide lens on a difficult year.

Robinson agreed that an increase in gang activity and the "mental impact" of telling young adults they had to stay indoors likely contributed to the violence. But separately, he cited the toll the pandemic took on police agencies. Many officers fell ill with Covid, forcing their agencies to reduce patrols and other crime prevention efforts.

The mass protests that followed George Floyd's murder by a Minneapolis police officer last May also diverted resources, said Robinson. And the anger directed at police made it tougher for some officers to do their jobs.

"When there's this call to defund police, it has an impact on the mentality of the men and women doing the job," he said, adding that constant criticism can cause officers to "become more reactive than proactive."

Robinson echoed other law enforcement officers in noting that thousands of inmates were released early from state prisons and county jails during the pandemic to stem Covid outbreaks. He said he thinks research eventually will show a correlation with the surge in homicides.

Leap disagreed. "If you get two shoplifting charges, it's a felony," she said. "That's who they're releasing. They're not releasing people from death row."

With mass vaccinations taking place across the state and nation, more places are reopening and young adults have more options to engage in something positive. But Leap said it will take a broad effort to bolster jobs and education, along with short-term intervention aimed at those still hurting from the pandemic, to improve the social conditions that contributed to the increase in homicides.

"As much as we've never dealt with a global pandemic in modern times, we've never dealt with the aftermath of a global pandemic," she said.

Reaser, in Los Angeles, is nonetheless optimistic. After a year of shutdowns, his youth softball league is starting up again. Finally, instead of trying to work out conflicts over the phone or online, Reaser can get young adult rivals to talk, face to face, and bond in a positive way.

"I really think that a lot of programs will open up," he said. "A lot of violence will slow down."

Methodology: This story draws on data from three sources. The data from these sources matches closely, but not precisely. Cause of death and population figures for 1979 through 2018 come from the federal Centers for Disease Control and Prevention. Cause of death figures for 2019 and 2020 come primarily from the California Department of Public Health and are based on death certificates. The exception is 2019 data for eight largely rural counties with few homicides. CDPH did not publish specific 2019 homicide figures for those counties due to data privacy rules. For those counties, 2019 homicide data comes from the California Department of Justice.

This story was produced by KHN, which publishes California Healthline, an editorially independent service of the California Health Care Foundation.

52. Despite Pandemic, Trauma Centers See No End to "The Visible Virus of Violence"*

GILES BRUCE

CHICAGO—On an early March day at the beginning of the Covid-19 pandemic, the emergency room at the University of Chicago Medical Center teemed with patients.

But many weren't there because of the coronavirus. They were there because they'd been shot.

Gunshot victims account for most of the 2,600 adult trauma patients a year who come to this hospital on the city's sprawling South Side. And the pandemic hasn't dampened the flow.

"The visible virus of violence continues unabated," said trauma chief Dr. Selwyn Rogers Jr.

The Chicago hospital's experience mirrors what's happening at other metropolitan trauma units around the nation, where the number of patients seeking care for injuries caused by what's known as penetrating trauma—gunshot wounds or stabbings—appear to be holding steady, straining hospitals already busy fighting Covid-19.

The Hyde Park hospital's Level 1 trauma center has been bustling since it launched in May 2018. On that day in March, about a half-dozen gowned staffers in the unit—which is separated from the rest of the ER by a set of double doors—hurriedly worked on a patient who had just been brought in through the ambulance bay.

"We pretty much opened and became one of the busiest trauma centers in the city," Rogers said.

Much of that is because of its location, he said. The South Side of Chicago is home to busy expressways and vast manufacturing plants, but also some of the most violent neighborhoods in the city. About a third of the University of Chicago Medicine's adult trauma patients are gunshot victims, Rogers said.

The volume has remained steady despite the city and state issuing a stay-at-home order March 21 in response to the coronavirus pandemic. In fact, Rogers said, domestic violence incidents appear to be on the rise as people shelter in place.

"It's not surprising that penetrating trauma has kind of stayed stable," said Dr.

*Originally published as Giles Bruce, "Despite Pandemic, Trauma Centers See No End to 'The Visible Virus of Violence,'" *Kaiser Health News*, May 14, 2020. Reprinted with permission of the publisher. *Kaiser Health News* is a nonprofit news service covering health issues. It is an editorially independent program of the Kaiser Family Foundation that is not affiliated with Kaiser Permanente.

Kenji Inaba, trauma chief for the Los Angeles County-USC Medical Center. "One could surmise there's a lot of potential for this: people being at home, in close contact with others. There's still potential for that human-on-human interaction to occur."

Trauma Care Affected Everywhere

Overall trauma statistics appear to be on the decline nationally, driven by a decrease in blunt trauma from fewer car crashes as people drive less during the pandemic, said Jennifer Ward, president of the Trauma Center Association of America.

"You would expect that to be down," she said. "Less people are going out. You would expect them to be doing less dangerous things than they're doing on other days, less traffic, things like that."

But injuries from gunshots and stab wounds are not dropping.

"As far as domestic violence, I think communities are in a heightened state of awareness," said Kathleen Martin, a board member for the American Trauma Society. Also "gun sales are up. People are looking at protecting themselves."

These trends are playing out across the nation.

At the Los Angeles trauma center, early spring is generally quieter than other times of year. Inaba, the trauma chief, said the unit usually has about 60 to 70 patients weekly with blunt injuries, such as those caused by car or construction accidents. That number has recently been down to as low as 10 to 25 cases as fewer people are driving and working.

But the number of gunshot and stabbing victims has effectively remained static—and maybe even ticked up a bit—hovering around 10 to 15 cases a week, Inaba said.

"Trauma is an interesting thing," he said. "Here at USC, we have for weeks now stopped all of our elective surgeries. This is one specialty you can't stop. We need to have surgeons available 24/7."

At Houston's Memorial Hermann-Texas Medical Center, which has been called the busiest trauma center in the country, blunt trauma cases dropped by about 5 percent while penetrating trauma incidents rose by roughly 3 percent in the three weeks after the city started its March 16 shutdown, according to trauma chief Dr. Michelle McNutt. Although she has anecdotally seen cases of intrafamily violence, she said, it's too early to have solid data showing whether domestic violence is up.

Metropolitan Family Services, a Chicago-area nonprofit with locations on the South Side, has had a steady number of domestic violence victims seeking services, according to spokesperson Bridget Hatch.

"There's just less mobility for victims," said Melanie MacBride, a legal aid attorney with the nonprofit. "People are down to one income or no income. Even when you're in a domestic violence situation, that might make you more reticent to upend your situation."

Renata Stiehl, who supervises domestic violence court advocacy for Metropolitan Family Services, said the stay-at-home orders and economic stress could exacerbate tensions and make it harder to report cases before they escalate.

"It's really like a forced hostage situation," Stiehl said. "When you have these ingredients and you have someone who has the propensity to commit this type of abuse, you're creating the perfect environment for it to thrive."

Stiehl noted that in Cook County, however, accusers are now able to file and have remote court hearings for orders of protection.

And neighbors may be more likely to call the police about a domestic disturbance because they're home to hear it.

Pandemic's Toll on Trauma Staff

As trauma center staffers continue to treat injuries inflicted by violence, they are also being pulled in other directions because of the pandemic.

Trauma surgeons are often certified in critical care, so they're helping pulmonologists with Covid-19 patients. Trauma nurses are assisting in now overwhelmed intensive care units. Trauma data collectors have instead been asked to help compile coronavirus statistics.

To soak up the overflow demand, pediatric trauma units are increasing the age limits of patients they treat from the usual 18 to 21. The pandemic has also forced other changes for trauma patients. Family members generally can't visit their traumatically injured loved ones because of the coronavirus. Violence-prevention activities have been limited by the outbreak.

Even though protective gear has been hard to come by doctors and nurses in the trauma centers are having to outfit themselves with personal protective equipment for every patient. "We have to assume they're Covid-positive until proven otherwise," Martin said. Trauma staffers are so specialized that if any of them get infected, it can set the whole unit back.

Dr. Brian Williams, a University of Chicago trauma surgeon, said he and his colleagues also work to reduce their patients' infection risk, putting masks on them when they arrive and housing them in an ICU separate from the one used for treating Covid-19.

"It's as if nothing has changed as far as the volume and acuity of the traumatic injuries we are seeing," he said. "What has changed is how we approach our job in taking care of patients who come in and making sure patients and health care workers are mutually protected without diminishing the level of care we provide."

Some doctors fear the situation could get worse.

In Cleveland, Dr. Glen Tinkoff, who heads trauma for University Hospitals and sits on the board of the American Trauma Society, said that although his system's trauma volume has been down about 10 percent lately, he expects that number to go in the opposite direction once sheltering-in-place restrictions begin to be lifted.

"We'll see a spike as desperation, despair and hopelessness increase," he predicted. "There's a lot of people out of work. I fear that. You can sense the desperation around the city right now. People are wandering. You see individuals that are just kind of looking for trouble now on the streets."

A septuagenarian was recently brought to the hospital after being beaten with a baseball bat at an ATM, Tinkoff said.

He noted that while shooting injuries were down initially in Cleveland, he doesn't believe that will continue there or anywhere in America.

"You're going to see many of us be very busy as the spring and summer months start to come upon us," he said. "The aftermath is going to be tough. I hope I'm wrong."

54. Federalism and Its Discontents

*Guns, Germs and Insurrection**

ALAN H. KENNEDY

Has federalism failed? Donald F. Kettl answers in the affirmative in his book The Divided States of America: Why Federalism Doesn't Work, and regarding inadequate responses to the Covid-19 pandemic, in his Public Administration Review article, "States Divided: The Implications of American Federalism for Covid-19." Kettl argues that federalism causes inequalities stemming from policy differences between states. In this article, I go further than Kettl, finding evidence of failures of federalism not only in the context of Covid-19, but also in how federal inaction on guns caused jurisdictional externalities and how Electoral College flaws underpinned the insurrection.

Federalism and Gun Policy

Alexander Hamilton wrote in 1787, in, "Federalist No. 1: General Introduction," that the system of federalism framed in the new Constitution would avoid another, "Unequivocal experience of the inefficiency of the subsisting federal government." Hamilton was wrong. The inability of Congress to enact any meaningful laws designed to prevent gun violence, even after successive mass shootings in recent years, reflects systemic failure of federalism with deadly consequences. A century later, Woodrow Wilson observed in a seminal article, "The Study of Administration," that it is difficult to, "Run a constitution," efficiently if Congress abdicates the legislative branch's responsibility to enact legislation that allows execution of tasks necessary to protect the public.

Paralysis of Congress on what Joshua Newman and Brian Head termed a "Wicked problem," in a 2017 article, "The National Context of Wicked Problems," is the opposite of good governance. In the absence of congressional action, state and local governments enacted a patchwork of gun laws that vary in their aims and effectiveness. Some jurisdictions banned assault rifles, imposed magazine limits and passed "red flag" laws, while other jurisdictions made it easier to buy, sell and transport guns. The consequences of disparate gun laws have included both legal and illegal movement of guns across state

---

*Originally published as Alan H. Kennedy, "Federalism and Its Discontents: Guns, Germs and Insurrection," *PA Times*, https://patimes.org/federalism-and-its-discontents-guns-germs-and-insurrection/ (February 28, 2021). Reprinted with permission of the publisher.

and city borders, resulting in deaths from guns that originated in places with fewer restrictions. In short, federalism has spawned havoc with regard to gun policy.

Federalism and Covid-19 Policy

Inadequate national and state responses to the Covid-19 pandemic in the United States, where more than 400,000 people have perished from the novel coronavirus, have been exacerbated by systemic failures similar to the failures which have plagued American gun policy for decades. As Kettl noted in, "States Divided," in 2020, former President Donald Trump and Congress mostly left decisions regarding how to respond to the pandemic to the states, some of which in turn left decisions to individual cities. Such decisions included whether to mandate the wearing of masks, whether to restrict public institution and private business capacities to enforce social distancing, whether to require testing and contact tracing and whether to mandate Covid-19 vaccinations.

Due to inaction by the federal government, with even Covid-19 relief packages subjected to avoidable delays and partisan bickering, governors, mayors and health departments became key actors. Some governors based their decisions on pandemic trends, while other responses to the spread of Covid-19 were based on ideology or business considerations, leading to variation between local jurisdictions more aligned with partisan pressures than with scientific evidence. This resulted in increased inequalities along racial and class lines exacerbated by jurisdictional policy differences. According to Kettl, governors resorted to, "Accepted patterns of the political culture and policy decisions," as former President Donald Trump downplayed the pandemic as a "hoax."

Federalism and Incitement of Insurrection

Evidence of failure of federalism appears not only with regard to jurisdictional disparities in gun policy and disparate responses to the Covid-19 pandemic but also in Electoral College flaws that contributed to the insurrection incited by Trump. After losing dozens of legal challenges to the 2020 presidential election, supporters of Trump stormed the United States Capitol on January 6, 2021, in a violent bid to stop Congress and former Vice President Mike Pence from approving results from the Electoral College. As a presidential elector for President Joe Biden and Vice President Kamala Harris, I intervened in a lawsuit by Republican would-be electors that encouraged Pence to reject Democratic electors based on a contorted interpretation of Electoral College procedure.

The American Society for Public Administration stated that Trump, "Concretely and egregiously," violated his oath, "As he exhorted a mob to disrupt the constitutionally mandated certification of the Electoral College vote." ASPA noted that Trump even pressured, "Public servants to commit election fraud," which the Electoral College, enabled by Trump, offered multiple paths to victory despite losing nationwide by seven million votes. A national popular vote, instead of the arcane Electoral College, would have made it more difficult for Trump and his supporters to bring legal challenges and would better reflect the will of the voters. Trump's impeachable actions mark an extraordinary break from existing constitutional processes that resulted in deadly consequences.

Rethinking Federalism

In sum, evidence of failures of federalism are apparent in jurisdictional externalities, inequalities and undemocratic outcomes in the context of gun policy, Covid-19 response and insurrection. Fortunately, these disparities have drawn renewed consideration of the systemic problems with American federalism. Unfortunately, solutions have proven elusive due to entrenched interests. For scholars of public administration, the need for systemic changes to address what Hamilton might have viewed as, "Inefficiency of the subsisting federal government," should motivate more examination of jurisdictional disparities and inequalities arising from the failures of federalism.

55. Keeping Our Neighbors Safe*

Sarah Sweeney

Over the past year there has been a significant uptick in gun related violence across the county, which has led me to wonder, where does public administration have the opportunity to make a difference? According to a report by NBC news, just this year alone there have been 160 shootings from January to April, compared to 90 shootings during the same time in 2020 that included loss of life of at least 4 individuals per event. As pandemic related fears of safety, tighter gun control laws and changes in policing measures rise, so too has the sale of handguns across America. As public administrators it is our duty to ensure an informed public understanding of the rights and responsibilities of gun owners and to protect our vulnerable neighbors at the same time. It is vital that we have secure gun laws that both uphold the amendment rights of our communities within reasonable limits and also maintain secure operation of those weapons for the safety of all.

Greater access to handguns, especially to first time or untrained owners, can often lead to increased incidents of violence and suicide; especially during times of high stress, anxiety and depression. During the pandemic, where there has been an increase in unemployment, poor health indicators and harder-to-access support services, there has also been higher rates of domestic violence and suicides, as people have become more isolated, angry and frustrated with their circumstances. According to the Coalition to Stop Gun Violence, merely having a gun in the home immediately increases the likelihood it will be used, whether it is for self-defense or self-inflicted injury. These are some the stories we have seen in the news: curious children exploring cabinets or closets at home and finding a handgun, bullied youth who see no other option than retaliation with force and domestic violence victims reaching for their only hope of self-defense. An astonishing 60 percent of deaths by gun are self-inflicted suicides; staggering numbers such as this are avoidable with targeted policy and legislative work through which we can make a difference.

As public administrators, it is important to explore how we can have impacts against growing numbers of gun violence across America, and part of that work involves addressing drivers of inequity in our communities; poverty, income inequality, under-performing schools and under-resourced public services. Working toward improving access to services, quality of life for neglected communities and improved health outcomes, as well as interrupting domestic violence trends are all vital to this process.

*Originally published as Sarah Sweeney, "Keeping Our Neighbors Safe," 55, *PA Times*, https://patimes.org/-keeping-our-neighbors-safe/ (May 8, 2021). Reprinted with permission of the publisher.

These are the prime areas in which we can have significant impacts, and as policymakers and community leaders it is our duty to make our communities safer for everyone. Even if this means limiting access to deadly weaponry by those looking to gain greater access. Some of the safety measures that have been put in place to protect citizens from gun violence include universal background checks, gun licensing, banning assault style weapons and outlawing the sale of high-capacity magazines. Increasing safety measures around gun control could have a direct impact on decreasing the number of gun-related deaths in our nation, and it is up to us to direct those conversations and provide education on how we can do this together.

If we are to draw a comparison to something so simple as becoming a licensed driver, we know that to get behind the wheel of a vehicle we must study traffic laws, pass a written and driving test, obtain insurance and register our vehicles in a timely manner. So why is it such a stretch to understand and implement guidance and laws related to safe gun handling and ownership? Through increased regulations we could potentially decrease the incidents of gun related violence and better facilitate safe gun handling, and ensure healthy, safe communities moving forward. We have the opportunity as advocates and leaders to encourage those in positions of power to move toward increased oversight of gun control. We must continue to fight for our communities and their safety, and make potentially unpopular but realistic decisions when it comes to regulating access to deadly weapons. We live in a time of great uncertainty and have the unique opportunity to make our mark on the future of legislation. I would thus encourage you to advocate for the safety of your neighbors and those you represent.

PART III

The Future

56. What Makes a "Smart Gun" Smart*

Donald Sebastian

Every time a toddler accidentally shoots a friend or family member, a teen kills himself via gunshot or a shooter perpetrates an act of mass violence, public discussion circles back to "smart gun" technology. The concept has roots in a 1995 National Institute of Justice (NIJ) study that recommended a technology-based approach to reduce the incidence of police officers killed in gun-grabs by assailants. More recently, President Obama's message on gun violence included specific recommendations on federal actions designed to promote the development and commercialization of electronic gun-safety systems.

The term "smart gun" has been embraced by the popular press as a catchall for all forms of electronic personalized safety technology. The idea is to make sure a gun can be fired only by its authorized user. But the different scenarios in which a gun could be inappropriately discharged call for fundamentally different safety systems.

The metaphor of a common door lock is a useful way to think about the various technological approaches. The key serves as the personal identifier. The pin tumblers that recognize the key inside the lock serve as the authenticator. And the latch serves as the block. All electronic gun safety systems must accomplish all three of these basic functions—identify authorized shooters, authenticate their credentials and then release the block to the firing mechanism.

How one satisfies those needs is subject to the performance constraints of the application environment and the physical constraints of the weapon itself. These differences create distinct branches on the family tree of personalized-weapons technology.

Proximity Sensors—Can You Hear Me Now?

One group of solutions owes its heritage to the NIJ study focused on protecting police weapons from takeaway during a close quarters struggle. It suggested a token-based proximity sensor using Radio Frequency Identification (RFID). A number of working RFID prototype guns have been demonstrated, beginning with Colt's 1996 handgun and including Triggersmart, iGun M-2000 and the Armatix iP1.

In a badge, wristband or ring, a user wears a passive RFID tag, like those embedded

*Originally published as Donald Sebastian, "What Makes a 'Smart Gun' Smart," *The Conversation*, https://theconversation.com/what-makes-a-smart-gun-smart-52853 (January 11, 2016). Reprinted with permission of the publisher.

in products to prevent shoplifting. It's the "token" and serves as the key in the front door metaphor. Like a physical key, it can be duplicated or shared. What matters is possession of the token, not the identity of the token holder.

A wireless RFID reader is built into the gun and serves the role of authenticator. It generates a signal that activates the RFID tag to respond with an embedded code. If there's a match, the electromechanical components unblock the weapon firing system and the gun functions normally. The response time of these systems is generally dependent on the choice of electromechanical components used in the blocking system (e.g., servomotors, solenoids, shape memory metals), but are generally less than half a second. By design, the gun can remain active as long as there is a signal link, or in some configurations as long as pressure sensors detect the gun is being held.

If the tag is too far away from the transmitter to self-activate and respond, then it's like losing your key to the front door—the gun remains locked down. The Armatix iP1, for example, specifies a range of 15 inches. If you try to spoof the transponder with a signal that does not contain the individual code, it's like using the wrong key—it may fit the slot but cannot be turned because it does not match the tumblers—and the gun remains locked down.

Various designs interfere with the mechanical firing mechanism in different places—from trigger bar to firing pin. There are also different technologies including solenoid actuators, shape memory alloy-based components and even electronic firing systems that serve as the deadbolt to be released upon receiving an authentication system. The details are proprietary to the individual products on the market and reflect design trade-offs in power consumption, free space to accommodate components and response time.

Proximity of gun to token is not an absolute determinant of rightful possession during a close-quarters struggle. But the technology does offer simplicity of operation, easy weapons exchange across permitted users (i.e., partners) and reliably disables a weapon from use if the officer has been overpowered and the duty weapon taken.

Biometrics—Do I Know You?

The benefits of a token-based system in a street encounter become a liability in the home. The viability of the approach is wholly dependent on the owner securing the token where it cannot be accessed by denied users. But guns used for home protection are more likely to have token and weapon stored together to prevent any delay in the event of an intrusion. And anyone who has both the token and the weapon can fire it.

A second group of technologies evolved in response to child-safe handgun legislation adopted in New Jersey and Maryland in the early 2000s, designed to prevent unauthorized use of personal firearms stored in the home. Biometric authentication systems eliminate the physical token. Instead, a measurable physical characteristic of any authorized user becomes the key. It can't be taken without permission, counterfeit or otherwise transferred.

To date, fingerprints have been the primary attribute used in biometric systems. Kodiak Arms Intelligun and Safe Gun Technology's retrofit for rifles use fingerprint detection as a primary mode of security. If the fingerprint is the key, then the sensor and pattern matching software are the pin tumblers that perform the authentication function in these guns.

The most widely used sensor technology relies on capacitance imaging of the fingerprint. The variation in distance between the ridges and grooves of the finger and the sensor plate creates a distribution of electrical charge storage (capacitance) that can be measured in an array of conductor plates in the sensor. Other fingerprint sensors rely on infrared (thermal) imaging, and some use pressure detection to create a digital pattern that is a unique representation of the print.

The sensor software needs to be trained to store acceptable patterns that may represent different fingers of a single user or various fingers from multiple authorized users. After that, any pattern that doesn't match within some specified tolerance is rejected. The reliability of the authentication process is influenced by the resolution of the sensor, the extent and orientation of the exposed finger, and physical factors that can interfere with the mapping. For example, moisture on the finger can defeat a capacitive detector, cold fingers can reduce the reliability of thermal imaging, and dirt, paint or gloves can obscure the fingerprint beyond recognition.

There are other types of biometric security being explored. One prototype sponsored by NIJ adopted vascular biometrics that detect the blood vessel structure below the skin surface. An emerging class of biometrics are dynamic or behavioral and combine some element of individualized physicality amplified by learned patterns of behavior. For instance, voice identification combines the structure of one's vocal chords with the breath patterns of speech learned in infancy. Electronic signature authentication captures the speed and pressure of pen on LCD pad (and not the image of the signature) as the signer executes handwriting in a pattern ingrained early in life.

Over the last 15 years, our research team at NJIT has developed a gun safety system based on a novel behavioral biometric called Dynamic Grip Recognition™ (DGR). The team demonstrated that changes over time to the pressure pattern created on the grip of a handgun as one counter-braces the force of trigger pull were individual to the user, reproducible and measurable.

Our prototype detects grip patterns during the first 1/10th of a second of trigger pull and unlocks the weapon with no apparent lag to the shooter. Because DGR works during trigger pull of a properly held weapon, the approach can also reduce accidental firings during mishandling of a loaded weapon.

Reliability—Can I Trust You?

Reliability is always a concern raised in discussions of electronic gun safety systems.

The interior of a firing weapon is not a friendly environment for electronics, but there is now a sufficient history of ruggedized circuitry that failure rates of the underlying electronic hardware are orders of magnitude less than the predicted failure rates of the mechanical weapon (somewhere between 1 in 1000 and 1 in 10,000 depending on the precision and quality of the weapon).

Power is clearly a concern here, too. But advances in microprocessor technology and battery storage that have been driven by smart phones and portable electronics remove this issue as a show stopper. Motion detection and wake-up software can reduce battery drain during storage. Integrating the power supply to the ammunition clip and even charging by mechanical cycling are all ways to address power loss as a mode of failure.

In biometric systems, there is another element to consider: failure of the identification algorithm. Those are false negatives in which a rightful user is not recognized, or false positives in which an impostor is wrongly authenticated. The recognition rates for fingerprint detectors have been claimed to be as high as 99.99 percent (1 in 10,000 failure rate).

As the array of sensor technologies grows, one might expect a multisensor or multispectral approach to be the ultimate choice for biometric-based systems. These have the advantage of multiplying reliability rates when independent measures are used. For example, a fingerprint sensor with a 1-in-10,000 failure rate, coupled with a dynamic grip recognition with a failure rate of 1 in 1000, would produce a combined reliability of 1 in 10,000 × 1000 or 1 in 10,000,000.

Will We Ever Be Able to Buy One?

Throughout the 20-year-long discussion of "smart guns," the topic has been a lightning rod for debate between pro- and anti-gun lobbies. But too often, there isn't substantive knowledge of the underlying technologies, their appropriate use and their design limitations.

Personalized weapons technology can make a contribution to reducing death and injury from accidental or unauthorized weapons use. It is not a panacea—the technology can't stop shootings like Virginia Tech, Aurora or Sandy Hook, where lawfully purchase weapons were used. But it can be an option for gun buyers to ensure their weapons never fall into the wrong hands.

The existing platforms show that smart guns are not science fiction and could be a commercial reality much sooner than later. A recent survey by the NIJ identified 13 different personalized weapon systems, at least three of which were deemed to be in commercial preproduction. Obama's initiative could be an important step to accelerate development and promote private sector investment necessary to mature these technologies to the point of reliability and affordability that will spur consumer adoption.

57. Do Americans Want to Buy "Smart" Guns?*

Lacey Wallace

Recently legislators and special interest groups have pushed for greater availability of "smart" guns as a safety and crime-reduction tool. Then-President Barack Obama called for more research into "smart" gun technology in January 2016, and that April issued a memorandum calling for government-led research into smart guns as well as potential use by some federal agencies.

"Smart gun" refers to firearms that include some sort of safety device designed to make sure that the gun can be fired only by an authorized user. These safety devices include fingerprint recognition, wearable "tags" that a gun can recognize and other similar features. Smart guns are not yet widely available on the market.

They are not a new concept. In the 1970s, Magna-Trigger marketed a magnetic add-on feature for revolvers. This prevented the gun from firing unless the user was wearing a specially designed magnetic ring. Due to controversy and politics, however, smart guns have been very slow to come to market. Smart gun manufacturers and gun retailers have faced boycotts and protests in years past.

But Would Americans Actually Buy Smart Guns?

My own research focuses heavily on gun purchasing and teen gun carrying. Previous research on Americans' willingness to purchase smart guns has found mixed results. So I set out to try to better understand how Americans feel about smart guns and why they might feel that way.

Past Research Doesn't Tell Much

There isn't very much research about attitudes toward smart guns, and the limited research that does exist has drawn different conclusions.

For instance, one study in 2015 by Julia Wolfson at Johns Hopkins and colleagues at

*Originally published as Lacey Wallace, "Do Americans Want to Buy 'Smart' Guns?," *The Conversation*, https://theconversation.com/do-americans-want-to-buy-smart-guns-71765 (January 29, 2017). Reprinted with permission of the publisher.

Harvard and Northeastern University asked respondents about their willingness to purchase a "childproof" gun. Results showed that most Americans were willing to buy this type of gun, with high interest from people self-identifying as liberals, people who do not currently own guns and those with children in the home.

Another study by the National Shooting Sports Foundation (NSSF) in 2013 asked respondents a similar question, but found that Americans were largely against purchasing smart firearms.

So why did these studies find such different results?

Past research has struggled with a number of problems. I examined existing studies as part of my own research, and found that none specifically ask whether a person would choose a smart gun or a traditional firearm if both were available. Instead, most just ask whether individuals feel favorable toward smart guns or willing to purchase them. With such a controversial issue, there is the risk that certain groups will use question wording or sampling strategy to sway results.

I also found that the existing studies define the term smart gun very differently. Some use the term "childproof" while others do not. This was a key difference between the Wolfson and NSSF studies.

The difference in terminology makes it difficult to compare results across studies, and it may explain why results are so different. Last, existing studies often look only at a few characteristics of respondents. This makes it unclear how different subgroups of Americans might feel.

What Do People Really Think About Smart Guns?

In February 2016, I conducted a nationwide web survey of 261 gun owners and 263 nonowners. My sample was located by Qualtrics, a survey and market research company.

Although my survey was not nationally representative, my sample was very similar to the U.S. population on characteristics like age, political leaning and income.

In my survey, I asked: If you were purchasing a firearm, and this [smart gun] technology were available, which type of firearm would you purchase? Respondents could choose from four answers: a smart gun; a traditional firearm; say they were unsure; or say they would never consider purchasing a firearm. To be consistent with the Wolfson study, I chose to give respondents a smart gun definition without the term "childproof."

I found that current gun owners were significantly less likely to favor smart guns over other firearms than nonowners. About 46 percent of gun owners preferred a smart gun compared to 62 percent of nonowners. Males and individuals with pro-gun attitudes were less likely to prefer smart guns to traditional firearms. Overall, males were less than half as likely as females to prefer a smart gun, and male gun owners were about a third as likely as female gun owners to prefer smart guns.

Pro-gun individuals agreed with statements like "My community would be safer if more people owned guns" or "People who own guns are more patriotic than people who do not own guns."

But not all gun owners had the same views. Gun owners who also have a history of victimization, have moderate political views or live in the Northeast were all more likely to prefer smart guns.

Education or income level, race, marital status, presence of children in the home and willingness to discuss smart guns with a doctor had no significant association with willingness to buy a smart gun over a traditional firearm.

Nonowners were much more likely to support smart guns than gun owners. However, they were also more likely to have no preference for gun type or to say they would never consider purchasing a gun.

What Does This Mean?

Overall, I found that gun owners and people who were more "pro-gun" were less likely to choose a smart gun over a traditional firearm. This is important because estimates suggest that a small number of Americans own most of the guns in the U.S. A 2015 unpublished survey from Harvard and Northeastern University estimated that just 3 percent of Americans owned half of the nation's guns. Other estimates suggest that gun owners today own more guns per household than they did in years past. So those likely to go out and purchase a firearm—current gun owners—may not be willing to choose a smart gun.

There is no national database of all gun owners. This means we can only estimate how many people actually own guns, and what kinds, so most estimates are based on surveys or criminal background checks. And in my own study, respondents said they felt uncomfortable sharing information about whether they owned a gun with strangers and people they did not know very well. For this reason, it is possible that individuals underreport owning a gun or how many guns they own. Without a national list of all gun owners to double-check, we rely on additional research with other samples, like federal background checks, to make sure the patterns we see are consistent.

We need more studies with larger, nationally representative samples and more detailed questions about smart guns. However, my study sheds light on how subgroups of Americans feel about the issue. Not all gun owners or nonowners feel the same way about smart guns. Support is not evenly divided by political party. American attitudes toward smart guns are complex and do not necessarily follow the patterns we might expect.

58. License and Registration, Please

How Regulating Guns Like Cars Could Improve Safety*

Keith Guzik *and* Gary T. Marx

In the midst of the Senate's failure to agree on measures designed to tighten controls around the sales of firearms, a new idea is emerging.

Last week, U.S. Representative Jim Hines, a Democrat from Connecticut, appeared on "The Daily Show with Trevor Noah" and said, "we ought to probably test people and make sure there is as much licensing and regulation around a gun as there is around an automobile."

He is not the first political figure to suggest this idea. Before the shooting in Orlando, President Obama proposed the same approach at a town hall meeting earlier this year:

…traffic fatalities have gone down drastically in my lifetime. And part of it is technology. And part of it is that the National Highway Safety Administration does research and they figure out seatbelts really work. And then we pass laws to make sure seatbelts are fastened.

Regulating guns like cars is an interesting idea. And, it wouldn't require congressional approval.

Compared to the measures proposed in Congress, which amount to prohibitions against socially undesirable persons like terrorists and people who suffer from mental illness, a regulatory approach goes further by focusing on the technology itself. It would create a regulatory framework promoting responsible use of guns.

As sociologists who have studied the relationship between technologies and social control in a variety of settings, we believe the history of the automobile shows how such a strategy can make dangerous objects safer, while also preserving private property, individual liberty and personal responsibility.

How Cars Were Made Safe

The motor vehicle, like the firearm, is a quintessential American object. It expresses values of freedom, individuality and power. And like guns, automobiles were once a major threat to public health and safety.

*Originally published as Keith Guzik and Gary T. Marx, "License and Registration, Please: How Regulating Guns Like Cars Could Improve Safety," *The Conversation*, https://theconversation.com/license-and-registration-please-how-regulating-guns-like-cars-could-improve-safety-61257 (June 26, 2016). Reprinted with permission of the publisher.

Early vehicles regularly struck horses and pedestrians in the streets, gave birth to roving criminals like Bonnie and Clyde, and became common settings for sexual assaults. But through a combination of traffic codes, civil liability laws, insurance policies and administrative requirements, the automobile was eventually made manageable.

Subsequent eras of reform have addressed traffic safety in additional ways by targeting vehicle design (seatbelts and airbags), drunk drivers and distracted driving. As a result, the rate of traffic fatalities has decreased from more than 15 per 100 million vehicle miles traveled in the 1930s to just above 1 per 100 million today.

Regulating Guns Like Cars

What would regulating guns like cars look like?

In some regards, we are already there. Operating a firearm, like operating a motor vehicle, requires a license in many jurisdictions. Certain types of criminal offenses—domestic violence in the case of firearms, drinking and driving in the case of automobiles—can result in a suspension or revocation of that license. These rules focus on the competency of users.

But, the regulation of cars goes beyond this by establishing a larger web of regulatory relationships around the technology itself.

As anyone who owns and operates a car knows, it must also be titled to establish ownership, registered to allow use of public roads and insured to protect owners and victims in the case of vehicle accidents. These requirements create an incentive for responsible conduct by drivers looking to avoid traffic tickets and insurance premium increases. It also helps finance a network of public and private entities, including police officers and insurance companies, to help keep track of cars.

Trips to the DMV notwithstanding, the regulatory burden of owning and operating a car has done little to diminish Americans' love affair with the automobile.

Regulating guns like cars would thus require a new set of regulations that would reward the responsible purchase, possession and operation of guns, and build the regulatory framework to enforce it.

This is a more tried and true approach to managing dangerous technologies than the simplistic prohibitionist logic of simply keeping guns away from those we categorize as "the bad and the mad."

But, Guns Aren't Cars

Some challenges to such an approach can easily be anticipated.

Legally speaking, gun rights supporters would point to the Second Amendment and argue that no mention of motorized vehicles is made in the country's founding document. But the Fourth Amendment does pronounce "the right of people to be secure in their persons, houses, papers, and effects, against unreasonable searches and seizure," a protection arguably violated by ordinary traffic stops. We as a society have still been able to craft a legal framework that balances this individual liberty with the public interest in vehicle safety.

There are practical differences, too. Cars are highly visible, which facilitates their control. Handguns are largely invisible, with their invisibility increasingly protected by law. This makes their regulation more difficult.

Cars on private property are not subject to state regulations. Yet, most gun deaths take place at home in the form of suicides. That means regulating guns like cars would likely not impact the greatest harm caused by firearms.

A Way Around Gridlock?

Regulating guns like cars would provide additional safety against guns in the public spaces where the worst mass shootings have occurred—schools, the workplace, churches, dance halls and movie theaters.

Perhaps the best endorsement for regulating guns like cars is that it wouldn't require congressional approval. States have the latitude to craft the requirements for owning and operating vehicles that suit them best. They could do the same with guns. Following the Supreme Court's recent decision to not hear a challenge to Connecticut's ban on assault weapons, states should be emboldened to try more innovative approaches on gun control.

Representative Hines and President Obama are thinking outside of the political box in addressing gun violence. Regulating guns like cars would be neither perfect nor easy. But as Congress continues to debate measures that largely look past the weapons themselves, it would be a welcome move in the national effort to prevent the next Columbine, Virginia Tech, Aurora, Newtown, Charleston, San Bernardino or Orlando.

59. People Who Shoot Risk Unhealthy Levels of Lead Exposure*

Mark A.S. Laidlaw, Andrew Ball, Brian Gulson, Gabriel Filippelli, *and* Howard Walter Mielke

A gun is a dangerous weapon for obvious reasons. But there are less obvious risks to those who use them. New research shows people who shoot, for work or leisure, risk lead poisoning.

Our just published review shows how exposure to lead from bullets, airborne particles in shooting ranges and other sources shows up in shooters' blood at levels we believe pose a health risk.

Who's at Risk?

Security personnel, police officers and members of the military who fire guns at shooting ranges for work, and members of the public who shoot at firing ranges for recreation, are at risk.

Large numbers of shooters are involved, particularly in the U.S., where there are about 16,000–18,000 indoor firing ranges. In the U.S., about one million law enforcement officers train regularly at indoor firing ranges each year and 20 million people practice target shooting as a leisure activity.

The Geological Survey calculated that in 2012 about 60,100 metric tons of lead were used in ammunition and bullets in the U.S. Given that lead is the dominant metal in bullets and primers (which initiates the combustion of gunpowder in the bullet cartridge), there are large numbers of people exposed by firing bullets.

It's difficult to estimate how many Australians shoot at ranges and are exposed to lead. While the Sporting Shooters Association of Australia says it has 180,000 members, not all use shooting ranges.

How Are Shooters Exposed to Lead?

Shooters are exposed to lead when firing lead bullets. The bullet primer is about 35 percent lead styphnate and lead dioxide (also known as lead peroxide). When a shooter

*Originally published as Mark A.S. Laidlaw, Andrew Ball, Brian Gulson, Gabriel Filippelli, and Howard Walter Mielke, "People Who Shoot Risk Unhealthy Levels of Lead Exposure," *The Conversation*, https://59.com/people-who-shoot-risk-unhealthy-levels-of-lead-exposure-68220 (April 5, 2017). Reprinted with permission of the publisher.

fires a bullet, lead particles and fumes originating from the primer discharge at high pressures from the gun barrel, very close to the shooter.

Shooters are also exposed to lead from the bullet itself as some parts disintegrate into fragments due to misalignments in the gun barrel. The extreme heat during the firing of a bullet results in some vaporization of these lead fragments.

Shooters inhale lead particles emitted during the firing of a gun, whether that's from the primer or the bullet itself. Once deposited in the lower respiratory tract, lead particles (and different chemical forms of lead) are almost completely absorbed into the bloodstream.

Lead dust from the shooting range also sticks to shooters' clothes and can potentially contaminate vehicles and homes. Shooters can also ingest lead particles by transferring them from their hands into their mouths when they smoke, eat or drink.

Shooters' blood lead levels tend to be higher the more bullets shot, the more lead in the air at shooting ranges and the increased caliber of weapon.

What Our Review Found

We reviewed 36 studies that measured blood lead levels at shooting ranges. The studies were from 15 countries, but most were from the U.S. About two-thirds of the studies looked at people who used shooting ranges for work.

We found blood lead levels of at least one of the participants in 31 of 36 studies had an elevated blood lead level. This means more than the current adult blood lead reference level of 5μg/dL, or 5 micrograms of lead per deciliter of blood, as recommended by the U.S. Centers for Disease Control and Prevention and National Institute of Occupational Safety and Health.

Importantly, we found elevated blood lead levels (greater than 5μg/dL) in shooters using both indoor and outdoor shooting ranges, consistent with the release of the fine-grained primer-based lead close to the shooter's face and body.

How Does Lead Affect the Body?

The U.S. National Toxicology Program reviewed the evidence for health effects associated with chronic lead exposure in adults and children at levels identified in our literature review.

They found such blood lead levels were associated with a range of neurological, psychiatric, fertility and heart problems.

While studies have not specifically investigated all these outcomes in shooters, it is biologically plausible these conditions are associated with raised blood levels resulting from exposure to lead at shooting ranges. But few studies have been conducted on the shooting population to be sure.

There is a particular risk to women of child-bearing age exposed to lead at firing ranges because of the uptake and storage of lead in the mother's bones where it substitutes for calcium.

This is a particular problem for pregnant women, because the fetus requires calcium from her bones. So the fetus could be exposed to the mother's lead stores during critical times in development. This could cause serious neurological disorders when born.

Female shooters can also pass on the lead exposure to their children through breast milk. Additionally, multiple studies have shown raised blood lead levels in children shooting guns at firing ranges due to direct exposure. Studies show raised blood levels in children are linked with range of health problems. These range from being inattentive, hyperactive and irritable, to delayed growth, decreased intelligence, and short-term memory loss.

How Do We Limit Lead Exposure?

The ultimate solution to protect the health of shooters is to replace all primers and bullets with lead-free substitutes, which are already available.

We recommend measures such as ensuring adequate exhaust ventilation and wet-cleaning of surfaces at firing ranges, requiring people who work at firing ranges to have their blood lead levels checked, and for similar testing for frequent shooters.

We also recommend shooters be aware of the risks of lead exposure and follow guidelines recommended by health organizations such as the Council of State and Territorial Epidemiologists or Safe Work Australia.ost in the clash of ideological soundbites.

60. Gunning for Understanding

*Facebook and the Gun Control Debate in America**

Maggie Callahan

The idea that a Facebook group could be used to forge consensus and mutual understanding of gun rights in the United States seems farfetched at best. Using a social media platform that has been charged with unraveling democracy to discuss one of the most divisive and salient issues in American politics appears almost destined for failure. This seemingly hopeless project, however, was undertaken by Advance Local who partnered with Spaceship Media, Newseum, Essential Partners, and Reveal from the Center for Investigative Reporting and Time with success.

Following the Parkland shooting in which 17 high school students were killed and 14 were injured, civil unrest over guns in America has been amplified to new heights. In 2018 alone, there were nearly 58,000 incidences of gun violence and 340 mass shootings in the United States, with nearly one mass shooting every day of the year. These deaths are executed by a weapon for which ownership is codified as an individual right in the American Bill of Rights. This incredibly divisive issue became the subject of Advance Local's ongoing mission to build mutual understanding across America in 2018 following the Parkland shooting. The title of this specific project was Guns, An American Conversation.

Twenty-one candidates were recruited for a two-day intense workshop at the Newseum in Washington, D.C. During this workshop, Essential Partners, a nonprofit specializing in building peaceful conflict resolution strategies and healthy relationships, taught selected candidates effective partner exercises dealing with how to relay their grievances and questions in ways that furthered and enriched the discussion.

These 21 candidates were joined by 130 other participants in a closed Facebook group. Advance Local selected candidates from a variety of backgrounds that spanned the full spectrum of opinion on the gun debate. 51 percent of these participants felt strongly for or against gun control, and the remaining 49 percent represented viewpoints between these extremes from neutral to somewhat supporting or against gun control. Participants included victims of gun violence, teenagers, mothers, ex-offenders, lawyers and hunters.

The group discussion relied primarily on the methods and strategies of dialogue journalism. This method uses journalism to better democracy by opening a platform for

*Originally published as Maggie Callahan, "Gunning for Understanding: Facebook and the Gun Control Debate in America," *PA Times*, https://patimes.org/gunning-for-understanding-facebook-and-the-gun-control-debate-in-america/ (April 30, 2019). Reprinted with permission of the publisher.

civic communication, which reduces polarization by creating a structured environment. This structured environment emphasizes the need for participants to express their view without the insults that typify polarizing political debates.

In addition to dialogue journalism, strong moderation was used to maintain peaceful, thoughtful discussion. Seven moderators were chosen to build personal relationships through introductions with the outcome each hoped for during the discussion. Then, moderators worked to establish guidelines on etiquette and the management of "explosive comments." This process involved quieting some viewpoints and amplifying others while refraining from making or deleting too many comments. This moderation technique allowed for insightful discussion in which each participant was given the tools to voice their opinion without being talked over or down to.

The initiative achieved its intended effect: creating a deeper understanding of differing views regardless of personal opinion. Participants, though not always reaching an agreement on the issue, and with 3 members removed from the group, were largely able to understand opposing viewpoints. The process also debunked the stereotyping that is common for opposing position members. For example, a Latina member of the NRA served to debunk the typical persona of an NRA member as old, white and male and demystified her position.

Mirroring efforts have been launched by participants following this discussion in their local communities across America, and the participants have created a book club to continue their discussion beyond gun control. The Facebook group connected geographically and ideologically distant viewpoints and enhanced mutual understanding in an unexpected and unprecedented way.

Guns, an American Conversation has served to demonstrate that technology can be used for noble aims in democratic participation. Facebook's ability to connect individuals who may have never otherwise met proved essential in humanizing and depolarizing the gun debate for participants. This project further highlights how accessible the tools of democratic participation are if citizens are gunning for understanding and have the tools to constructively moderate and discuss topics. Understanding is no more than one enlightened Facebook group away.

To learn more about this case visit https://participedia.net/en/cases/guns-american-conversation-0. To read more about other innovative applications of public participation visit, www.participedia.net.

Appendices

Appendix A

*Glossary of Gun Safety Terms and Acronyms**

Alan R. Roper

Action—The working mechanism of the firearm. This action includes items like the breech bolt, the frame, or the receiver.

AIWB—Appendix Inside the Waistband

Ammo—A slang abbreviation of ammunition

Ammunition—Projectiles that include a case, primer, powder, and a bullet.

AO—Adjustable Objective

A.R.—Arma-Lite Rifle (Not Assault Rifle)

Assault Rifle—Often used by the military or police, this is the technical term for a selective-fire rifle that fires reduced-power ammunition from a detachable magazine. Examples of an assault rifle include the AK-47 and M16 models.

ASR—Advanced Sniper Rifle

ATF—Bureau of Alcohol, Tobacco, Firearms and Explosives

Automatic—A firearm that offers the continuous feed of ammunition while depressing the trigger.

Backstraps—The rear part of the pistol grip. Some models of handguns, like Glocks, feature interchangeable backstraps.

Ballistics—The scientific study of the motion and effects of projectiles shot from firearms. Factors affecting ballistics include the trajectory, velocity, caliber, and barrel rifling relating to a shot.

BC—Ballistic Coefficient

Beaver-Tail—The rear of the grip of a gun that fits into the space between your thumb and forefinger.

Bench rests—A form of shooting and an accessory where competitors fire from fixed positions to get the best shot grouping on targets.

Bird-Shot—Referring to shot projectiles with diameters under .24-inches.

BJHP—Brass Jacketed Hollow Point

Black-Powder—The first form of firearm projectile repellant used in the firing of ammunition in antique guns.

---

*Published with permission of the author.

Blank Cartridges—These cartridges have primer and powder, but no projectile. They are common in movies and other faux applications for stuntwork.

Bluing—A blue or black finish to steel that occurs through exposure to an acid bath.

Boat-Tails—Bullets that feature tapered edges to improve flight efficiency and accuracy over distance.

Body Armor—Protective armor like Kevlar or steel plates to protect you from projectiles

Bolt Action—This is a type of action that fires one round at a time. After the bullet is fired, the empty shell is unloaded by the user manually pulling back on the bolt before loading another round into the chamber.

Bore—The interior of the barrel of the firearm.

Boxer Stance—Standing square in front of the target.

Breech—The rear of the barrels bore.

BT—Boat Tail

BTHP—Boat Tail Hollow Point

Buck Shot—Projectiles found in shotgun cartridges.

BUIS—Back Up Iron Sights

Bullet—The head of the cartridge, expelled through the barrel of the firearm.

Butt—The rear of a rifle or shotgun.

Caliber—The diameter of the projectile, expressed in hundredths of an inch.

Carbine—A type of semi-automatic rifle.

Casing—The brass cartridge that holds the primer, powder, and the projectile (bullet).

CCW—Concealed Carry Weapon

Chamber—The region of the barrel where the firing pin engages the ammunition.

Charging Handle—The rear of the AR-style rifle where you pull back to prime the weapon.

Choke—A compensator near the muzzle that disperses the energy of the shot.

Clear—An expression describing clearing the ammunition from the chamber and feed of the firearm.

Clip—Slang for the magazine.

CLL—Cowboy Lead Load

Cock—To charge the firearm and make it ready for firing.

Comb—The part of the stock for the shooter's chin rest.

Compensator—An accessory for the front of the pistol to reduce recoil.

Competency—Your knowledge and experience in handling forearms

CRO—Chief Range Officer

CT—Copper Tip

Dampeners—Accessories added to the stock of the rifle to absorb recoil shock.

Derringer—A short-barrel pistol named after Henry Derringer.

Discharge—To fire a live round through a handgun or rifle.

Double-Action—A trigger action that cocks and fires the firearm.

Double-barreled Shotgun—Shotguns feature dual side-by-side or over-and-under configurations. These are typically breakneck models that you load at the hilt.

Double-Set Trigger—One trigger cocks while the other fires.

Double-Stack—Magazines that stack bullets in a staggered arrangement instead of directly on top of each other allow more rounds per mag.

Double Tap—Two shots fired rapidly back-to-back in succession. Typically, the shooter doesn't aim at another target between shots.

Dry Fire—Discharging the firearm in an unloaded state with no ammunition in the chamber or feed.

Dud—A cartridge that fails to fire. Ammunition malfunctions can include hang-firs, misfire, and squib loads.

EDC—Everyday Carry

Ejector—The mechanism in the firearm that ejects the casing after firing the projectile.

EMJ—Enclosed Metal Jacket

Eyes and Ears—The necessary PPE for your time at the range—ear muffs and shooting glasses.

Feed—The part of the gun that moves the ammunition from the magazine to the chamber.

FFL—Federal Firearms License

Fiber Optics—A fluorescent front sight for handguns like Glocks.

Firearm—The term describes pistols, rifles, shotguns, and bolt-action rifles.

Firing Pin—The part of the trigger assembly that punches the cartridge, igniting the primer.

Flash Suppressor—This attachment lessens the flash of light as a round exits a gun's barrel by allowing hot air and gas to escape. It attaches directly to the end of a firearm's barrel.

Floating Barrels—A bedded barrel avoiding contact with the stock of the gun.

Floor Plates—The removable bottom of the magazine.

FMJ—Full Metal Jacket

FN—Flat Nose

FNEB—Flat Nose Enclosed Base

45 ACP—An abbreviation for the ammunition for a .45-caliber automatic colt pistol.

FP—Full Patched

FPS—Feet Per Second

Frame—The lower receiver of a handgun.

FTE—Failure to Eject

Gauge—The size of the bore of the barrel on a shotgun.

Glock—This is a series of popular semi-automatic, short recoil-operated pistols designed and produced by the Austrian company, Glock Ges.m.b.H. Although this term is sometimes incorrectly used as slang for any handgun, it should only be used when referring to the Austrian branded pistols.

Grain—A unit of measure for powder and bullets. One grain equals 1/7000 of a pound; or 64.799 milligrams. It's important to note that grain is not the same as a "granule" or pieces of gun powder.

Grip—The part of the firearm held by the trigger hand.

GSSF—Glock Sport Shooting Foundation

Gun Belt—A specialized belts that hold your tactical holster, personal medical kit, ammo side-cars, and knife.

Gun Control—Something you want to vote against as a responsible firearms owner.

Gun Lock—A system that encases the trigger, preventing the discharge of the firearm.

Gun Powder—The powder in the cartridge created the explosion that drives the projectile through the firearm's barrel.

Gun Smith—An individual skilled in the repair, modification, design, and production of firearms.

Hammer—The mechanism in the gun that launches the firing pin.

Hammer Block—A safety device separating the hammer and firing pin until you pull the trigger.

Hammerless—A striker-fired pistol with automatic reloading and no safety or cocking mechanism available.

Hangfire—An ammunition malfunction that's describing delayed discharge of the primer or powder. A defective impact on the cartridge by the firing pin.

Heel—The base of the firearm stock.

Hollow Point—A type of ammunition with a hollow center in the head of the bullet, filled with material designed to deform the bullet on impact, causing maximum damage to the target.

Hoplophobe—A new slang for individuals irrationally afraid of firearms.

HP—Hollow Point

HSP—Hollow Soft Point

Jacket—The layer of material, usually brass or synthetic, surrounding the core of the bullet.

JHP—Jacketed Hollow Point

JSP—Jacketed Soft Point

Lead—The substance used in the production of firearms projectiles.

Leading—The particles that remain in the barrel of the firearm requiring cleaning.

Less Lethal—Firearms systems launching rubber bullets or tear gas.

LHP—Lead Hollow Point

Loaded—A description of a firearm with the bullet in the chamber, ready to fire.

Loading Gate—The spring-loaded or hinged cover on the frame, allowing you to load a firearm like an A.R. or shotgun manually.

LOS—Line of Sight

LRN—Lead Round Nose

LSWCHP—Lead Semi Wad Cutter Hollow Point

LWC—Lead Wad Cutter

Machine Gun—A type of military-style fully-automatic, hand-held forearm popular in movies.

Magazine—The component of the firearm that houses the ammunition.

Mainspring—The firing spring storing the striker or hammer of the weapon.

MC—Metal Case

ME—Muzzle Energy

MIL-SPEC—Military Specification

Misfire—A type of ammunition malfunction relating to a cartridge failure.

MOA—Minute-of-angle

MOLLE—Modular Lightweight Load-carrying Equipment

Mouth—The end of the magazine that accepts the cartridge.

MR—Mean Radius

MRT—Mid-range Trajectory

Muzzle—The business end of the firearm that releases the projectile.

Muzzle Discipline—The practice of pointing the muzzle in a safe direction.

MV—Muzzle Velocity

NBRSA—National Bench Rest Shooters Association

Negligent Discharge—The accidental discharge of a firearm when the owner does not have total control over the rifle or gun.

NFA—National Firearms Act

NICS—National Instant Criminal Background Check System

Nose—The tip of a handgun or rifle bullet.

NRA—(National Rifle Association) is a public organization fighting the legal battle for America's gun rights.

NRMA—National Reloading Manufacturers' Association

NROI—National Range Officers Institute

NSSF—National Shooting Sports Foundation

OAL—Overall Length

Optic—A type of handgun or rifle sight. The optic produces a green or yellow dot on your target.

PALS—Pouch Attachment Ladder System

Partition Bullet—A dual-chambered and jacketed bullet. The front provides penetration while the rear remains unexploded to drive the round through armor plating.

Patch—A cloth used in the cleaning of the barrel of your firearm. You wrap it around a ball before plunging it in the barrel to clean the gun.

PCC—Pistol Caliber Carbine

PDW—Personal Defense Weapon

PG—Partitioned Gold

Pistol—Any variety of handguns.

Pistol Grip—Describes a type of grip on an automatic rifle or assault shotgun portion of a shoulder-operated gun.

Plinking—Firing at inanimate objects like bottles and cans.

Primer—The part of the casing that ignites the powder.

Propellant—Powder or gas igniting the powder.

PSCA—Professional Sporting Clays Association

PSP—Pointed Soft Point

PTHP—Platinum Tip Hollow Point

Pump Action—A cocking mechanism on a pump-action shotgun.

RCO—Range Conducting Officer

Recoil—The reaction from the explosion of the prodder and the firing of the projectile. Recoil is heavier in shotguns and least noticeable in handguns.

Red Dot—A type of rifle and handgun sight.

Reload—A previously exhausted cartridge repurposed as a new round.

Revolver—A type of pistol using manual loading and a cylinder instead of a magazine.

R.F.—An abbreviation for Rimfire.

Rib—A raised surface is located along the top of a gun barrel and used as a sight.

Ricochet—When the projectile deflects away from its original flight path after striking a surface.

Rifle—A type of automatic or self-loading firearm, also known as a long-gun.

Rifled Slug—A cylindrical slug designed to shoot through a rifled barrel.

Rifling—The spiraled grooves cut into the bore of a rifle or handgun barrel. The rifling helps to start the rotational spin of the projectile to the target.

RM—Range Master

RMI—Range Master Instructor

RO—Range Officer

Round—A slang or colloquial word for a cartridge.

RSO—Range Safety Officer

SAAMI—Sporting Arms and Ammunition Manufacturers Institute

Safe—A gun safe is where you store your firearms.

Safety—The most important part of firearms ownership.

Safety Catch—The catch on a double-action pistol preventing it from firing. Most striker-fired guns don't have this feature.

SBR—Short Barreled Rifle

Scope—A telescopic sight, commonly called a scope, is an optical sighting device that is based on a refracting telescope for magnifying a target.

SCSA—Steel Challenge Shooting Association

Sear—The part of the firearm keeping the hammer cocked until you pull the trigger.

Semi-Automatic—A firearm that discharges a round with each trigger pull, without the need to cock the gun between shots.

Shooter Ready—A call during competitive shooting signaling the start of your round.

Shotgun—A firearm that relies on cartridge ammunition that disperses and versatile range of the projectile, from buckshot to rubber pellets.

Silencer or Suppressor—A fitting screwing into the barrel of your gun. The suppressor dampens the noise of the shot, saving your ears. Suppressors are useful in hunting to stop the shot alerting animals nearby.

Single-Shot—A firearm that requires manual loading between each shot.

SJHP—Semi Jacketed Hollow Point

SJSP—Semi Jacketed Soft Point

Skeet—A shooting competition involving participants attempting to shoot clay discs with shotguns.

Slide—The top of a semi-automatic pistol that moves along the barrel. You pull the slide to cock the gun.

Slide-Action—A type of semi-automatic firearm action where the slide moves with the explosion of the cartridge.

Slide Release—The levers on the side of the gun returning the slide to the firing position after inserting a new magazine.

Sling—Found in 2-point, 3-point, and single-point variations to suit user comfort. The sling reduces operator fatigue when on duty for extended periods.

Sling Swivel—The metal loop on the rifle that connects to the sling.

Small Arms—Firearms with small calibers.

Snub-Nosed—Handguns with short barrels.

Soft Point—A bullet featuring a metal jacket with an exposed nose. As a result of this configuration, the bullet expands on hitting the target.

SP—Soft Point

Spray—Firing multiple shots in an erratic pattern to hit a target.

Squib—When the cartridge propellant is only sufficient to move the projectile partially down the barrel.

STHP—Silver Tip Hollow Point

Stippling—A type of grip enhancement.

Stock—The part of the gun attaching to the tang or handle of the weapon.

Stove Jam—when a cartridge fails to eject and sticks in the ejection chamber.

SWC—Semi Wad Cutter

Takedown Levers—The levers on the gun or rifle help you separate the frame and slide or upper and lower receivers.

Tang—The part of the receiver that fits into the stock behind the hammer.

TFSP—Total Fragmenting Soft Point

TMJ—Total Metal Jacket

TOF—Time of Flight

Trigger—The part of the frame that causes the gun to fire when depressed.

Trigger Guard—The part of the frame surrounding the trigger.

Trigger-Lock—Prevents the accidental discharge of a firearm.

TTSX—Tipped Triple Shock X

USCA—U.S. Carbine Association

USPSA—United States Practical Shooting Association

VAF—Voluntary Appeal File

Velocity Feet-Per-Second (FPS)—A measurement of the projectile's speed as it's leaving the barrel of the firearm.

The Wall—The part of the trigger pull where you feel the tension as the firing pin is ready to release.

WC—Wad Cutter

WCF—Winchester Center Fire

Weapon—Referring to a rifle, handgun, or any type of gun that causes injury.

Weaver Stance—A type of shooting stance where the dominant foot is in the rear.

WFN—Wide Flat Nose

WFNGC—Wide Flat Nose Gas Checked

YSSA—Youth Shooting Sports Alliance

Zero—The farthest distance at which the firearms projectile hits the target accurately. Also known as the practice of aligning a rile or handguns sights.

RESOURCES

The Four Golden Rules of Firearms Safety, (2017), Vinjatek/Kooc Media LTD. Retrieved from https://vinjatek.com/gun-terms/.
Gun Acronyms, (2020), Armsvault. Retrieved from https://armsvault.com/gun-information/gun-acronyms/.
The Range 702, (2019), Glossary of Basic Firearm Terms. Retrieved from https://www.therange702.com/blog/glossary-of-basic-firearm-terms/.

Appendix B

Proclamation Declaring June 4, 2021, National Gun Violence Awareness Day*

CITY OF LAFAYETTE, COLORADO

This proclamation declares June 4, 2021, to be National Gun Violence Awareness Day in the City of Lafayette, Colorado, to honor and remember all victims and survivors of gun violence and to declare that we as a country must do more to reduce gun violence.

WHEREAS, every day, 100 Americans are killed by gun violence and more than 300 have sustained non-fatal firearm injuries over the last 5 years; and

WHEREAS , Americans are 25 times more likely to be killed with guns than people in other developed countries; and

WHEREAS , protecting public safety in the communities they serve is a mayor's highest responsibility; and

WHEREAS , mayors and law enforcement officers know their communities best, are the most familiar with local criminal activity and how to address it, and are best positioned to understand how to keep their residents safe; and

WHEREAS , June 2, 2021, would have been the 24th birthday of Hadiya Pendleton, a teenager who marched in President Obama's second inaugural parade and was tragically shot and killed just weeks later; and

WHEREAS , to help honor Hadiya—and the 100 Americans whose lives are cut short and the countless survivors who are injured by shootings every day—a national coalition of organizations has designated June 4, 2021, as National Gun Violence Awareness Day; and

WHEREAS, the idea was inspired by a group of Hadiya's friends, who asked their classmates to commemorate her life by wearing orange; they chose this color because hunters wear orange to announce themselves to other hunters when out in the woods and orange is a color that symbolizes the value of human life; and

WHEREAS , anyone can join this campaign by pledging to Wear Orange on June 4 to help raise awareness about gun violence; and

WHEREAS , by wearing orange on June 4, Americans will raise awareness about gun violence and honor the lives and lost human potential of Americans stolen by gun violence; and

WHEREAS , we renew our commitment to reduce gun violence and pledge to do all we can to keep firearms out of the wrong hands and encourage responsible gun ownership to help keep our children safe.

NOW, THEREFORE BE IT RESOLVED that the Mayor and City Council of the City of Lafayette, Colorado, do hereby declare June 4, 2021, to be National Gun Violence Awareness Day.

---

*Public document originally published as City of Lafayette, Colorado, *Proclamation Declaring June 4, 2021, National Gun Violence Awareness Day.*

We encourage all residents to support community efforts to prevent the tragic effects of gun violence and to honor and value all human lives.

PASSED AND ADOPTED THIS 1st DAY OF JUNE, 2021

ATTEST: CITY OF LAFAYETTE, COLORADO

Lynnette Beck, City Clerk   Jamie Harkins, Mayor

Appendix C

Expressing Support for the Designation of June 4, 2021,
as "National Gun Violence Awareness Day" and June
*2021 as "National Gun Violence Awareness Month"**

117TH CONGRESS
1ST SESSION
S. RES. 242

IN THE SENATE OF THE UNITED STATES
May 26, 2021
Mr. DURBIN (for himself, Ms. DUCKWORTH, Mrs. FEINSTEIN, Ms. KLOBUCHAR, Mr. BLUMENTHAL, Mr. BOOKER, Mr. MURPHY, Mr. MARKEY, Mr. CARPER, Mr. VAN HOLLEN, Mr. MENENDEZ, Ms. SMITH, Mr. CASEY, and Mr. MERKLEY) submitted the following resolution; which was referred to the Committee on

---

RESOLUTION

Expressing support for the designation of June 4, 2021, as "National Gun Violence Awareness Day" and June 2021 as "National Gun Violence Awareness Month."

Whereas, each year in the United States, more than—

(1) 38,500 individuals are killed and 85,000 individuals are wounded by gunfire;
(2) 14,000 individuals are killed in homicides involving guns;
(3) 23,000 individuals die by suicide using a gun; and
(4) 480 individuals are killed in unintentional shootings;

Whereas, since 1968, more individuals have died from guns in the United States than have died on the battlefields of all the wars in the history of the United States;

Whereas 2020 was one of the deadliest years on record for the United States, with an estimated 19,300 individuals killed in gun homicides or nonsuicide-related shootings, a 25-percent increase over 2019;

Whereas unintentional shooting deaths by children increased by nearly $1/3$, comparing incidents in March to December of 2020 to the same months in 2019;

Whereas, by 1 count, in 2020 in the United States, there were 610 mass shooting incidents in which at least 4 individuals were killed or wounded by gunfire;

---

*Public document originally published as United States Congress, Senate Resolution 242, Expressing Support for the Designation of June 4, 2021, as "National Gun Violence Awareness Day" and June 2021 as "National Gun Violence Awareness Month.

279

Whereas, every year in the United States, more than 3,000 children and teens are killed by gun violence and 15,000 children and teens are shot and wounded;

Whereas approximately 8,800 individuals in the United States under the age of 25 die because of gun violence annually, including Hadiya Pendleton, who, in 2013, was killed at 15 years of age in Chicago, Illinois, while standing in a park;

Whereas, on June 4, 2021, to recognize the 24th birthday of Hadiya Pendleton (born June 2, 1997), individuals across the United States will recognize National Gun Violence Awareness Day and wear orange in tribute to—

(1) Hadiya Pendleton and other victims of gun violence; and

(2) the loved ones of those victims; and

Whereas June 2021 is an appropriate month to designate as "National Gun Violence Awareness Month": Now, therefore, be it

Resolved, That the Senate—

(1) supports—

(A) the designation of "National Gun Violence Awareness Month" and the goals and ideals of that month; and

(B) the designation of "National Gun Violence Awareness Day," in remembrance of the victims of gun violence; and

(2) calls on the people of the United States to—

(A) promote greater awareness of gun violence and gun safety;

(B) wear orange, the color that hunters wear to show that they are not targets, on "National Gun Violence Awareness Day";

(C) concentrate heightened attention on gun violence during the summer months, when gun violence typically increases; and

(D) bring community members and leaders together to discuss ways to make communities safer.

Appendix D

*Prohibiting Firearms at Work, LMC Model Policy**

LEAGUE OF MINNESOTA CITIES

League models are thoughtfully developed by our staff for a city's consideration. Models should be customized as appropriate for an individual city's circumstances in consultation with the city's attorney. Helpful background information on this model may be found in Firearm <u>Regulation and Cities</u>.

City of _____, Minnesota
Firearms at Work Policy

The City of _____ hereby establishes a policy prohibiting all employees, except sworn employees of the Police Department, from carrying or possessing firearms while acting in the course and scope of employment for the city. The possession or carrying of a firearm by employees other than sworn Police Officers is prohibited while working on city property or while working in any location on behalf of the city. This includes but is not limited to:

- Driving on city business;
- Riding as a passenger in a car or any type of mass transit on city business;
- Working at city hall or any other city-owned work site;
- Working off-site on behalf of the city;
- Performing emergency or on-call work after normal business hours and on weekends;
- Working at private residences and at businesses on behalf of the city;
- Attending training or conferences on behalf of the city;

An exception to this policy is that city employees may carry and possess firearms in city-owned parking areas if they have obtained the appropriate permit(s). Therefore, if a city employee must drive his or her personal vehicle on city business, he or she may check a firearm with the city Police Department during the workday and retrieve it after work. The Police Department will establish procedures to ensure that the firearm is locked up and is not able to be retrieved by anyone other than the owner/employee.

When responding to on-call work from home after regular work hours, an employee is prohibited from bringing a firearm in their private vehicle unless the vehicle remains in a parking lot and is not needed in order to respond to the call.

Violations of this policy are subject to disciplinary action in accordance with the city's disciplinary procedures policy.

*Originally published as League of Minnesota Cities, "Prohibiting Firearms at Work, LMC Model Policy," https://www.lmc.org/resources/firearm-regulation-and-cities/ (August 10, 2020). Reprinted with permission of the publisher.

About the Contributors

Abe **Aboraya** covers health care for WMFE, an NPR affiliate in Orlando.

Michelle **Andrews** is a correspondent for *Kaiser Health News*.

Cara **Anthony** is a *Kaiser Health News* Midwest correspondent.

Christie **Aschwanden** is a reporter for *Kaiser Health News*.

Andrew **Ball** is a professor of environmental microbiology at RMIT University.

Michelle **Barnhart** is an associate professor of marketing at Oregon State University.

Lois **Beckett** is a ProPublica reporter covering politics, big data and information privacy issues.

Sean **Britton** is a deputy county emergency medical services coordinator in Broome County, New York.

Jack **Brown** is a senior associate at the Center for Public Safety Management, and director of the Office of Emergency Management in Arlington County, Virginia.

Giles **Bruce** is a contributor to *Kaiser Health News*.

Samuel **Brunson** is a professor of law at Loyola University Chicago.

California Department of Justice is a statewide investigative law enforcement agency and legal department of the California executive branch under the elected leadership of the California Attorney General.

California Office of the Attorney General ensures that the laws of the state of California are uniformly and adequately enforced.

Maggie **Callahan** is a master's student of public diplomacy at Syracuse University and a graduate assistant for the Participedia Project at the Maxwell School of Citizenship and Public Affairs.

Ron **Carlee** is a visiting assistant professor of public service at Old Dominion University and former city manager of Charlotte, North Carolina.

Center for Public Policy at VCU's Wilder School advances research and training that informs public policy and decision-making to improve our communities.

Ann **Christiano** is the Frank Karel Chair in Public Interest Communications at the University of Florida.

City of Lafayette, Colorado, is a home rule municipality located in southeastern Boulder County, Colorado.

Emily **Costa** is a master's student in public administration at Roger Williams University in Rhode Island.

Brian **DeLay** is an associate professor of history at the University of California, Berkeley.

Gabriel **Filippelli** is a professor of earth sciences and director of the Center for Urban Health at the Indiana University–Purdue University Indianapolis.

Lisa Aronson **Fontes** is a senior lecturer at the University Without Walls, University of Massachusetts Amherst.

Chaseedaw **Giles** is the social media manager for *Kaiser Health News*.

Evan V. **Goldstein** is a doctoral candidate at The Ohio State University.

Amanda Michelle **Gomez** is the *Kaiser Health News* Peggy Girshman Fellow reporting on how public health policy impacts everyday people.

Joaquin Jay **Gonzalez** III is the Mayor George Christopher Professor of Public Administration at the Edward S. Ageno School of Business of Golden Gate University in San Francisco, California.

Rod **Gould** is the senior manager for training at the Center for Public Safety Management in Greenbrae, California.

Brian **Gulson** is with Macquarie University.

Keith **Guzik** is an associate professor of sociology at the University of Colorado Denver.

Michael **Hirsh** is a professor of surgery and pediatrics at the University of Massachusetts Medical School.

Aimee **Huff** is an assistant professor of marketing at Oregon State University.

Neal H. **Hutchens** is a professor of higher education at the University of Mississippi.

Roger L. **Kemp** is a distinguished adjunct professor at Golden Gate University and has worked as a city manager in the largest council-manager governments in California, New Jersey, and Connecticut.

Alan H. **Kennedy** is a Ph.D. candidate at the University of Colorado Denver and 2020 ASPA Founders' Fellow.

Adam G. **Klein** is an assistant professor of communication studies at Pace University.

Don **Klingner** is a distinguished professor and director of the MPA program at the University of Colorado, Colorado Springs.

Mark A.S. **Laidlaw** is a Vice Chancellors Postdoctoral Fellow at RMIT University.

League of Minnesota Cities is a membership association dedicated to promoting excellence in local government, serving more than 800 member cities through advocacy, education and training, policy development, risk management, and other services.

Suevon **Lee** was an intern at ProPublica and has previously worked as a reporter for the *Ocala Star-Banner*, where she covered courts and legal issues.

Gary T. **Marx** is a professor emeritus of sociology at the Massachusetts Institute of Technology.

Kerry B. **Melear** is a professor of leadership and counselor education at the University of Mississippi.

Howard Walter **Mielke** is a professor in the department of pharmacology at the Tulane University School of Medicine, Tulane University.

National Shooting Sports Foundation is the trade association of the firearms industry, leading the way in advocating for the industry and its businesses and jobs, keeping guns out of the wrong hands, encouraging enjoyment of recreational shooting and hunting and helping people better understand the industry's lawful products.

Annie **Neimand** is a Ph.D. candidate in sociology at the University of Florida.

Molly **Pahn** is a research manager at Boston University.

Aneri **Pattani** is a *Kaiser Health News* correspondent reporting on a broad range of public health topics, with a focus on mental health and substance use.

Laura **Prater** is a postdoctoral fellow at The Ohio State University.

Phillip **Reese** is a data reporting specialist and an assistant professor of journalism at California State University–Sacramento.

Meghan **Reilly** is a legislative analyst at the Office of Legislative Research of the State of Connecticut.

Alan R. **Roper** is a distinguished adjunct professor of public administration at Golden Gate University.

Veronica **Rose** is the principal research analyst at the Office of Legislative Research of the State of Connecticut.

Elisabeth **Rosenthal** is the editor-in-chief of *Kaiser Health News*.

Joaquin **Sapien** is a reporter at ProPublica covering criminal justice and social services.

Donald **Sebastian** is a professor of chemical, biological and pharmaceutical engineering at the New Jersey Institute of Technology.

Michael **Siegel** is a professor of community health sciences at Boston University.

Ian **Smith** is a first year science teacher at Clewiston Middle School in Hendry County, Florida.

Timothy M. **Smith** is a professor of sustainable systems management and international business at the University of Minnesota.

Sarah **Sweeney** is a professional social worker and public administrator in Washington State.

Laura **Ungar**, Midwest editor/correspondent, covers health issues out of *Kaiser Health News*' St. Louis office.

U.S. Bureau of Alcohol, Tobacco, Firearms and Explosives or ATF is a law enforcement agency in the United States' Department of Justice that protects our communities from violent criminals, criminal organizations, the illegal use and trafficking of firearms, the illegal use and storage of explosives, acts of arson and bombings, acts of terrorism, and the illegal diversion of alcohol and tobacco products.

U.S. Congress is the legislative branch of the United States government.

U.S. Department of Justice enforces the law and defends the interests of the United States according to the law; ensures public safety against threats foreign and domestic; provides federal leadership in preventing and controlling crime; seeks just punishment for those guilty of unlawful behavior; and ensures fair and impartial administration of justice for all Americans.

Utah Department of Public Safety is a law enforcement agency in the State of Utah.

Lacey **Wallace** is an assistant professor of criminal justice at Pennsylvania State University.

Washington Office of Superintendent of Public Instruction, or OSPI, is the state education agency for the State of Washington implementing state laws regarding education.

Sandy **West** is a correspondent for *Kaiser Health News*.

Tom **Wickizer** is a chair and professor of public health at The Ohio State University.

Index